FIELDS OF FIRE

W/D BOOKSALE 07/08

FIELDS OF FIRE

THE GREATEST FOOTBALL MATCHES EVER

JOHN LUDDEN

MAINSTREAM
PUBLISHING

EDINBURGH AND LONDON

For Christine, the measure of my dreams

www.johnludden.co.uk

First published in Great Britain in 2001 by
MAINSTREAM PUBLISHING COMPANY (EDINBURGH) LTD
7 Albany Street
Edinburgh EH1 3UG

ISBN 1 84018 461 2

A catalogue record for this book is available
from the British Library

Typeset in Confidential and Garamond
Printed and bound in Great Britain by
Mackays of Chatham

CONTENTS

1. The Greatest Story Never Told
    Dinamo Kiev v The Nazis, 1942   7

2. Hat Harom
    England v Hungary, 1953   15

3. The Magyars' Last Stand
    Hungary v West Germany, 1954 World Cup final   31

4. Snowflakes in the Sun
    Real Madrid v Manchester United,
    *   1957 European Cup semi-final*   45

5. A Solid Gold Watch
    Manchester United v Red Star Belgrade,
    *   1958 European Cup quarter-final*   55

6. The Second Coming
    Real Madrid v Eintracht Frankfurt, 1960 European Cup final   65

7. Sunset over Guadamarra
    Barcelona v Real Madrid, 1961 European Cup   77

8. The Panther and the Gypsy Curse
    Benfica v Real Madrid, 1962 European Cup final   85

9. The Summer of '66
    England v West Germany, 1966 World Cup Final   95

10. Celtic Nights
    Celtic v Inter Milan, 1967 European Cup final   107

11. The Son of Dondinho
    Brazil v Italy, 1970 World Cup final   117

12. Fool's Gold
    Scotland v Holland, 1978 World Cup   133

13. A Fistful of Dollars
    Argentina v Peru, 1978 World Cup   145

14. The Prodigal Son
    Italy v Brazil, 1982 World Cup   151

15.   Scopa
      Argentina v England, 1986 World Cup quarter-final   167

16.   Tears of a Clown
      England v West Germany, 1990 World Cup semi-final   181

17.   The Treasure of San Genaro
      Italy v Argentina, 1990 World Cup semi-final   195

18.   Dancing with Tears in Red Eyes
      Manchester United v Bayern Munich,
        1999 European Cup final   209

1.

THE GREATEST STORY NEVER TOLD

DINAMO KIEV V THE NAZIS

1942

If you win, you die.

Many claim it never took place. That it was just a figment of some Communist's imagination – another example of exaggerating the strong spirit and righteousness of the great Soviet Union. Nobody talks about it today. Now that the Communists have upped and run, or rather changed their leopard-like spots, people tend to forget. However, in the city of Kiev there resides a man who many claimed took part in the alleged event and is still alive today to tell this extraordinary and moving tale. Sadly he has little to say. Sensibly, in the current climate, Makar Honcharenko keeps himself to himself, and also his memories. The true facts are remarkably sketchy. What is known is that some kind of football match did take place and that the prize for the winners was no trophy. It was no medal. It was not even a handshake or the words 'Well done'. The prize for victory was death. And yet they still played to win. As the bullets from the grinning Nazi SS troops slammed into their legs, the Ukrainians across the field fell down on their knees. But they still refused to bow down. The German High Command looked on in horror as the players of Kiev roared out in defiance. This was a myth that had to be snuffed out. Read on.

THE BEGINNING

The story begins in the early hours of 21 June 1941. At three o'clock the German war machine rumbled ominously in all its might across the Ukraine's western border. For the Soviet border troops it was a hopeless cause. Caught totally unaware they were swiftly overrun. Above, in the dark Ukrainian skies, the Luftwaffe hurtled east; hundreds of bombers intent on crushing Josef Stalin's Red Army whilst it slept. The Germans trampled arrogantly through the vast terrain. They left in their wake scenes of death, misery and destruction. The Ukrainians' belief that the Germans would liberate them from their persecution under Stalin was to prove tragically mistaken. Hitler and his henchmen regarded these Eastern Slavs as cannon fodder and, indeed, slave labour; for in the wake of the Wehrmacht came the sinister units of the Einsatzgruppen. These were SS brigades committed to wiping out all Jews, and Ukrainians deemed undesirables. Hundreds of thousands of innocent people were slaughtered with chilling efficiency, as Himmler's death squads went to work. The systematic butchering of an entire race was under way.

Some of the worse excesses took place beyond a steep wooded ravine, at a place called Babi Yar, just outside the Ukrainian capital of Kiev. The city fell to the Germans on 19 September 1941. Eight days later the executions began. The SS began to round up all the Jewish inhabitants of the city. Men, women and children were herded together, stripped naked and marched off in long winding columns to the outskirts of Kiev. Marshalled by SS guards with dogs and armed with whips and pistol butts, they were beaten and pushed towards freshly dug mass graves. Then the SS opened fire with heavy machine-guns. At Babi Yar alone, 33,771 Jewish Ukrainians were butchered. Watching from high up on the craggy hills of the ravine, SS officers congratulated themselves on the smoothness of the proceedings. The rich black soil of the Ukraine was being drenched with its people's blood.

Ukrainian freedom fighters found themselves surrounded by enemies. The Russians to the east and the Germans to the north were equally hated. The partisans fighting for a free Ukraine sometimes found themselves having to fight both at once. During the '30s the area had suffered intolerably under Stalin's regime. An estimated four million people were killed during the Communists' purges. Moscow employed a systematic policy of starvation in a cold-blooded attempt to starve the Ukrainians into submission and onto the dreaded collective farms.

In the early days of June 1942, in Kiev, the invaders took a breather from the looting and killing to indulge themselves in a spot of public relations. The Nazi hierarchy believed that for propaganda purposes a football match between themselves and a local side would do wonders for morale. How amusing it would be to witness a superior team of the 'Master Race' humiliate these Ukrainians in front of their own countrymen. The side chosen for this Nazi circus act was the pride of all Ukraine, Dinamo Kiev. The Kiev players had all been in captivity for some time. Many of them were badly undernourished and dreadfully thin. Illness had taken a heavy toll. The

Germans treated prisoners of war on the Eastern Front with scant regard for their well-being. The values of the Geneva Convention were not adhered to here on the killing fields of Russia. Indeed mostly prisoners were not taken by either side. This was a war of ideologies, a war to the finish.

When the Germans rolled into Kiev the Dinamo players had been extremely fortunate. Captured all together, a Wehrmacht officer recognised them. A football supporter, he contacted his superiors who ordered the officer to keep the Ukrainians alive until further notice. The footballers were put to work in a bakery, but any chance that came their way Dinamo would practise their formidable skills in an empty yard at the back of the kitchen. There they would be watched intently by German guards high up on a watchtower. Shaking their heads, they failed to hide their admiration of the talents shown by these supposedly inferior Slavs. The Kiev players were approached by the Nazis and told in no uncertain terms of their participation in the upcoming 'friendly'. They were also informed that they could not play under the name of Dinamo. They chose instead the name of Start. But in their hearts the Ukrainians were and always would be Dinamo Kiev.

On 12 June, posters began to appear on every Kiev street corner. They announced: Football. Armed Forces of Germany versus Kiev City Start. During the build-up the local commandant, Major General Eberhardt, informed the local population that this match would help to promote good relations between the German Army and the citizens of Ukraine. In a perverse act of friendship, Eberhardt promised to go easy on the home side. It was to be a German team made up from the ranks which would take on the bedraggled Kiev. The game would be held in the Zenith stadium, and would take place amidst much Nazi triumphalism. In front of a full house made up of an enthusiastic Ukrainian crowd, the match got under way. The watching Eberhardt could not help but smile when the German Army side took an early lead.

The crowd made their views known. They booed the Germans all the way back to the halfway line. Kiev regrouped. As the match restarted they slowly began to rediscover their touch. It wasn't long before they had equalised and, to the delight of the terraces, taken the lead. The half-time whistle blew and Major General Eberhardt exploded in fury at the Kiev players. 'What the hell do you think you are doing?' roared the Nazi commandant. 'I am warning you, if you do not ease off you will face a firing squad.' With this he turned and left the room, followed by two SS stormtroopers. One of the Ukrainians threw a bottle that smashed against the door after the Germans had departed. With renewed determination they prepared to rub the Nazis' noses in the dirt.

The second half saw Dinamo Kiev hammer their massively outclassed opponents. Within a short period they had made it 4–1. It all proved too much for the fuming Eberhardt. He ordered the referee to finish the game and with this he left the stadium. He dared not carry out his threat of shooting the Ukrainian players. First he had to see them beaten and put in their place. They would be allowed to live. At least for now. Around the ground the citizens of Kiev cheered their team off the pitch. Many were crying, whilst others mocked the German soldiers who watched them intently, hoping to receive orders to fire into the crowd.

Three days later a rematch took place. This time the German team had been reinforced with players brought in especially to secure victory. Once again the Zenith stadium was packed to the rafters. The Kiev side took the field to be greeted by raucous applause from their home supporters. They would not disappoint. Ninety minutes later the Ukrainians had romped home 6–0. It appeared that the Aryan supermen were human after all. The red-faced Eberhardt knew he had badly underestimated the Dinamo players. For although their fitness had waned, their skill and technique was far superior to anything he had available. Headquarters would be furious. With the sound of thousands of Ukrainians singing their national anthem ringing in his ears, the commandant made his plans.

Into Kiev came the Hungarian team MSG Wal. MSG was made up of Hungarian professional footballers who had been fighting alongside the Germans on the Eastern Front. They were a top-class outfit. A colleague of Eberhardt had recommended them with the words, 'They will get you off the hook.' Eberhardt was not about to let the Ukrainians have any respite. He had already cut their rations and banned them from training. The game against MSG would take place only two days after the previous match. On 19 July 1942, Dinamo Kiev entered the Zenith stadium for a third time. With their city behind them they prepared to take on the Hungarians of MSG. Eberhardt nervously took his seat. The scenes around the ground filled him with fear. This was a situation that had to be controlled, otherwise he could find himself in deep trouble. Many of his fellow officers had been shot for less. The next 90 minutes was for this German an absolute nightmare. Kiev smashed the Hungarians 5–1.

Already the whispers had started. The Kiev players sat exhausted in their dressing-room. They knew they were living on borrowed time. Theirs was a no-win situation. The Germans would let them live as long as they continued to beat them. For they had to be seen to have their revenge. But there was a flipside to this coin. After each victory for the Ukrainians, the Germans became more and more agitated, whilst the crowds grew in defiance. Kiev was a city on fire with admiration for their footballers. Very shortly something would have to give. The German administration were outraged with the situation. Eberhardt's superiors ordered him to arrange an immediate rematch. Again Dinamo triumphed, this time by 3–2. The Hungarians were packed off in disgrace. Eberhardt was deep in the mire. He visited the Kiev players at the bakery. By this time they were a sorry sight.

The effort put into the games and their starvation diet had left them close to collapse. Eberhardt found it hard to believe that this rag-tag bunch had managed to keep up such a show of defiance. His promise of better rations and medical help cut no ice with the Dinamo stalwarts. None of them spoke when he had finished talking. They simply stared straight at him. This unnerved the German. He began to think that maybe they were not human. Human or not, Eberhardt would take no chances in the next encounter. The call went out for the best of the best. The crack German Army side Flakelf courtesy of a Luftwaffe transport plane arrived. Flakelf had never been beaten.

The epic tale of Dinamo Kiev's resistance had spread through the whole of the Ukraine and beyond. Already the story of this football team that was defying the Nazis had reached the gates of Moscow and Josef Stalin himself. Sadly the fairy tale was set to come to a horrific end. On 9 August 1942, the German Army formed a ring of steel around the Zenith stadium. They had run out of patience. This was the day the story would end. There would be few locals allowed to watch this time round. The crowd would mostly be made up of German Wehrmacht soldiers eager to intimidate and scream abuse at the Ukrainians. Around the pitch Nazi SS guards would patrol with their fearsome Alsatian dogs. Others set up machine-guns and aimed them onto the football field.

Shortly before kick-off an SS officer visited the Ukrainians' dressing-room. It was there that they were made the offer. 'The situation is this,' snarled the German. 'Victory for us is not essential, for we already know that we are vastly superior to vermin like yourselves. It is obvious to everybody that you have cheated your way to your various wins. No, all that matters to us now is that you obey this one simple command. Lose the match! For if you win, you die. This I truly promise you,' whispered the German. 'Nothing is more certain. Win and you die.' Win the game and they would be executed. Lose and they would be allowed to live. Exist with dishonour? For a people as proud as the Ukrainians this would be akin to death itself. As they discussed their situation it was clear that the idea of giving in was out of the question. They had come too far and suffered too much simply to throw in the towel.

The game began. At first Flakelf had the upper hand. Kiev looked half-hearted with their challenges, although in such intimidating circumstances this was hardly surprising. The Germans quickly took advantage and stormed into a two-goal lead. The Wehrmacht soldiers on the terraces were loving it. After having their noses rubbed continuously in the dirt recently, this was most definitely pay-back time. The citizens of Kiev amongst the crowd looked sadly on. It was a sorry spectacle. Their lads were being put to the sword. The jeering and catcalls of the Germans, however, had a stirring effect on the Ukrainians. The more the Nazis mocked, the more determined they became to get back into the contest, and damn the consequences. Soon they were level and threatening to go in front. Their football was laced with a passion and zeal that defied the no-win situation they found themselves in. Kiev were playing like a team in a hurry for their own funeral.

The Flakelf defence began to crumble under the incessant attacks of the Ukrainians. The local German High Command, who had travelled to the capital to witness the end of this saga, sat fidgeting in their seats. As Dinamo continued to race forward a third goal looked a certainty. Finally it arrived. A Kiev forward burst through and almost broke the back of the Flakelf net with a stunning shot; 3–2 for the Ukrainians. Now was the moment of truth. The SS were nothing if not true to their words, for as soon as the ball hit the net the shooting began. At first the guards aimed short of the Dinamo players. It was a warning. Start losing or die. Showing unbelievable courage, the Ukrainians refused to curtail their efforts and continued to attack the Flakelf goal. The order came from Commandant Eberhardt to open fire at the legs of the Kiev players.

The clatter of machine-gun fire rang out. Two Ukrainians fell to their knees. Their comrades carried on the fight. More shots rang out and down went another. The Kiev footballers dropped one by one under a hail of bullets. Some tried to get back on their feet. The Flakelf players stood dumbfounded with shock and fear. The call came from the stands for the frightened referee to signal the end of the match. The pitch was scattered with Ukrainians lying injured in pools of blood. The Kiev team was rounded up, dragged off and thrown into the back of a waiting army truck. Covered in dirt and bleeding profusely from their wounds, they had remained defiant to the last. 'You were warned,' screamed the SS officer who had entered the dressing-room before the game. 'Now you pay the price.' The truck headed off in the direction of Babi Yar.

Once there the Ukrainians were lined up on the edge of a huge crevasse. The German officer in charge was the same one who had originally recognised the Kiev team when they were captured. For reasons known only to himself, he showed a little heart and spared three of the players. They were forced to watch as their team-mates, still in their blood-stained football kits, prepared themselves to die. In a murderous shower of machine-gun fire Dinamo Kiev finally lay down. For what it was worth the Germans had their victory.

TODAY

Outside the home of Dinamo Kiev there stands today a statue dedicated to the memory of these brave young men. Standing ten feet tall, it depicts a band of footballers standing arm in arm. If you were to ask the majority of people in Kiev about the statue they would tell you that the games never happened. The whole story was made up by the Communist party after the war. However, something must surely have taken place. You could simply not make up such a story! The Ukrainians are proud of their past, but they are equally proud of their present. Such tales of so-called Communist valour and ten-foot statues belong to another age.

On 24 August 1991, the Ukraine finally won its independence from the Russian Bear. Today Dinamo Kiev are once more the pride of the nation. Only one man knows the truth and Makar Honcharenko is saying nothing. This frail, 90-year-old former Kiev player refuses point blank to tell his story. The truth of 'The Greatest Story Never Told' looks certain to die with him, but the legend will undoubtedly live on.

2.

HAT HAROM

ENGLAND V HUNGARY

1953

Amongst the ancient cobbled back streets of Budapest that lie in the shadow of the Danube, there stands a bar called Hat Harom. It is frequented by a dwindling band of proud old men. When they gather together to reminisce, the conversation almost inevitably turns to a murky November afternoon back in 1953. A time when Hungarians ruled the roost in world football. A time when these wizened old men reached a unique peak of football perfection. The time of Hat Harom. The time of 6–3.

It was the early dawn of Wednesday, 25 November 1953. Wembley stadium stood hushed and expectant, its Union Jack fluttering high and proud over the home of English football. The previous night had witnessed a fierce storm lash out in fury at the capital's famous monuments. Now as a new day broke all was quiet. A thick swirling mist had descended on London. The sound of freight trains beginning their journeys scattered in echoes through the brisk winter air. As the morning wore on the sky cleared and bright specks of sunlight appeared through the gloomy clouds. For English football the day of reckoning had dawned.

At their first glimpse of the white cliffs the Magyars suddenly realised the full extent of the task ahead. Their mood, from being jovial, became pensive as the journey over the English Channel drew near its end. Their coach and Deputy Minister of Sport, Gustav Sebes, had preached to them endlessly the importance of victory in the forthcoming match with England. 'Uncle Gusti', as he was nicknamed by his players, had been allowed by his Communist superiors to play his team at Wembley only after promising them that victory was inevitable. This promise worried Sebes. The Prime Minister, Matyos Rakosi, was not a man who made idle threats. The English had to be beaten.

Something special had occurred behind the grim shadow of the Iron Curtain. Hungary had given birth to an extraordinary generation of footballers. Foremost amongst these was a man whose talent belied his physical appearance. It was said by critics of the player in question that he was too fat, too slow, weak in the air and hopelessly one-footed. Ferenc Puskas, they claimed, would never be good enough to pull on a shirt of his motherland. How wrong these people would prove to be. For what he possessed in his left peg alone was enough to see Puskas carve out for himself a place in the annals of the game's greats. Here was a footballer who in technique and attitude was the heartbeat of a truly outstanding Hungarian team. From his position of centre-forward Ferenc Puskas would direct operations around him as his fellow Magyars wreaked havoc amongst opposition defences.

Sheltered till then from all western eyes, the Hungarians first appeared upon the scene at the 1952 Olympic Games in Helsinki. There they enthralled as they swept to the title destroying everyone in their path. The Magyars' sophisticated playing system introduced a deep-lying centre-forward. The bold, incisive Nandor Hidegkuti was a player performing in a manner years ahead of his time. His ability to drop back into midfield and create gaps for others was a tactic which had been tuned to perfection in the Hungarian first division. With all the country's best players placed by the authorities under the umbrella of the club side Honved, Sebes and his coaching staff were handed ample opportunity to refine this ploy. As Hungary's finest grew in confidence many a side were crushed. Nandor Hidegkuti was the perfect player to pull off such innovative moves. His penetrating passes carved the way forward for stupendous performers such as Puskas, Josef Bozsik, Zoltan Czibor and Sandor Kocsis.

Josef Bozsik in particular was highly regarded by Sebes. This swashbuckling midfielder cut an impressive sight on a football field. Bozsik shared an unerring relationship with Ferenc Puskas on the pitch. These two had been best friends since the age of three. As youngsters they had played football on the bombed-out wastelands of Budapest. They had watched as swarms of Russian bombers headed towards Germany to hammer the final nail into the Nazis' coffin. Whilst Bozsik was a devout Communist party member, Puskas tended not to extol the virtues of such ideology. For him serving his country did not extend to kissing the backside of Mother Russia. Football was all that mattered. Everything else, including politics, came a very poor second. Sandor Kocsis was Ferenc Puskas's partner in crime up front. His nickname of 'Golden Head' had a double meaning – blond locks and an outstanding ability in the air. His partnership with Puskas blossomed. With the mesmerising wing play of Zoltan Czibor, Kocsis received service of such distinction that he could not help but deliver. This was a front line sprinkled liberally with gold dust. In goal stood the commanding Guyula Grocsis. His swift kicks and clever distribution helped create many a Magyar opportunity. Strong and agile, he provided a formidable barrier to opposing forwards. In front of him lay a no-nonsense back line which took no prisoners. Buzansky, Lorant, Zakarias and Lantos were not defenders to be messed with. As their much heralded team-mates received all the plaudits the defence went about their jobs in a quiet, efficient and, when necessary, ruthless manner.

It was in December 1952 that the idea of a Hungary–England showdown was first raised. Both Gustav Sebes and the head of the English FA, Stanley Rous, were in Switzerland for a European football conference. The Magyars were in the midst of an epic unbeaten run. Already they had begun to be touted as potential champions in the upcoming World Cup in Switzerland in two years' time. The English, with almost unbelievable arrogance, believed that they remained masters of the world game; this despite an almighty embarrassing defeat by the minnows of the USA in the 1950 World Cup finals. These Magyars needed to be put in their place. Stanley Rous laid down the challenge to the Hungarians to take them on at Wembley. Rous declared to the Magyars' coach, 'Mr Sebes, I do think it is time that you chanced your hand and brought your lads to London.' Although highly tempted, Sebes could not possibly shake on such a proposal. For although he agreed in principle, any decision of this magnitude would have to be rubber-stamped by the higher echelons of the Hungarian Communist hierarchy. They then would need to seek approval from the Kremlin. Finally, a pensive Gustav Sebes found himself summoned to the office of Prime Minister Rakosi. Rakosi informed him that permission would be granted for such a contest, but woe betide Sebes and his team if events went awry. Defeat would not be tolerated. The consequences of that could not even afford to be contemplated. The icy snowbound wilderness of Siberia was a long way from Budapest. And so preparation was allowed to get under way. Contact was made with the English FA and a provisional date was decided upon by both countries – 25 November 1953.

Gustav Sebes travelled over to England. This was a man renowned for his thoroughness. He paid a visit to Wembley stadium. Watched only by a curious ground staff, Sebes measured out the length and width of the pitch. He cut a lonely figure in the vast expanse of this famous old ground, as he and his tape measure prepared with minute detail the derailing of an empire. Leaving nothing to chance, a meticulous Sebes checked out the bounce of the ball, and even stood trying to judge where the sun would be on the afternoon of the game. Uncle Gusti could not help but smile to himself. 'One day,' he thought, 'they are going to look back on all this and wince.' With this he set about bringing the English Bulldog to heel.

Sebes managed to acquire footballs similar to what would be used in the big match. Five in all were shipped back to Budapest. It was important that the Hungarians quickly acclimatised to this far heavier version. Once back home, Uncle Gusti ordered that all the Magyars' opponents in practice matches play in the English style. As Puskas, Bozsik, Hidegkuti and co ran amok, a feeling began to emerge amongst the Hungarians that the three lions of England were in big trouble.

The Hungarians had proved in the past that big-shot reputations meant little to them. The previous May they had travelled to Rome to take on the powerful Italians. It was a game played to inaugurate the new Olympic stadium. The Magyars had not beaten the Azzuri for 28 years. It was an embarrassing stain on their record, and one which they badly wanted to cleanse. This they would do in quite magnificent style. For on an unforgettable, warm, sultry Roman evening they put Italy to the sword with an incredible 3–0 victory. Nobody ever beat the Azzuri at home. It was a rare event if they were even held to a draw, but to be mauled in such a way! With Puskas in searing form scoring twice, and Nandor Hidegkuti completing the rout, the Magyars romped home in front of a full house of 80,000 nonplussed Italians. The team left the arena with the sound of an ovation from the Roman crowd ringing in their ears. The reputation as well as the popularity of the Hungarians was soaring. As they attempted to cross back over the border to Hungary, the Magyars found themselves recognised by Italian rail workers as their carriage came to a halt, who insisted on meeting the Hungarian footballers and showing them their new engine. Sebes at first looked on in amusement, but when he spotted Puskas driving off down the track with his new friends, he quickly lost his sense of humour. Although a man of many talents, Ferenc was no train driver! Happily no damage was done and after many embraces and signings of autographs the team continued unhindered home to Budapest.

The English press waited for the Hungarians with bated breath. The newspapers had already billed the contest as 'The Match of the Century'. Ten days before, the Magyars had their final warm-up against Sweden in Budapest. The Football Association despatched a party of officials to check on their forthcoming opponents' form. The Swedes were no better than average and the Budapest crowd were expecting blood. Nine times out of ten this would have been the case. But luckily for the Scandinavians, Gustav Sebes had insisted that the Wembley-type match ball be used for the first time in an international. His players hated it. With the home crowd baying for goals the Magyars were awful. They struggled desperately to find any resemblance of their normal play. At half-time they pleaded with Sebes to be allowed to use their normal ball. But the Hungarian coach was having none of it. 'Come Wembley you will thank me,' he told them. Sensing their worries, Uncle Gusti changed tack: 'Trust me,' he said to them, 'just trust me.' The second half saw little improvement. A 2–2 draw was the final result, with Puskas even missing a penalty. The Budapest crowd yelled derision at the captain of the Magyars. When the Swedes grabbed a last-minute equaliser, catcalls and whistles reverberated around the stadium.

The Englishmen abroad, all jolly splendid in their FA suits and ties, watched with some glee. It appeared that these much hyped Magyars were not that special after all. The proud, unbeaten home record looked under little threat from this lot. They returned to London to inform all that come 25 November, the Union Jack would still be flying high over Wembley stadium. And as for the little fat guy up front, he even missed a penalty! Matthews, Finney, Mortensen and co would pulverise these sad, shabby, highly overrated Commies. Such opinions were widely shared amongst the Hungarian newspapers. The press were livid with their team's limp showing against the Swedes. Headlines screamed that it was not worth turning up at Wembley, for they would be soundly thrashed. Sebes took this all on board. Did they think he was a fool? Outwardly he accepted the criticism whilst inside his stomach churned. For the master plan to beat the English was already laid. He was damned if he was going to show his hand so close to the big day. 'If they want to moan and groan then let them,' he thought. Uncle Gusti schemed and let others shoot their mouths off, 'for humble pie tastes nicer when other people have to eat it'. He would have his day in the sun.

En route to London the Magyars stopped off in Paris for a few days' rest and preparation. Gustav Sebes had arranged a low-key practice match against a Renault car factory team. The idea was to rid the Hungarians of the bad vibes they had felt after the Swedish débâcle. It worked, for in front of 15,000 Parisians a third-gear Magyar team smashed 15 goals past their hapless opponents. Self belief and confidence had begun to flood back into the Hungarians' play. Suddenly Wembley could not come fast enough. Sebes sensed this. The nagging thought that the effects of the Swedish game would linger in the confrontation with the English vanished completely. Uncle Gusti relaxed. His lads were back in business. On their departure from Paris, hundreds gathered at the railway station to wish them well against England.

On their arrival in London the Magyars were met by Stanley Rous. During their stay they would reside at the Cumberland Hotel. Here they would make their final preparations. Gustav Sebes sought permission from the English FA to train on the Wembley surface. Rather surprisingly this was refused. Privately this sour and unsporting act saddened and irritated the Hungarian coach. He could not understand such bad manners. He detected a lack of respect. Instead they were despatched to West London, to Loftus Road, the home of Queen's Park Rangers. Sebes had a full-strength squad to pick from. Nobody wanted to miss out. If any of the Magyars was injured they were keeping it to themselves. Only Grocsis gave cause for concern, but the keeper was renowned for being a hypochondriac. Sebes tended to listen to his goalkeeper moan about his ailing health, then play him anyway.

Come the day of the match, the Magyars awoke to a dense fog that had engulfed London. Many of the Hungarians had suffered a sleepless night due to howling gales lashing their windows. Around 9 a.m. a tired and bleary-eyed group of footballers gathered together in the hotel foyer. They were in mixed mood. Some were excited about the day's events, others rather pensive about what lay ahead. Sebes appeared armed with an abundance of diagrams. He and his assistant, Guyula Mandi, ushered the lads into a private room. It was time to lay down exactly what was expected of them on this most momentous of days. He asked for quiet. When everyone was settled he began. 'England are great opponents,' he declared, 'but they can be defeated.' He spoke first to his wingers, Budai and Czibor. 'Attack their defenders, wear them down, but never forget defence is an essential part of your job. You must get back to cover.' Sebes spokes about the dangers of the only Englishman deemed by the Magyars capable of winning a place amongst their ranks. 'Track Stanley Matthews wherever he roams,' warned Sebes. 'Do not let him out of your sight.'

To Nandor Hidegkuti, the man who was to almost single-handedly destroy English football, Uncle Gusti spoke in great detail of how he must start in traditional mode, but then move deep and set up attacks from the middle of the pitch. 'This will confuse the English,' said Sebes, with possibly the understatement of the decade! 'Josef Bozsik!' Sebes's eyes met Bozsik's and a smile broke out on the face of the coach's favourite. 'Your job will not be easy, Josef, although the English will pay less attention to you than to our forwards. You must make every effort to break and shoot for goal, but never forget, defence is also an important part of your task.' Bozsik listened intently as Sebes explained his role to him. He had total respect and huge fondness for the old man. He had no intention of letting him down. For he and his team-mates knew of the rash promise made to Rakosi by their coach. England would be beaten, and they would be beaten well.

For two hours Gustav Sebes spoke about the weaknesses of the English and of how the Magyars could take advantage of them. At times his excitement threatened to overwhelm him as he talked of the importance of victory, and of how it could be achieved. Watching from the back was Ferenc Puskas and the president of the Hungarian FA, Sandor Barcs. Finally, when Uncle Gusti wrapped up the proceedings, Puskas turned to his president and asked him if he had understood a word of what Sebes had been saying. 'No,' said Barcs. 'Neither did I,' replied Puskas, 'neither did I!' The last words of the tactical conference were to be spoken by Josef Bozsik. He waited until Sebes had finished and in a manner that moved all present said quietly, 'Fear not, Uncle Gusti, for that is how it is going to be. We will not let you down.' The Magyar forward had in his own way lit the flame that was set to engulf the English.

Around midday the Hungarians boarded the coach that was to take them to Wembley. The day had brightened with the sun breaking through. The Magyars were tense, their faces etched with concentration. A police motorcycle set off in front of them and they were on their way to the Twin Towers. Along the route some took up a rather tuneless version of the Hungarian national anthem. Others sang old country folk songs, anything just to help them relax. Puskas sat next to Bozsik. The two friends didn't talk. Their minds were focused intently on the game. As they approached the stadium, the Magyars gazed out of the coach windows at the thousands of English supporters winding their way to the ground. From around the country they had arrived in droves. The opportunity of seeing the much vaunted Hungarians with their own eyes was just too good to miss. For most, players such as Ferenc Pushas existed only as grainy images on Pathé newsreels. It was difficult to appreciate their genius when encased in the drab and dreary Pathé newsreels. Happily these black and white pictures would soon come to life in stunning Technicolor.

Come 1.15 p.m. and 100,000 people had crammed into Wembley. The Royal Air Force marching band was busy striding across the famous turf, all glitter and sparkling uniforms as they performed to a huge, appreciative audience. Tension was beginning to rise. On their arrival the Hungarians had turned down a request to inspect the pitch. They had instead headed straight for their dressing-room. The defender Josef Zakarias stated rather ominously in earshot of a group of nearby journalists, 'Who is interested in seeing the operating theatre before the operation?' With this he stalked off to rejoin his team-mates. When these comments were translated for the nearby English newspapermen they appeared to find them quite hilarious. Others who knew better felt a cold shiver run down their spine.

Once inside their inner sanctum the Magyars steadied themselves. Sebes sensed a confidence about his team. The talking and preparations were complete. He could do nothing more. Now it was down to the players. Sandor Kocsis decided to lighten the atmosphere. He challenged his fellow

Magyar Puskas to a duel. Kocsis claimed that he could keep the ball up in the air 100 times. The captain of Hungary took him up. A considerable amount of cash was bet, and the contest began. On reaching 98, Kocsis appeared a certainty to triumph. In his moment of glory, however, Zoltan Czibor lunged towards him to send the ball spinning away. The Hungarians fell about laughing. Happily Sandor Kocsis saw the funny side, whilst Puskas paid up anyway. The captain decided to stretch his legs and soak up the atmosphere in the Wembley tunnel. Outside the English dressing-room he spotted the diminutive figure of Blackpool's Ernie Taylor. Noticing Ernie's size, Puskas headed off back to his team-mates to announce with a huge grin on his face, 'We are going to be all right today, lads, they have someone playing who is even smaller than me!' On hearing this the Magyars collapsed again into hysterical laughter. If the Hungarians were nervous at facing such supposedly daunting opponents they were doing a fine job of hiding it.

Back in Budapest and across Hungary, people huddled in groups around their radios waiting for battle to commence. Electricians had been kept busy all week setting up outside broadcasting transmitters for the unfortunates who had to work. Come kick-off the entire country would come to a standstill, and the only voice heard would be the excitable tones of the radio commentator George Szepesi. Szepesi was in his own way as big a star in Hungary as any of the Magyars. Now he prepared to bring life to the motherland's finest hour. Directed to his commentary berth Szepesi felt his stomach churning. Sebes and the players were all close friends. He prayed for the day to go well.

As the time approached 2 p.m. the referee blew his whistle to signal for the players to line up in the tunnel. On sizing up the Magyars alongside him, the English captain, Billy Wright, appeared shocked at the state of their kit. He looked in disbelief at their low-cut boots in comparison to the footwear worn by the home team. He could not help but smile. Turning to his centre-forward Stan Mortensen, Wright said quietly, 'We are going to be all right here today, Stan. Look at them, they have not even got any decent kit!' Ninety minutes on and Billy Wright, captain of Wolves and England, was to have changed his opinion drastically. For the English would not be all right. They were about to be slaughtered.

A HUNGARIAN RHAPSODY

Seconds before kick-off, Ferenc Puskas flicked the ball onto his left foot and rolled it up the length of his leg. Ever the showman, the Hungarian captain flipped it onto his back heel and clipped it off to a smiling Nandor Hidegkuti. Not wanting to be outdone by his fellow Magyar, Hidegkuti went on to perform his own little party trick. There were gasps from the Wembley crowd. It was but a mere aperitif. There would be no excuses for England if events were to go awry. For 90 years the unbeaten home record had stood. Others had become tired of hearing of their alleged invincibility. The English were playing with the true facts. For had not the Republic of Ireland beaten them only a few years before? They had claimed their record was still intact by stating that Eire was a British team. This attitude irked other countries who itched to see them knocked off their arrogant perch.

Well, Hungary was not British. There would and could be no excuses if Puskas and the Magyars handed them a defeat on their precious home turf. There was only one way to finish off a legend. That was to kill it dead, once and for all. The age of the British Empire was drawing to its close. Hungary would do their bit to hurry it along. The year 1953 would see the coronation of Queen Elizabeth II, Gordon Richards winning the Derby, and New Zealander Sir Edmund Hillary scaling Mount Everest. Defeat by the Hungarians was unthinkable. The footballers of this small island prepared once more to repel 'Johnny Foreigner'. This time, however, it would be different.

At the first whistle Nandor Hidegkuti, as planned, dropped deep into midfield. The Magyars flitted like red ghosts into their assigned positions. The centre-half allocated to mark Hidegkuti was Blackpool's centre-half Harry Johnston. Immediately Johnston was confused. Should he stay in his position or should he follow the Hungarian up the field? Before he had time to ponder the problem, Bozsik set up Hidegkuti to lash home a tremendous drive from 25 yards. Not 90 seconds on the clock and the Magyars had first blood. England wobbled as Hungary swarmed all over them. With their five forwards effortlessly interchanging positions, they stormed the bastion of English football. The Magyar style of lightning one-twos and blistering, accurate long balls had the home side chasing shadows. A second goal quickly came with magical approach work from Bozsik and Puskas setting up Hidegkuti again to smash past the helpless England goalkeeper Gil Merrick. England were in tatters. Luckily the Dutch referee, Leo Horn, appeared to take pity on them and disallowed Hidegkuti's strike, much to the annoyance of the bewildered Magyars.

It mattered little. Czibor, Bozsik, Kocsis, Budai, Puskas and the ghosting Hidegkuti continued to press forward. And yet it was the home side who struck next. Breaking out from the onslaught, Sewell levelled the proceedings in the 14th minute. His low shot beat a diving Grocsis: 1–1. From being toyed with for the first quarter of an hour the English had grabbed a fine equaliser. With the home crowd roaring their side on, the three lions were back in the game. Five minutes later Hungary were back in front. Refusing to panic and sticking to their battle plan, they charged. Ferenc Puskas, with his deft left peg, caressed a pass that sent Zoltan Czibor racing down Wembley's wide-open spaces. From Czibor the ball flew to the distinctive blond head of Sandor Kocsis. His astute flick to the deadly feet of Nandor Hidegkuti could have only one consequence. With great skill Hidegkuti steered his shot into the English goal. Harry Johnston was in the midst of a nightmare. His decision to follow his man wherever he roamed had resulted in huge gaps which the Magyars exploited with relish. He implored his captain for advice on how to deal with his tormentor. But Wright had his own problems. All across the pitch his team were being overrun. Gustav Sebes looked on with huge pride. His lads were doing him proud. The Magyars were playing at their peak. From all angles Hungarians were rampaging forward with victory in their eyes. Shots rained down on Gil Merrick from every conceivable and, indeed, inconceivable position. More goals appeared a certainty. However, the one which followed would almost defy description; and indeed belief.

THAT GOAL

On 25 minutes one of the great footballing images of the twentieth century occurred. With one piece of magic from his illustrious armoury, Ferenc Puskas joined football's immortals. Receiving the ball on the English six-yard line, he dragged it clear from a hurtling Billy Wright and smashed an unbelievable rising shot into the net. It was an outrageous piece of sublime skill from the Hungarian which captivated the Wembley crowd. Down the other end of the pitch, behind Grocsis's goal, the Magyar reserves danced a jig of delight at seeing their captain score such a momentous goal. This slightly bulky, some would say podgy, figure with his oily hair plastered down his head was a most unlikely looking athlete. But in the blink of an eye Ferenc Puskas had opened a million wide. Commentating on the game for BBC television was Kenneth Wolstenholme. His immediate reaction to Puskas's moment of wizardry summed up the sheer amazement of everyone present: 'My goodness!' shouted the startled Wolstenholme. 'If he can do tricks like that, we ought to have him on at the music hall!'

The lesson continued. With Wembley still buzzing from Puskas's work of art, the Magyars cut loose and went straight for the English jugular. Minutes later, Ferenc Puskas scored again. Josef Bozsik, happily torturing England with his devastating thrusts from midfield, set up his best friend, who effortlessly flicked a shot with his heel past the hapless Merrick. His heel! Not 30 minutes had passed and the home side resembled an army in disorganised, chaotic retreat. With whiplash precision and delightful ease the Magyars pinged the ball around, amongst, and even, when required, over the top of the chasing English. It was a massacre.

Minutes before half-time England rallied; and Stan Mortensen roared through the Hungarian rearguard and crashed in a fine shot to give the scoreline a more respectable appearance. A typical bullish effort from the barnstorming Mortensen which gave heart for the second half. The whistle blew for the end of the first period. Coming off the pitch the English discussed animatedly how to deal with the tactics employed by the wily Hungarians. In the dressing-room the debate raged on. 'Do I go with him or should I stay?' implored a clearly flustered Harry Johnston, but neither his captain nor indeed his manager, Walter Winterbottom, could supply him with a sufficiently good answer. For the truth was they simply did not have a clue. This was uncharted territory for the three lions. The Magyars had led them down a road which they had never been down before. It was a strange world inhabited by red dervishes that sprang gleefully amongst them.

Meanwhile, across the corridor, the Hungarians were in seventh heaven. Gustav Sebes urged his lads to keep playing the same way and victory would be theirs. The goalkeeper Grocsis was jokingly warned by his forwards that if he let any more goals in they would beat him up after the match! Puskas stood up and declared, 'Come on, we've got them. Just keep going, relax, play your normal game, and by God we've got them!' Sebes sounded a note of warning. 'The English will never give up,' he said. 'It is not in their nature. Be wary, do not get complacent.' Uncle Gusti had little need to worry. For the unbeaten home record of the English would finally be put to rest shortly into the second half. A shell-shocked Gil Merrick watched in dismay as a thunderous shot by the magnificent Bozsik whistled past him to make it 5–2. Shortly after, Nandor Hidegkuti completed a grand hat trick when he smashed home from an incredibly accurate Puskas-volleyed pass. In the shadow of the Twin Towers the Magyars were rewriting history. It was a sumptuous performance. Hungary had outclassed, out-thought and outmanoeuvred a technically inept home team who, though bristling with effort and determination, were found sadly lacking in finesse. With a full half-hour left to play the visitors decided it was time to have some fun. Out came the party hats as the Magyars took it in turns to show off their dazzling skills.

As the goal tally mounted, mayhem reigned in the Wembley commentary box. George Szepesi was in a state of euphoria. He, like his fellow Hungarians on the field, had the English journalists in raptures. Szepesi's unashamedly patriotic way of greeting every Magyar goal, 'Goal. Goal. Goal. Goallll!' had colleagues in the press area smiling widely. At one stage a supporter offered the breathless Szepesi a small glass of whisky from his flask, encouraging this excitable and hugely affable Hungarian to even higher levels of euphoria. It was all great fun. For despite seeing their side cut to ribbons on the football pitch, the home fans realised they were in the presence of something special.

Back home in the motherland people went to great lengths to keep up with their lads' battle with the English. Miners deep in the bowels of the earth were kept in touch by having the constantly changing scoreline scrawled onto coal buckets, which were then lowered down towards them. The streets of Budapest lay bare and still. Trams stood empty, whilst shops and cinemas had shut down for the afternoon. All Hungarians listened in disbelief to Szepesi's awe-inspiring commentary, as he painted pictures of Puskas, Bozsik and Hidegkuti tearing England to pieces. With a job well done, and their point proved, the Magyars took their foot off the gas. Around the stadium spontaneous applause rang out in tribute to their performance. With time running out, Grocsis risked a beating in the dressing-room when he brought Mortensen down and conceded a penalty. Up stepped Alf Ramsey of Ipswich Town to lower the deficit, if not the humiliation. For as Puskas put it in his own inimitable way after the match, 'We murdered them. We should have scored ten.' The final whistle was the sign for the whole ground to rise as one and salute these extraordinary Hungarian footballers. The English fans cheered them as if they were their own.

Puskas and his team took the acclaim from the centre circle. They bade farewell to a truly appreciative audience. These Magyars were gifts from the footballing gods, forever to be cherished and respected. Across Hungary the 6–3 scoreline was greeted with unreserved joy and elation. The sensational news of their team's thrashing of the English spread like wildfire across the countryside. In every village and town parties were held in their honour. Like Christmas and New Year's Eve rolled into one the Hungarians indulged and opened up the wine caskets. There was to be many a sore head in Hungary the following day.

Events following the final whistle are forever ingrained in the soul of every Hungarian football fan. Intent on congratulating his fellow countrymen on a wonderful victory, George Szepesi set off for the dressing-room. Entering, the sight which confronted him was one which stayed with Szepesi for the rest of his life. For expecting to find the Magyars celebrating, instead the scene was one of 11 footballers sitting quietly and totally exhausted. The only sound was a spluttered cough, or the rattle of studs on a concrete floor. The Hungarians themselves were finding it almost impossible to come to terms with their momentous achievement. Szepesi gazed around at the players' faces. To a man they looked drained of all energy. He watched in silent admiration as Nandor Hidegkuti kissed both his boots. Bozsik sat with his head in his hands. Touched by this, Szepesi decided this was not the time for festivity and quietly slid back out the door. Shortly after the sound of the Hungarian national anthem was heard from the direction of the Magyars' changing-room. With tears of pride falling down his cheeks, Szepesi decided to head onto the Wembley turf. Only the groundsman and his assistants remained. He walked over to the spot where Ferenc Puskas had sent Billy Wright spinning. Gazing around at the vast, now-empty terraces, Szepesi thought to himself that they should place a memorial here on this exact spot. It should read: This is where Hungary defeated England.

On rushing to congratulate his players, Sandor Barcs got himself lost! By accident he stumbled into the English dressing-room. On spotting Barcs, Billy Wright jumped up out of the players' bath and walked over to shake his hand. 'I congratulate you, Mr President,' said a dripping wet England captain. 'You have a wonderful team.' Barcs was touched by such sportsmanship, especially from a man like Wright who had suffered more than any at the hands of the Magyars. Billy Wright would later say, 'They were not just a cut above us, they were miles above us. We did our best and worked hard, but they were truly fabulous. It was a real privilege to play against them.' Stanley Matthews, long after, spoke in similar vein: 'They were by far the best team I ever played against,' he declared. 'That most wonderful Hungarian team – Puskas, Hidegkuti and those fantastic team-mates. They were the best ever.' The newspapers mirrored the admiration of the English players. They heaped praise on this marvellous team from behind the Iron Curtain. It was they who gave the nickname of 'Galloping Major' to Ferenc Puskas, a near-perfect description of this Napoleonic figure who had led the assault which finally breached the walls of English football.

The following day a delightful event occurred back at the Cumberland Hotel, where the Hungarians were recovering from over-indulgence at the post-match banquet. Stanley Rous arrived on the doorstep with a suitcase literally stuffed full of cash. His intentions were honourable. Armed with the takings from the previous day's game, he wished only to reward the Magyars for their splendid showing. He was ushered through to a private reception room, where waiting to greet him was the bemused figure of Gustav Sebes. Also present were George Szepesi and Sandor Barcs. The head of the English FA shook the hands of all present and explained to Sebes the purpose of his visit. Uncle Gusti was horrified! There was no way on earth he could accept

the money. He and his Magyars were amateurs. It would go against everything
they believed in if he accepted this generous offer. Rous turned to the
president, Sandor Barcs, but the reply was the same. Szepesi looked on wide-
eyed as his fellow Hungarians refused even a penny from the Englishman. All
Sebes asked was that England agree to a return match in Budapest the
following year. This staggered Rous. For after seeing his team humbled out on
the football pitch, he himself felt humble. He agreed wholeheartedly to Sebes's
request for a rematch, happily oblivious to what waited on the banks of the
Blue Danube.

It was a jubilant Hungarian party which boarded the train at Victoria
Station to begin the long journey home. Eight thousand congratulatory
telegrams had been sent to them. Waiting to wave them off were hundreds of
English supporters. As the train departed a huge cheer went up from the
crowds. The players waved back at the well-wishers. As he watched his lads
bask in the glory of their performance, Gustav Sebes felt enormous pride. The
pressure placed upon him by Rakosi to guarantee victory had never managed
to intimidate his team. As Josef Bozsik had promised beforehand, they had
not let him down.

Uncle Gusti watched as Ferenc Puskas foraged joyfully through the heaps
of telegrams. His thoughts returned to the Sweden game when his captain had
been pilloried and made a scapegoat for the Magyars' inept performance by
the Hungarian newspapers. He hoped that the same journalists who had
enjoyed twisting the knife deep on that occasion were now choking on their
humble pie. It was not in Gustav Sebes's nature to gloat. But the notion of
these characters having to backtrack on their spiteful words filled him with
glee.

The Magyars travelled to Paris where once more they were mobbed. It
appeared that the whole of Paris had turned out to applaud their epic win.
Whilst there the Hungarian party went to see the famous Parisian show, *Folies
Bergère*. After settling into their seats whispers began to echo around the
packed theatre. Their presence had been noted. Across the aisles people began
to stand and applaud the Magyars. The names of the players were shouted by
the cheering French – Puskas! Hidegkuti! Bozsik! The Hungarians were
invited to go up on stage and take a bow. They waved sheepishly at their
admirers. All looked slightly embarrassed, except for Puskas, who basked in
the adulation, milking the moment for all it was worth.

Finally they began the last part of their journey home to Budapest. What
awaited them as they crossed the Austro–Hungarian border was nothing short
of remarkable. For at every station en route to the capital, thousands of their
countryfolk waited impatiently to greet the returning heroes. The first port of

call was a tiny town called Hegyeshalom. Here countless Hungarians had gathered, eager to be amongst the first to glimpse a sight of the 'Golden Squad'. As the train carrying the Magyars appeared the local brass band began to play the national anthem. Scenes of hysteria awaited Gustav Sebes and his men. They found themselves submerged under a tidal wave of goodwill. Flowers and gifts were thrown. It was the same everywhere. At Gyor, Komarom and Tatabanya, the Magyars looked on in astonishment at the tremendous receptions. However, all would pale into insignificance compared with what awaited them in Budapest.

A hundred thousand citizens awaited the return of the Magyars. People went to incredible lengths to secure the best vantage points. Many clung grimly to the top of lamp posts. Others sat precariously on tree branches. Keleti railway station found itself under siege. As the train appeared the sense of excitement grew. The order was given to begin playing the anthem. When the train finally came to a halt the crowds exploded with joy! The highly impressive stained-glass roof of the station threatened to shatter into a thousand pieces with the noise that greeted the return of Budapest's favourite sons. The Magyars were back amongst their own. As they disembarked the footballers found themselves mobbed, and they quickly vanished under a flurry of backslapping and over-enthusiastic bear-hugs.

Families and friends were not allowed to be the first to welcome Puskas and his men home. That honour belonged to Communist party officials and members of the Hungarian FA. This was a photo opportunity that these men were prepared to die for. Puskas and Hidegkuti were among the favourites embraced and hailed as heroes of the motherland. Many a photograph was taken of ageing overweight men in shabby grey suits with their arms wrapped tightly around Magyar footballers. These would appear on the front page of every Hungarian newspaper the following morning. This was a wonderful opportunity to extol the virtues of the Communist endeavour. Propaganda did not come any better than this. Moscow would be delighted.

Two days later, in memory of Hungary's finest sporting hour, the Magyars were handed the motherland's highest honour. The Order of Merit was awarded collectively to the team. Under dazzling photo floodlights this moment was captured forever. Amidst the imperial surroundings of the Hungarian Parliament building, Prime Minister Matyos Rakosi bestowed on Ferenc Puskas the honorary title of major in his country's army. Rakosi treated the Hungarian footballers like long-lost brothers, but the irony of the situation was not lost on the Magyars, for they knew that if they had been beaten by England, their return to home soil would not have been such a good experience. As Rakosi praised their endeavours to the hilt, Gustav Sebes remembered vividly his Prime Minister's veiled threat. Expectations for his team had now reached such proportions that his fellow countrymen considered them unbeatable. But Uncle Gusti knew well that this was not the case. One day his side would be beaten, and he greatly feared the consequences.

But that was a worry for the future. Right now he would enjoy the team's success. For the Hungarians had undertaken the long journey to London in the hope of extinguishing a myth. Unbeknown to them, in doing so they had created their own legend. The systematic destruction of the English on that never-to-be-forgotten November afternoon had been simply awesome. Puskas and his cohorts had strode into Wembley stadium and succeeded beyond all their expectations. Hat Harom, 6–3. Here endeth the lesson.

3

THE MAGYARS' LAST STAND

HUNGARY v WEST GERMANY

1954 WORLD CUP FINAL

Every dream must end. Gustav Sebes pondered this thought as he watched his captain, Ferenc Puskas, complete a medical check on his injured ankle. The signs were good. Although Sebes sensed Puskas was putting on somewhat of a brave show it appeared that Hungary's favourite son would be fit to take on the Germans in the World Cup final. He, the doctor and the other coaches all agreed it was a gamble worth taking. Sebes desperately wanted Puskas back to renew his deadly partnership with Sandor Kocsis. For 'Golden Head' was showing signs of fatigue. The two matches against the South American giants of Brazil and Uruguay had drained much from the centre-forward. Although magnificent in both encounters Kocsis had received one hell of a pounding, and was in need of support.

His fellow Hungarians waited eagerly to hear if their captain would be fit to help them in the showdown against the hated Germans. As Puskas appeared from the treatment room he gave his best friend Josef Bozsik a knowing wink. The grin on his face showed that it was good news. Bozsik ran to embrace his life-long companion. Inseparable since the age of three, they would now prepare together for the biggest match of their young lives. It would mean handing back the captaincy, but this mattered little to Josef Bozsik. To have his friend back alongside him meant so much more. For Puskas, seeing his team-mates having to fight and overcome the challenge of the Brazilians and the Uruguayans without him had been too painful for words. His desire to rejoin the Magyars' crusade for glory was such that he would be willing to go through any pain barrier to achieve it. He had already missed too much. It was time to step back in.

The Hungarians stood on the brink of their finest hour. In 1938 they had reached the final only to lose, albeit highly controversially, to an Azzuri side playing in Paris under the threat of death from the Fascist dictator Benito

Mussolini. A telegram with the words 'win or die' had arrived in the Italians' dressing-room only minutes before the match. Against such desperate foes the Hungarians not surprisingly went down by four goals to two. But in the summer of 1954 they were convinced their time had come. Already the Magyars had slaughtered their fellow finalists 8–3 in the qualifying rounds. The West Germans' cynical taking-out of Puskas in that particular game had left a foul taste in Hungarians' mouths. A whiff of revenge was in the air, not only for their captain, but for events a decade before which had absolutely nothing to do with football. During the war many Hungarians had suffered intolerably under Adolf Hitler's sadistic regime. They had neither forgiven nor forgotten what they were forced to endure. The Jewish population of Hungary had been all but exterminated under German occupation. Up to 750,000 men, women and children had been shipped out en masse to meet their fate in the death camps of Auschwitz and Belsen. The frightful memory of Hungarian Jews being forced to wear the yellow star of David on their arms on the streets of Budapest had cut deep. Now, before the eyes of a watching world, the Magyars would attempt in their own small way to seek retribution. It was sadly beyond them to bring back the dead, but if the day went well, they intended to humiliate the Germans.

Gustav Sebes did not underestimate the threat the West Germans posed, but he in no way feared them. He knew well of Herberger's tactical ploy of saving his best hand for the final. Players would come in who had not featured when the Magyars had beaten the Germans earlier in the competition. Sebes admired his brave counterpart. Any man who attempted the gamble that Herberger had undertaken deserved to be respected. But there was something about this cunning German that worried Uncle Gusti. He appeared lucky, and this when playing on such a stage was a very dangerous weapon. The Magyars had gone 42 games unbeaten. They stood one game away from immortality. Was it really asking too much for just one more victory? Logically there was little for Sebes to be concerned about. On paper Hungary were in a different class to the Germans. And yet . . .

They called it the crazy folly of a foolhardy man. A lunatic scheme dreamt up by a madman. The critics declared that it was not so much dancing close to the fire, but more akin to dancing naked through the flames. Sepp Herberger had embarked on the biggest gamble of his career. He and his assistant Helmut Schoen had studied the film of the Magyars running amok at Wembley until it was almost worn out. The plan was relatively simple. After having been drawn against the Magyars in the qualifying rounds the German manager saw his chance. Knowing that they had the beating of the other danger in the group, Turkey, he would purposely play a weakened line-up against the all-conquering Hungarians, thus keeping his strongest team for a possible showdown with the Magyars later in the competition. It proved a painful, bloody experience. With a team minus half of its regulars, West Germany found themselves the victims of a rampant Hungarian forward line which delighted in smashing a staggering total of eight goals past them. As each one slammed into the back of the net Herr Herberger winced. He had expected defeat, but not wanton slaughter. The Hungarians had seemed almost possessed in their eagerness; a willingness tinged with memories of events past. There had been one bright spot for the West Germans, though, for they managed to do Puskas.

Whether the taking out of Ferenc Puskas was pre-planned is argued over even today. From the opening whistle the Major had been subjected to a series of disgraceful challenges by the German defenders. In what seemed an orchestrated campaign to bring the Hungarian hero to earth, the tackles multiplied. Finally he was had. The tall, blond centre-half Werner Liebrich scythed Ferenc Puskas with a foul made long after the ball had gone. Sebes and the rest of the Hungarian bench ran to the touchline, enraged at the treatment of their fellow Magyar. The team doctor, Lazlo Kreisz, sprinted over to inspect the damage inflicted on the sprawling Puskas. It was bad. Kreisz signalled to Sebes that there was no way that he could continue. The Major's ankle was badly swollen, and the worst fears of all Hungarians were confirmed when shortly after the final whistle it emerged from the Magyar camp that he was almost certainly out of the competition.

Puskas was furious. He accused the Germans of deliberately setting out to eliminate him from the tournament. Years later he would mellow in his opinion, but at the time he felt bitter. There was, however, a deeper, darker whisper that involved West Germany. Throughout the competition rumours abounded that whatever the German trainer put in his sponge it most definitely was not water. The fitness level of Herberger's team astounded all who watched them. They appeared almost superhuman. Whether this was achieved through legal methods was shrouded in doubt.

It was a full-strength West German team which lined up against Turkey in the decisive play-off. The Germans romped home by seven goals to two. Much to the relief of Sepp Herberger, his version of Russian roulette had paid off. It was a joyful man who hugged his players at the end of the game. To play with a loaded gun, spin the barrel, pull the trigger and still be standing showed he had nerve, and plenty of it. The first phase of the master plan was complete. West Germany would now go forward to play Yugoslavia in the quarter-finals. Herr Herberger began silently to fancy his team's chances. He knew well that somewhere over the other side of the hill the Hungarians lay in wait. If the World Cup were to be won this wily old crow realised that the Magyars would have to be overcome. There would lie the ultimate challenge

The final was made with considerable ease. The Yugoslavians were despatched 2–0, whilst in the semi-final a remarkable 6–1 drubbing of an uninterested Austria put them through at a canter. The routing of the Austrians saw for the first time the Germans lay down their marker as potential world champions. It was a result which startled many people, but not Gustav Sebes. His high opinion of Herberger had proved correct. This was a worthy opponent.

The earlier story regarding Ferenc Puskas's ankle injury had proved untrue. The Major's return to action was greeted with unreserved joy when it was announced back home. Hungary stood ready to hail the greatest day in her history. Defeat was unthinkable. Huge street parties were planned for as soon as the final whistle sounded. Any feelings of uncertainty had been dispelled when the exuberant broadcaster George Szepesi had declared over the radio that Ferenc Puskas was back to lead the team to glory. And how they deserved it! The abundance of skill, heart and determination they had shown in reaching the final had at times reduced him to tears during his commentaries. Szepesi was convinced that come the end of the match against the Germans, he would be broadcasting on a momentous victory for the motherland.

On the day of the final in Berne, the Hungarians awoke after an uncomfortable night. A Swiss brass band had performed until three o'clock in the morning, keeping the Magyars awake. Sebes had stormed down to demand that the band cease playing. But his plea fell on deaf ears. From their hotel windows the bleary-eyed Magyars watched as their manager fought their corner, only to be met with looks of derision from people who seemed, some thought, to be acting under orders. Finally Sebes prevailed and they managed to grab a few hours' sleep. Around midday Gustav Sebes sent his players back up to their rooms to get some more rest, but almost on cue the brass band magically reappeared. The Magyars gave up.

Arriving at the stadium, the Hungarians couldn't believe the scenes that awaited them. Thousands of people stood milling around, many desperate to get hold of tickets. The Swiss police were proving hopeless at coping as events threatened to spiral out of control. The Magyar coach was surrounded by hordes of German supporters who were letting the Hungarians know exactly what they thought of them. An infuriated Puskas was quick to reply and from him and his team-mates gestures and comments were hurled back. The Magyars were taking no rubbish from these people. They had already seen enough of their antics to last a lifetime. This time the war would be fought on the level platform of a football field. No guns, no gas chambers, no yellow stars.

The ever-efficient Germans had arrived early, and were already busy preparing themselves for the task ahead. Back outside, the Magyars had left the coach and were struggling to make progress through the throng into the stadium. Gustav Sebes was getting worried that one of his players would be injured. It would only take a clumsy or, indeed, well-placed kick and disaster would be upon them. The authorities had totally lost control. As if things weren't bad enough, as the Magyars finally made it through to the entrance, they found their way blocked by burly Swiss soldiers. Quite inexplicably the guards refused to believe a by now frantic Sebes when he explained who they were! It was all turning into a farce. Suddenly panicking, one of the soldiers raised his rifle butt and smashed Gustav Sebes to the ground. Outraged at seeing the old man attacked, the Hungarian players surged forward. It was only the swift intervention of a FIFA official which prevented further chaos, and even bloodshed. On recognising the Magyars he quickly ushered them through the gates and relative peace was restored. A dazed and staggering Uncle Gusti was helped by his players to the dressing-room. This was no way to prepare for a World Cup final.

The rain was crashing down in torrents. The terraces of the Wankdorf stadium swarmed with thousands of drenched German supporters. The short distance which separates the two countries meant close to 30,000 Germans had made the journey to cheer on their team. The black, red and yellow tricolour enveloped most of the stadium. The Hungarians fought steadfastly to make themselves heard amongst fanatical backing for the West German team. In the shadow of the snow-capped peaks of the Alps, with dark, gloomy clouds looming overhead, the two teams came into view. In front of 60,000 people Ferenc Puskas and Fritz Walter led their respective countries out of the tunnel and onto the pitch. Both sets of players lined up for the national anthems. Already they looked soaked to the skin. With the ceremonies completed, Hungary and West Germany broke away to begin their short warm-up. Puskas and Walter shook hands in the centre circle. They exchanged pennants. The English referee, Bill Ling, flicked the coin which was to land in the Magyars' favour. The Hungarian captain decided to hand the Germans the privilege of kicking off the World Cup final. The formalities now complete, it was time for the Magyars' last stand.

The game began at a frantic pace. Herberger had sent his men out with instructions not to let the Hungarians settle, to get in amongst them. An early corner was gained as West Germany took the game to their illustrious opponents. The opening moments saw possession changing hands constantly. On five minutes Josef Bozsik won the ball in the centre circle and sent Sandor Kocsis into the penalty area. Golden Head's early strike was fumbled badly by the German goalkeeper Turek. He was forced to look on in horror as the ball fell loose to a lurking Ferenc Puskas. From eight yards out Puskas smashed it low into the goal. The Hungarians had the start they had craved. On the touchline the Magyars came flying off the bench in celebration of their captain's early strike. Gustav Sebes's decision to recall Puskas had been seen to be vindicated. Two minutes later, an awful mix-up between left-back Kohlmeyer and his keeper let in Zoltan Czibor to stab home from close range. The Germans were in tatters. Not eight minutes showing on the stadium clock and they looked on the verge of another monumental hiding. Turek punched the turf in despair. His defenders glared at him but said nothing. The ball was booted back upfield for the game to restart. Herberger looked glum. This was turning into a nightmare for the Germans.

As for the Hungarians, they appeared set for another rout. The mountain that West Germany now had to climb would be as high as the Apennine peaks that towered majestically above them. But this was a resilient bunch. It simply was not in their nature to give up. The captain and midfield playmaker Fritz Walter led the comeback. Inspired by their captain, the Germans swept forward. Minutes later they halved the deficit. The ever-dangerous forward, Rahn, smashed a low cross which was misjudged by a retreating Zakarias, who was left at the mercy of an oncoming Morlock: 2–1.

There was to be no 8–3 this day. On 18 minutes, with the Germans pressing hard, a corner was earned. From Fritz Walter's incoming cross a badly blundering Grocsis in the Hungarian goal was left panic stricken as Helmut Rahn thundered a close-range equaliser into the Magyar goal. German supporters roared out in relief at being back in the contest. Gustav Sebes's admiration of West Germany's comeback was tinged with feelings of deep suspicion. The power, pace and determination of the Germans astounded him. Never had he seen such phenomenal stamina in a team. They appeared almost possessed as they ran around like demons. Sebes motioned to his players to concentrate on the game as they gestured at him with looks of incredulity at their opponents' staying power. But still the Magyars created chances. Kocsis, with a marvellous flying header, brought a superb save out of Turek. Nandor Hidegkuti came close to putting his country back in front when he let fly with a low drive which rebounded off the inside of the German post. It was stirring stuff. West Germany refused to lie down. A frightful mistake by Grocsis almost let in Rahn, but his effort was cleared. As the half-time whistle blew both teams were going hell for leather for that third goal. This was a World Cup final to tell your grandchildren about.

In the German dressing-room a film crew pushed upon Fritz Walter a young Swiss boy intent on getting the captain's autograph. Herberger urged his captain to sign the little brat's piece of paper, to let them get on with planning their tactics for the second half. The cameramen were working on behalf of FIFA. Their job was to capture for posterity the events of the 1954 World Cup final. Eventually the crew departed. Across the way the Hungarians complained bitterly about the events that had befallen them. Ferenc Puskas was scathing in his comments about the referee. Bill Ling had been officiating when the two sides had come together in the qualifying rounds. Not surprisingly, Puskas was still bitter about the protection handed out to him back then. But here he had little reason to complain, for his marker, Horst Ekel, had hounded him incessantly but fairly.

Gustav Sebes preached to his players the importance of not losing heart, and to keep their attacking shape. For as sure as night follows day they would score again. Deep inside, a nagging feeling told him that this day would end in disaster, but he dared not let this show. Only God knew how much he loved this team. These were his lads. Sebes worried greatly about what would become of them if events went awry here in Switzerland. The Hungary of 1954 was no place for fallen heroes. These were troubled times. Moscow required winners. Anything else would be deemed absolute failure, and the price for that was high.

The Magyars, however, began the second half with all guns blazing. Turek was playing the game of his life. Twice he denied Ferenc Puskas, throwing himself at the captain's feet to prevent certain goals. When the German keeper was beaten, Kohlmeyer came to his team-mate's aid by clearing Josef Toth's shot off the goal-line. Further chances came and went. Toth crossed superbly for Sandor Kocsis to smash a superb header against the crossbar, whilst Zoltan Czibor became another victim of the magnificent Turek as he dived bravely at the Magyar's feet.

Ever so slowly, the Germans weathered the storm. Orchestrated by the skilful prompting of Fritz Walter, they began to create opportunities of their own. Rahn escaped from a sagging Hungarian rearguard and let fly a crashing drive which Grocsis was forced to turn round the post. The sight of the Magyars visibly tiring only served to increase morale amongst the West Germans. The fitness level of their players, which had epitomised their performances throughout, showed no signs of waning. And yet, with 12 minutes remaining, Nandor Hidegkuti should have buried them, once and for all. Czibor unleashed a ferocious shot which Turek found impossible to hold. He was forced to watch helplessly as the rebound fell at the feet of Hidegkuti. The Magyar hitman, with the entire goal to aim at, inexplicably put his effort into the side netting. For a second the Germans held their breath. It was the kind of chance that Hidegkuti usually put away with his eyes shut. At seeing their normally lethal comrade miss such an ideal opportunity, many of the Hungarians looked to the heavens. Nandor Hidegkuti slowly picked himself up off his knees. The Swiss rain that had all but drowned this World Cup final increased ten-fold. The scene was all set for a dramatic last twist.

Six minutes from time the sky caved in on the Hungarians. Josef Bozsik, who by now was performing from memory, found himself the victim of a midfield mugging by the robust Schafer. Schafer stormed off down the left wing. Alongside him half a dozen white shirts hurtled into the Magyar penalty area in support. The ball was flung across a crowded box, Lantos's attempted header clearance fell only to the deadly feet of Helmut Rahn. As Gustav Sebes closed his eyes, Rahn took aim, side-stepped a desperate Magyar lunge, and from the edge of the area shot low and good past a despairing Grocsis. The stadium exploded with the roar of the German supporters. Bedlam reigned on the terraces. The German banners and tricolours waved in honour of their side's staggering comeback. On the pitch Herberger's men had to be prised apart by the referee to continue the match. The Magyars appeared done for. In the lashing rain, with their shirts caked in mud and sweat, they resembled a team resigned to defeat. All except one.

Ferenc Puskas shouted encouragement at his comrades. 'Get your heads up,' roared the Magyar captain. 'Come on, get your heads up, there is still time. We are not done yet.' With clenched fist Puskas went amongst his team, demanding one final effort. Sebes stood on the touchline checking his watch. There were five minutes left. It was now or never. The Germans retreated into a defensive shell. They would sit and hold their lead. It would be up to the Magyars to break them down. Three minutes from time, the Hungarians thought they had succeeded. Josef Toth put Ferenc Puskas clear in the German penalty area. Showing great calm, the 'Galloping Major' took his time and calmly placed his shot past Turek: 3–3! Puskas had saved his country at the last moment. The little street urchin born and raised on the outskirts of Budapest disappeared under a flurry of red shirts. Gustav Sebes hugged and embraced all around him. Hungarian officials ran down to the bench to join in with their fellow countrymen.

But wait . . . The referee, after allowing the goal, noticed his Welsh linesman, Mervyn Griffiths, flagging wildly, desperate to attract his attention. At this stage a full minute had passed since the ball had hit the back of the net. The Magyars fell silent. Bill Ling went over to see what Griffiths had spotted. After a short discussion, Ling pointed to a free kick for West Germany. Puskas, it had been alleged, was offside when he scored. The Hungarians went berserk. Puskas walked towards Mr Griffiths and gave him what can only be described as a murderous glance. To the despair and anger of the Magyars their moment of redemption was wiped away. The game went on, the clock continued to run. Zoltan Czibor, in an emotional, frenzied finale, almost saved the day when he unleashed a tremendous low shot which appeared certain to beat Turek, only to see the inspired German keeper produce yet another magnificent save. For Czibor it proved too much. He collapsed to the ground with tears rolling down his face, pounding the grass in frustration. They could do no more.

The West German ribbons had been placed on the trophy. Off the pitch officials were busy preparing for the presentation. With the German players on the brink of exhaustion, Bill Ling blew the final whistle. Across the turf Hungarians dropped to their knees. Under rain-sodden skies, the Magyars' hearts lay broken. The West Germans ran across to their supporters to celebrate as one. A success earned by hard work. Teutonic cunning and no shortage of skill had been well rewarded. Sheltered by an umbrella, the president of FIFA, Jules Rimet, in his last act in office, handed over the trophy to a beaming Fritz Walter. A forlorn-looking Puskas stepped forward to shake Walter's hand. The players of both sides lined up for a final rendition of 'Deutschland Über Alles'. A penny for the thoughts of the Hungarian players at that moment. Sepp Herberger's ploy had succeeded beyond all expectation and he would return home a national hero.

But was their victory achieved using underhand methods? Ferenc Puskas would later remark that when he passed the West German changing-room 'it smelled like a garden of poppies'. Never one to mince his words, the Hungarian lit the fires of controversy when he went on to claim: 'That is why the Germans ran and chased like steam engines.' In his own inimitable way Puskas came out and said what everybody at the time was thinking but was too afraid to say, that, in short, Sepp Herberger's team played the 1954 World Cup final drugged up to the eyeballs on steroids. The fact that seven of the Germans went down with severe stomach cramps shortly after the final whistle fuelled the rumour. It is a strange tale told by Puskas, but one that to this day remains unproven. The dream was over. All that remains to tell is of the aftermath.

IN THE EYE OF THE STORM

Nobody spoke in the Magyar dressing-room. Words were worthless in such dire circumstances. Gustav Sebes sat with his head in his hands. He mumbled something to himself about bad luck. Aside from the odd curse aimed at linesman Griffiths, the silence was choking. In Hungary news of the disastrous defeat relayed by Szepesi's shell-shocked tones hit home with all the force of an exploding meteor. At first there was respectful mourning, but as the evening wore on the shock turned to anger. Riots erupted in the Hungarian capital. Shop windows were smashed and cars were overturned and set alight. Soldiers were sent to guard the homes of the players and manager after angry crowds gathered. Such is the fragility of footballing emotions, a team heralded as gods only 24 hours earlier were now pariahs. Gustav Sebes received instructions not to return home immediately as their safety could not be guaranteed. Instead, the train was met at the Hungarian border and accompanied by military escort to an army training camp where they would wait until feelings had calmed. They passed through deserted train stations. This time no one welcomed them home. Only the odd angry stare through the carriage windows demonstrated the feelings towards them. The true extent of their defeat had not yet struck home to the Magyars. They were totally unaware of what was happening in Budapest. At that moment trams were being derailed and overturned by rampaging mobs on its streets. Sebes was appalled when a government official grabbed his arm and said, 'Do not worry, comrade. We will defend your family and flat from attack.' The nightmare had begun.

Hungary was in turmoil. Demonstrations against the Magyars' defeat showed no sign of ceasing. Rumours abounded of wild parties on the eve of the final. One story that the Hungarian footballers had each accepted a Mercedes car in return for throwing the match was widely repeated. As events calmed momentarily, the team were allowed to return to their families. The anger and animosity that awaited astounded the Magyars. Hate mail was sent by the sackload to Ferenc Puskas. He and Gustav Sebes were deemed amongst the most guilty. Puskas could not step out of his flat without being savagely abused and having obscenities screamed at him. It even reached the stage where, when playing for Hungary in the Nep Stadium, his own fans would give him unmerciful stick whenever he was in possession. On one occasion, Puskas snapped and, turning to his baiters, dropped his shorts and flashed his backside at them. With that he stalked off the pitch. Gustav Sebes watched his captain's antics with a broken heart. This was not the glorious ending to the story he had envisaged. Sebes and his family were themselves under intolerable pressure. His son had to be assigned special protection after being badly beaten up on his way home from school. Death threats were delivered to his home. Every time Sebes travelled abroad with the Magyars, his family suffered immensely. In the summer of 1955 Sebes was relieved of his post by the Hungarian FA. They claimed it was because his familiarity with his players

had become unhealthy. The team had become stale. It was time to shake
things up. This was a decision which broke the old man's heart.

It was indeed the end of a glorious era for Hungarian football. For only a
short time later revolution would erupt in the motherland, and Soviet tanks
would emerge from across the border to crush all before them on the streets
of Budapest. The sparks which ignited the fire flared on 23 October 1956.
Two hundred thousand Hungarians marched through their capital
demanding independence from Moscow's grip. They were on their way
towards Parliament Square where a huge rally was being staged in protest
against the authorities.

On the way they had to pass Stalin Avenue, where stood a statue of the
Russian leader himself. Somebody had placed a placard around its neck. It
stated: Russian soldiers, take me with you when you go! The temptation
proved overwhelming. To huge cheers, students and workers set it alight. The
flames leapt high into the Budapest sky. There was to be no turning back. The
Hungarians had sent out a message which Moscow could not ignore. It could
not be allowed to go unpunished.

The Red Army attacked in all its might to crush the rebellion. Showing no
mercy they roared into Budapest to restore order. Hundreds of tanks, backed
by units of élite Soviet ground troops, began the assault. The Russian
leadership decreed that Hungary was to be made an example. It was nothing
short of wanton slaughter. Fierce resistance from Hungarian freedom fighters
proved no match for the well-drilled and ruthless Soviet war machine. As the
blue Danube turned red with the blood of Hungarian partisans, the
footballers of the motherland were locked away in a training camp outside
Budapest. When the fighting originally flared up, the Magyars had been
preparing to take on Sweden at the Nep Stadium. However, with events
hurtling madly out of control, the fixture became irrelevant as thoughts
turned to matters much more profound. All the players were anxious to return
home. The worry of family and friends caught up in the fighting saw the
Magyars heading off towards the firing of the guns. Puskas and Bozsik
returned to Budapest on 28 October. They walked warily out of Keleti railway
station and through the deserted surrounding streets, the rattle of gunfire
echoing eerily in the distance. Only a stone's throw away Russian soldiers were
lining up Hungarian fighters against a wall and shooting them dead.

Across Europe confusion reigned as to what was actually going on inside
Hungary. The press wires blazed that Ferenc Puskas had been killed in the
fighting. The BBC reported the death of this well-loved figure. For a short
period the football world was in mourning for one of the all-time greats.
Happily the story proved to be untrue. For with their close army ties, Honved

had managed to convince the Communist authorities to move Puskas and his fellow Magyars to a safer place. They were more use to the party alive than dead and were allowed to leave. On reaching the Austro–Hungarian border, the coach carrying the Magyars was surrounded by curious gun-toting border guards. On sighting Puskas, they appeared dumbfounded, for they had heard the rumours about him. Finally, after a lengthy session of autograph signing, the team were granted permission to pass through. In Vienna the Major was reunited with his wife and young daughter, who had been smuggled out amidst huge secrecy.

Now, Ferenc Puskas and the rest of his team-mates faced some soul-searching. The revolution had been all but crushed. The call had gone out from the authorities for the Magyars to return to Budapest. But return to what? Hungary was in ruins. People were disappearing daily, taken away by the Communist secret police, the AVH. Their beautiful capital, with its historic buildings and ancient monuments, had been virtually reduced to rubble by the Red Army. Sadly, most of the players' families had not managed to escape. It was an awful dilemma for the Magyars. To the west there was the lure of freedom, the opportunity to begin a new life; while back in the east were family and loved ones.

The Hungarian FA had shot themselves in the foot. Not only had the senior squad been evacuated, but also the under-21 team. These were the future Magyars; the next generation. The cream of the country's footballers had simply vanished over the horizon, many with no intention whatsoever of returning. It was a calamitous error by the authorities; and one for which even today they are still paying the price. Gustav Sebes was ordered to travel to Vienna in a vain attempt to convince the Magyars to come home. In an emotionally charged meeting, Sebes passed on the message from his superiors. It was to prove a wasted journey for Uncle Gusti. For despite holding the old man in huge esteem, the majority of the footballers had no inclination to return. Many of them had already made alternative arrangements. Europe's élite had already sent out feelers to various Magyars. Representatives of all the top clubs had besieged the hotel where the Hungarians had based themselves. Barcelona were among the first to make a move. Zoltan Czibor and Sandor Kocsis accepted the lure of Catalan gold and headed off to the Nou Camp, but others were more doubtful. Josef Bozsik found himself torn in two, and he and his comrade, Ferenc Puskas, talked long into the Viennese night about what to do. For Puskas everything was straightforward. He was all for trying his hand abroad. Wild horses could not have dragged him back to Budapest. As for Bozsik? Well, he was almost certain to return to the motherland. With his father having recently passed away, and his mother left with four young mouths to feed, he was left with little option. Also Bozsik's Communist beliefs weighed heavily on his conscience. Eventually, he made up his mind. He would go home. Puskas and Bozsik bade a tearful farewell. The life-long friends shared a final drink and said their goodbyes. The Major hugged the man who he considered his brother. They were never again to play together in the same team. Josef Bozsik died of a heart attack, aged 52, in 1978. Ferenc Puskas had sworn many years before not to return to Hungary. Technically still a deserter from the army, he would have been arrested by the Communist authorities as soon as he set foot on Hungarian soil. It was a broken hearted 'galloping Major' who fought back the tears on the day of his comrade's funeral. Such is life.

From 1956 to 1958 Puskas roamed across Europe looking for a club. His tendency to pile on the pounds when not playing put off many prospective buyers. It was only the empire-building president Santiago of Real Madrid who sensed the desire that still burned inside the Hungarian, went with his instinct and gambled on making the Major a Madrileno. The first meeting was the stuff of legends. With neither able to speak the other's native tongue, Puskas made his point with gestures. His pointed to his belly. 'Look!' he exclaimed loudly to Bernabeu in Hungarian. 'This is all very well, but look at me, I am at least 18 kilos overweight. I appreciate your offer, Mr President, but . . .' Don Santiago stopped the Magyar in mid-sentence. 'Enough,' he bellowed. 'Your weight, my friend, is not my problem, it is yours. It is of no concern. You will come with me to Madrid and you will be a star. End of argument!' In that instant Ferenc Puskas decided to join Alfredo di Stefano and the white knights of Real Madrid. But that is another story. The fact remains that the 1954 World Cup final was a magnificent opportunity for the Hungarians to carve their country's name on the greatest trophy of them all. Fate decreed it was not to be. The rain that fell in Berne as the dream died could well have been Hungarian tears. There was to be no happy ending. The Magyars' last stand.

4.

SNOWFLAKES IN THE SUN

REAL MADRID V MANCHESTER UNITED

1957 EUROPEAN CUP SEMI-FINAL

Matt Busby was never a man noted for superlatives, but on his first live sighting of the 'White Arrow' he simply could not help himself. Busby had flown over the Channel to France to cast an eye over his team's prospective opponents in their forthcoming European Cup semi-final. Real Madrid were deemed red-hot favourites to get through. They had beaten the French champions Nice 4–2 in the first leg in Spain. Now on French soil they only underlined this point with a performance that struck wonder and a little fear into the mind of the Manchester United manager. What he witnessed in Nice was to make Busby exclaim, 'Until today I thought that Peter Doherty and Alex James were the two of the best players I have ever seen. But now I have seen Alfredo the Great . . . ah, he is in a class of his own.' On hearing this, di Stefano was hugely moved. To be lauded by such a fine man was to him a marvellous accolade. When the two men finally met, di Stefano thanked Busby for his kind comments and jokingly asked him if he would consider becoming his publicity agent!

The blistering expulsion of Athletico Bilbao at the hands of the Mancunians was not lost amidst the imperial surroundings of Madrid. Bilbao had returned home bemoaning their bad luck but also full of praise for Busby's special young team. Tommy Taylor in particular had gained a reputation in the Spanish press for his ferocious performances over the two legs. His display against the esteemed Jesus Garay had caught the eye of Real's no-nonsense defenders. They knew they would have a hell of a fight on their hands with this bustling, rugged, but also tremendously talented centre-forward. Manuel Marquitos, the devil amongst the angelic white shirts, began in earnest to sharpen his studs.

Real Madrid had begun their defence of the trophy with a new face in their midst. Raymonde Kopa had joined from Rheims to add yet another fantastic string to an already golden bow. Real had been drawn against the Austrians of Rapid Vienna in the first round. In Madrid it was business as usual as di Stefano scored twice in a 4–2 victory, but in the Austrian capital of Vienna events were turned emphatically on their head when Rapid surprisingly thumped the Madrilenos 3–1. In front of an ecstatic home crowd, a complacent Madrid team were beaten by an Ernst Happel hat trick. These days Real would have been out, but back in those formative years a play-off could get them off the hook. Bernabeu sensed trouble. He simply could not allow his side to be eliminated at this early stage. The president made the call and off went the maker of deals, Don Raimondo Saporta, to talk to Rapid Vienna's hierarchy. As ever Saporta, armed to the teeth with a crock of Spanish gold, proved successful. For a sum of £25,000 Rapid agreed to the play-off game being held in Madrid. On 13 December 1956, in front of 100,000 screaming Spaniards, Real Madrid beat the champions of Austria by two goals to nil. The money had proved too much for the Austrians to turn down. As good as Madrid were on the pitch, their business acumen off it was equally impressive. In Saporta they possessed a man who could convince an angel to sell its wings.

After the demolition of Nice on away territory Madrid began to think about the growing threat from Manchester. President Bernabeu had been amazed by the English team's extraordinary show of defiance against the powerful Bilbao. Bernabeu's great sense of history told him this team raised from the crèche would be a formidable pointed thorn in the side of his beloved football team. Don Santiago would have to have a serious think about these previously unheard-of 'Busby Babes'. Manchester was a city overflowing with excitement at the prospect of their team playing Real Madrid. For weeks before the newspapers talked of little else. The opening leg was to be played in Madrid, and for the first time Old Trafford would stand ready to host that special night-time atmosphere of a European Cup match for the second leg. The mere thought of having to take on di Stefano and his wonderful team disturbed Busby, and yet at the same time filled him with awe. In normal circumstances he tended not to extol the virtues of opposing players in front of his own team. But in di Stefano's case he simply could not help himself. His lads listened with mixed feelings as their manager praised Alfredo to the high heavens. Just what on earth lay in wait for them in Madrid?

On a blazing-hot Spanish afternoon, Manchester United's aeroplane landed at Madrid airport. Shading their eyes from the blinding sunshine, the 'Babes' appeared and began to make their way down the gangway. They were met by a barrage of flashbulbs. Looking splendid in their club blazers with MUFC emblazoned upon each crest, the United lads were besieged by eager autograph hunters. The Real supporters had gathered in their hundreds to try to catch a glimpse of this much heralded English team. Tommy Taylor was the main target of their affection. Taylor, who had seen his reputation soar across Europe after his epic collision with Jesus Garay of Bilbao, found himself surrounded by hordes of Spaniards. Matt Busby watched with great pride as his boys were mobbed. To him this was what European football was all about. A brave new adventure in a far-off place. Madrid was only a plane ride from Manchester, but in so many ways it appeared as another world. The Madrid newspapers were fascinated by the Babes. They nicknamed the youngsters 'Los chicos' (the lads). During their stay in this wealthy, sophisticated city, United found themselves the focus of a press frenzy more suited to the arrival of a top Hollywood star. However, the opinion amongst the home supporters was that Manchester had had their day in the sun when they knocked out the Basques. It was time for di Stefano, Gento, Kopa and the rest to win back some Spanish pride.

The home of Real Madrid was set amidst a luxurious complex in the Chamartin district of the city. The stadium itself was built of white concrete and stone. It rose majestically, tier upon tier, towards the heavens, gleaming in the Spanish sunlight; a spectacle that was truly awe inspiring for the lads from Manchester. Compared to this Old Trafford resembled a garden shed!

Shortly before the game began an amusing incident occurred in the United dressing-room. Real officials sauntered in uninvited and demanded of Busby that he show them photographs of the United players taking part in the game. They had in their possession pictures of the Madrid men they said would be playing, which they duly showed to the United manager. Busby was lost for words. Temporarily taken aback, he recovered sufficiently to inform the Madrid deputation that his team's passports were all safely locked away back at the club's hotel, but they had his solemn word that the men set to perform for United were all genuine, and not ringers.

On 11 April 1957, the Busby Babes stepped out onto the home ground of the imperial Real Madrid. The arrival of the teams was greeted by a shower of white roses thrown from the highest bastions of the magnificent arena. The United players looked up in amazement as the cascade of flowers floated down onto the pitch. The Real side, led by their captain Miguel Munoz, applauded their supporters for what was a truly epic spectacle. Flashbulbs glittered around the stadium as the Bernabeu crackled to a symphony of firecrackers. Photographers scuttled around like ants, jostling each other to capture these historic moments for posterity. This was an afternoon that would be talked about in Madrid for many years. The Babes posed for a team photo on the pitch. Playing all in red, the English champions waited eagerly for the game to begin. The Real players, with the exception of di Stefano, appeared nervous. The White Arrow cut a composed figure amidst the bedlam on the field. In the grandstands the noise level was rising rapidly.

The pleasantries completed, both teams prepared for the kick-off. In its short history the European Champions' Cup had never experienced the like of what was unfolding here in Madrid. One hundred and twenty thousand people had paid out a world record sum of £55,000 for the privilege of being present at such a thrilling occasion. The famous Dutch referee Leo Horn signalled to his two linesmen, put his whistle to his mouth and began what was to be a fascinating encounter. For an hour Manchester United fought and defended like lions as Real penned them into their own penalty area. The red shirts found themselves pushed onto the back foot as Gento, Kopa, Rial and Mateos came at them repeatedly. In a white blur they roared forward. Backed by a fanatical crowd it appeared only a matter of time before they took the lead.

Di Stefano was followed everywhere by Eddie Colman. This little Salford urchin stuck like glue to the Argentinian. Much to the great man's distaste, Colman was having a stifling effect on his efforts to mastermind a Real breakthrough. When the Madrid talisman looked like blasting his man marker into orbit along would come Jackie Blanchflower to help out his team-mate and once more tighten the noose. Indeed an increasingly frustrated di Stefano was lucky not to be sent off when he scythed down Blanchflower only yards from a watching Mr Horn. However, it would be unthinkable for any referee to send off the leading man in his own personal theatre house. Much to the disgust of the protesting United players, Horn lost his nerve and the extremely perturbed Madrid number nine was let off with a warning.

Still the Babes held their ground. The captain, Roger Byrne, led by example from his left-back position. Up against the extravagantly talented Raymonde Kopa, Byrne held on tight to the flying Frenchman as he switched effortlessly into overdrive. It was a stirring battle between two vastly contrasting sides: the artistry and footwork of Real against the heart and sheer stubborn determination of Manchester United. Bill Foulkes over on the right was in the midst of a nightmare against the bolt of lightning masquerading as Paco Gento. Occasionally creaking, and indeed at times sliced wide apart, a brave United by some miracle survived to keep the rampaging marauding Spaniards at bay. At this stage Busby's tactics were holding firm. Just! Up the other end of the field Tommy Taylor found himself besieged by Madrid defenders, all intent on keeping him in hand. To achieve this no quarter was given. Taylor was hashed and slashed at throughout by the villainous Marquitos, ably abetted by the no-nonsense Zarraga and Real captain Miguel Munoz. They would not let themselves go the way of Bilbao. A harassed Taylor was shown no mercy. If the truth be known Manuel Marquitos did not require any assistance for a hatchet job, for this was a man who was more than capable of sending Tommy Taylor home on a stretcher. With a referee seemingly intent on turning a blind eye to any Madrid misdemeanour, Marquitos could have pulled a gun on the United forward and shot him dead, and still no punishment would have been forthcoming!

An hour gone and the European champions began to turn the screw tight. As United wilted under the relentless pressure the breakthrough finally occurred. The bolt was unlocked and Real Madrid came thundering through the door with all guns blazing. Paco Gento teased, jinked and then flew past a bemused Bill Foulkes. Without even glancing up, the man nicknamed El Supersonico by his adoring supporters delivered a perfect cross for Rial to stoop low and head the ball past Ray Wood. Around the stadium thousands of handkerchiefs were waved in delight, creating a wonderful scene. The Bernabeu was on fire! With the crowd baying for English blood the home side moved in menacingly for the kill. Alfredo di Stefano finally managed to rid himself of his Salford shadow. As Eddie Colman tired badly in his man-marking role, the chains loosened and the White Arrow broke free. With frightening acceleration di Stefano roared into the Manchester penalty area. Beating three red shirts, Alfredo cut past Roger Byrne and his chasing colleague and executed a heavenly chip over a stranded Wood in the United goal. Two goals down and the roof was caving in on Matt Busby's team. Like snowflakes in the sun the Madrilenos poured down onto Manchester United.

The crowd were buoyant. As a matador teases a dying bull so Real Madrid taunted their English opponents. Once more as in Bilbao chants of 'Ole!' were heard around the stadium. Byrne rallied his shell-shocked troops. In all their young and tender years the Busby Babes had never faced pressure such as this. Showing huge heart and determination they roared back at the Spanish. Duncan Edwards tore into the Madrid players determined to win back possession for his side. For the first time in the match United began to go forward with some menace. With Edwards seeing red mist and David Pegg beginning to take on and beat the uncertain full-back Beccerill the tide temporarily turned. As the Babes passed and moved, Madrid rocked. The home supporters began to whistle in frustration. Their anxiety rose when with only eight minutes remaining Tommy Taylor escaped from his hit squad and headed a goal back. As the ball struck the back of the net a deafening silence gripped the arena. Instead of holding on for just a one-goal deficit, the Babes threw caution to the wind and stormed forward in search of a dramatic equaliser. Pegg in particular was frightening the life out of the Spaniards.

Busby looked on in admiration as his lads continued to go for their opponents' throats. But there was to be a painful sting in the tail for the lads from the rainy city. As Manchester United romped forward, they were hit by a killer third goal only moments from the end, the brilliant Gento and Rial combining wonderfully to put away Mateos to score: 3–1. Once more the Bernabeu declared undying love for their team. On the final whistle, the Spanish players and supporters celebrated with great fervour and not a little relief at the game's outcome. It had been a fine and relatively even contest; and worrying for the Madrilenos that it was not over yet.

As was their wont, Madrid served up a sumptuous postmatch banquet for their visitors from England. Each United player was presented with a solid gold watch by Santiago Bernabeu in memory of their visit to the stadium named in his honour. It was a glorious evening and a wonderful display of generosity by Madrid's finest. One man particularly touched by Bernabeu's gift was Duncan Edwards. Edwards more than any treasured this prize acquired from his much vaunted opponents. He was to hold it dear for what remained of his tragically short life, for as he gazed proudly at his newly acquired gift, he little realised that time for him was running out. President Bernabeu made a heart-felt speech pledging the importance of friendship between the two great clubs. Busby was overwhelmed by Bernabeu's impeccable staging of the occasion. He realised it was something that Manchester United themselves would have to try to emulate. That night in Madrid a special bond began between the two cities. It was to endure in tragedy and finally in triumph. As the evening drew to a close and many a toast had been made in honour of eternal friendships a Real player cornered Busby and told him, 'If you were to come and manage us we would win every trophy in the world.' The United manager smiled and replied, 'Listen, my friend, if you were to give me di Stefano, we would win every trophy in the world!' With this the inquisitor moved sadly away. But this would not be the end of the matter. Real would try one more time to lure this genial Scotsman away from his adopted city.

Two weeks later Matt Busby stood with pipe and trilby in hand at Manchester airport to welcome the Spaniards onto English soil. As di Stefano emerged from the aeroplane he was immediately waylaid by eager young boys all desperate to have his signature in pride of place in their autograph books. The great one stood patiently scribbling as the crowds gathered wide-eyed around him. The Real players swaggered through customs after collecting their luggage. All eyes were on them as they chatted amongst themselves fully aware of the impression they were making. Dressed immaculately, they looked the epitome of class. Santiago Bernabeu stood smoking an enormous cigar as he chatted to waiting pressmen. This larger-than-life character declared with typical gusto that he was 'pleased to be in England and delighted to meet again my great friend Matt Busby'.

Madrid had pulled a fast one. Deeply disturbed at the ease with which David Pegg had gone past their full-back Beccerill in the first leg, they 'borrowed' from Real Zaragoza the Brazilian defender Torres. Torres was an accomplished player who would prove a vital asset to the Real back line. In the way the transfer was handled Madrid managed to stay within the rules of the competition by the skin of their teeth. Bernabeu had not forgotten what had become of their fierce primera liga rivals Athletico Bilbao. He was absolutely determined that the same fate would not befall his club. They would seek to hit the Babes early and be rid of this irritating hindrance to their superiority once and for all.

Busby had injury problems. Dennis Viollet had been put out of action and in to replace him was the blossoming inside-forward Bobby Charlton. He had watched the first leg in the Bernabeu from high up in the gods. Similarly to his manager Charlton had experienced an almost spiritual reawakening on his first viewing of di Stefano and his team. This was not the game he had been taught by Busby and Jimmy Murphy. These flashing white angelic figures streaking across the turf with lightning pace and precision were totally alien to anything he had ever seen. The Spaniards did not just pass the ball around the field, they caressed and cajoled it, conjuring up moments of skill that made the human eye blink in bewilderment. However, Matt Busby had great faith in Mrs Charlton's lad, confidently asserting that Charlton possessed the natural ability to be as good as the Argentinian master himself, Alfredo the Great.

On the day of the match, the United ground staff received orders from above to run on the sprinklers and start drowning the surface. Trouble arrived in the form of Real Madrid officials who appeared around mid-morning to inspect the pitch. They were horrified to see pools of water already gathering on the surface. Sensing what their Mancunian foes were up to, they immediately threatened to abandon the game if the sprinklers were not switched off. The game of one-upmanship had begun. United led 1–0, Busby's idea being that a soaked Old Trafford would hinder the sublime ball-playing skills of the Madrilenos. Sad for him that the Spanish, already paranoid about the forthcoming match, were on the lookout for such antics. As kick-off drew near, 65,000 people made their way to Old Trafford. From across the swing bridge that bestrode the River Irwell the red hordes swarmed. Could United do it? There was huge optimism in the air. They knew well the quality of this Madrid team. But after witnessing what their lads had done to

Athletico Bilbao in the previous round, anything was surely possible. For the first time in its history Old Trafford football ground welcomed with open arms the thrills and spills of the European Cup. Bathed in the dreamy haze of the newly installed floodlights an expectant crowd held its breath. With the temperature rising, the players made their way out of the dressing-rooms and lined up in the tunnel. The rattle of studs on a concrete floor and shouts of encouragement in both Spanish and English filled the air. Manuel Marquitos nodded across to Tommy Taylor. The lad from Barnsley acknowledged this with a huge grin. It was time to go back to war with this Spanish bull.

Alfredo di Stefano and his illustrious comrades ran out alongside the Busby Babes onto the Old Trafford pitch. With their white shirts glistening underneath the glow of the floodlights, a cold chill cut through the Mancunian air. The Madrilenos had entered the home of their closest rivals. It was time to show who was top dog. United, in their traditional red strip, looked brisk and businesslike. Duncan Edwards jumped around full of nervous energy, raging inside to tear into the Spaniards and get his team back in the tie. With the crowd close to a collective heart attack the game began.

For the home side it was to prove a disappointing evening. In the first half, with United throwing caution to the winds, Real hit them with two devastating counter-breaks. The Madrilenos struck like lightning. A sly di Stefano back-heel let in Raymonde Kopa for the first goal. A stunned Old Trafford looked on in dismay as the Spaniards celebrated. Kopa had finished wonderfully, placing his shot low past an advancing Ray Wood. When Rial added a second goal shortly before half-time, it was game, set and match. Manchester United were dead and buried. Like air seeping out of a hot-air balloon, the hopes of the Mancunians drifted far away into the dark dead of night. Madrid were almost home and dry, but it was not just beautiful football that had earned Real their interval lead. This was a night when the Madrilenos showed the other side of their game. At the back, their defenders fought tooth and nail to stem the Babes' attacks. No prisoners were taken as sly digs and cynical tackles were dished out to the United forwards. Touched by the angels up front, the touch of the devil at the back.

The second half saw United's incessant pressure on the Spanish defence finally reap dividends. Events threatened to turn sour as Real's defensive tactics outraged the Manchester players. With the crowd sensing a breakthrough, Tommy Taylor scrambled a goal back. Madrid wobbled slightly. Could United do the impossible? A feeling of optimism swept through the terraces. Maybe it wasn't all over? Waves of red shirts swarmed in and amongst the Real defence. Alonso in the Spanish goal performed heroics as shots rained in at him from all angles. To ease the pressure Madrid attempted to time-waste. The new man Torres blotted his braveheart copybook by pretending to be injured after a collision with David Pegg. As the United players tried to lift him off the field, the Real defenders blocked their path and attempted to drag Torres back onto the pitch. A nasty scuffle ensued as tempers momentarily boiled over. Enter Duncan Edwards. With one almighty shove the Spaniards were knocked aside and Torres was off the field of play! The Real players retreated. They had no wish to incur further the wrath of this powerful United midfielder.

With time almost up, Bobby Charlton stabbed home an equaliser from close range, but the tie overall was well beyond them. Madrid played out the dying moments by keeping wonderful possession, their skill and technique proving sufficient to keep any last mad dash for glory by United at bay. With the Babes still fighting manfully and praying for a miracle, the referee blew for full-time. Real Madrid had survived the Manchester onslaught. United were out of the European Cup, but only at the hands of the finest club side in the world. Santiago Bernabeu breathed a huge sigh of relief. His men had done him proud. There is a time when talent alone is not enough. You must also possess the guts and willingness for a fight. Clearly, the Madrilenos had these in abundance.

Before Don Santiago returned home there was one last task to be undertaken. At a post-match banquet laid on by Manchester United, Bernabeu attempted to woo Matt Busby. Using all his persuasive abilities, the Real president tried in vain to convince the Manchester United manager that his future lay in Madrid. He offered him 'untold riches, pleasures beyond your wildest dreams. Matt, I promise we shall make it heaven on earth for you.' Bernabeu's silky but powerful words made Busby seriously consider the offer, but only for a passing moment, for what he and Jimmy Murphy had at Old Trafford no amount of Spanish gold could ever buy. Later in the week he wrote to Santiago Bernabeu thanking him for his wonderful offer, but declining it. For as Busby so succinctly wrote: 'My heaven on earth exists right here in Manchester.' The matches against Real Madrid had shown Busby that it wouldn't be long before his team could take on the Spaniards and beat them. The wise Bernabeu was aware of this, thus the attempt to prise the United manager away and into the arms of the waiting Madrilenos. No other team in Europe frightened Bernabeu like Matt Busby's side. He knew that if his club were to be beaten it would probably be by these never-say-die young red devils from Manchester.

Madrid went on to retain their crown with a convincing 2–0 win over the Italians of Fiorentina. Playing on home soil in front of 124,000 people, Alfredo di Stefano and Francisco Gento scored the goals that sent their city soaring once more into fiesta mood. Miguel Munoz raised aloft the European Champions' Cup. Presenting Munoz with his prize was one of Real Madrid's most fanatical supporters – a certain General Franco. It was a relatively comfortable victory for the Madrilenos. Paco Gento remarked after the match that the real final for him and his team-mates was the two encounters against Manchester United. Gento was convinced that United would be their main rivals for further glory when battle recommenced the following season. The average age of the Real Madrid team was 28, whilst United's was only 21. Gento knew well, as did his president, that the Babes would be around for a long time yet. Time was surely on Manchester's side, but as events shortly proved, time was a luxury that the Busby Babes would not be allowed to have.

Fate was cruelly set to intervene and prove Paco's prediction dreadfully incorrect. The next time these two great clubs came together the red shirts would still be the same but tragically the men wearing them would not. The team that had stolen the hearts of the Madrilenos was no more. The Babes were all but dead.

> This Manchester United team made a magnificent impression on me. They had colourful and outstanding individual players, and as a team they were as powerful as any we ever met in the theatre of the European Cup. What a sad day it was for me when our treasurer Don Raimondo Saporta telephoned my home with the dreadful news of the disaster at Munich. None deserved more the fullness of a great career.
> – Alfredo di Stefano.

5.

A SOLID GOLD WATCH

MANCHESTER UNITED V RED STAR BELGRADE

1958 EUROPEAN CUP QUARTER-FINAL

On a misty Old Trafford evening, with pockets of fog swirling eerily across the pitch, the referee raised his whistle to his mouth and called time on the first leg of the European Cup quarter-final. The Red Star players punched the air in jubilation and relief. Although beaten by two goals to one, they had given themselves a good chance of pulling back the deficit in Belgrade in front of their own fanatical supporters. Matt Busby walked from his seat in pensive mood. It had been a tough encounter against a strong, determined, skilful team and it was only the power and sheer will of Duncan Edwards that had enabled them to scratch out a win. The return match in Belgrade would come only three days before a vital league showdown with the Wolves. Once more United's season was building to a gripping climax. Last season's endeavours, when they had gone for a treble and ended up with only one trophy, had shown Busby just how difficult it was to aim for European glory, as well as maintain the highest of standards at home. Inspired by the genius of their little inside-forward Sekularac, Red Star had produced a performance of gritty bravura and no little skill. What a performer this Sekularac was! During the first half he had tormented the home side with his beguiling play. Gasps of astonishment drifted down from the terraces as this magician from the Balkans, raised among Romany travellers, cast his spell over the Manchester crowd.

Luckily for Matt Busby and the 65,000 Mancunians watching, United possessed a few sorcerers of their own. Duncan Edwards was at his marauding best on that cold, murky Manchester evening. Three times in the first half he forced magnificent saves from the formidable 'black cat' Beara. Edwards at times was unplayable. For one so young he already resembled the finished article and it was he who ended the gypsy's marvellous, if short, cameo performance. An over-confident Sekularac was misguided enough to rob

Edwards of the ball with a well-timed interception. The next thing he knew he was airborne, finally coming to earth after a succession of cartwheels. After that little more was witnessed of the Yugoslav's box of tricks! Duncan Edwards drove his team relentlessly forward. Second-half strikes from Eddie Colman and Bobby Charlton gave United a slender advantage for their trip behind the Iron Curtain. But would it prove to be enough? The previous round had seen Busby's team take a three-goal lead back to Dukla Prague. There they had withstood a battering and a one-goal defeat to win through, but at times it had been more than a little hairy. After the second leg against Dukla, United were held up in Prague by fog in London. Eventually they were able to muster a plane to Amsterdam and from there they continued their journey by boat and train to arrive back in Manchester late Friday. This could not be allowed to happen again. From now on United would sort out their own travel arrangements, starting with the game in Yugoslavia.

The Red Star team arrived back in Belgrade full of hope following their impressive performance in Manchester. This club that was formed in 1945 as the official team of Belgrade University would give the Busby Babes the game of their lives when they travelled east for the return match, fielding players such as the fans' favourite Bora Kostic, a left-winger of blazing skill and pace, Rayko Mitic, captain of his club and country, and, of course, the enigmatic but brilliant Sekularac. Red Star waited impatiently for the battle with Manchester United to recommence on home ground.

Before they travelled to Belgrade, United had an important league match against Arsenal at Highbury. The Babes loved going down to London. On 1 February 1958, 63,000 people packed Highbury to see the Gunners take on the red devils. What they witnessed was one of the finest matches ever to grace that famous old ground. Manchester United, living up to their reputation for stirring, attacking football, sneaked home in a classic encounter. Goals from Edwards, Charlton and Tommy Taylor had given the club from the grim north a seemingly impregnable half-time lead. But Arsenal bravely clawed their way back to make it 3–3.

With Highbury ablaze with excitement, United picked themselves up, dusted themselves down and went up an extra gear to score twice more. Further goals from Dennis Viollet and a typical Taylor stroke looked finally to have made the two points safe, but the Gunners refused to let go of the Babes' coat-tails One last time they hit back to create a momentous finale: 5–4 was the final score. Every supporter in the stadium rose to applaud the teams off the field of play. The Busby Babes with their white shirts spattered and caked in mud left the arena with the cheers of the fans ringing in their ears. It had been a wonderful best-ever league performance, for the following week Manchester United would embark on a date with destiny.

Fate has a cruel habit of dealing the most horrendous of hands. It was during the second half of this epic contest that Duncan Edwards's card was indelibly marked. With one of his best shuddering challenges, Edwards waylaid an unfortunate Arsenal midfielder. So enraged was the stricken Gunner that he plotted instant revenge on his young provocateur. Luckily the Arsenal captain, Dave Bowen, managed to calm him down and the game continued at its furious pace. Had Bowen not intervened on behalf of his player, come the following Monday morning Duncan Edwards may well have been on the treatment table at Old Trafford rather than on that fateful trip to Belgrade.

Shortly after 8 a.m. on a misty, rain-sodden Monday morning, British European Airways flight number G-ALZU A857 soared off the end of a Manchester runway and headed south over the Channel and deep into Germany, to Munich. On board was the Manchester United team and a host of journalists, photographers and pressmen. The familiar bulldog features of assistant manager Jimmy Murphy were missing from the United party. Murphy had stayed behind to take charge of the Welsh national team who were involved in a vital World Cup qualifying match against Israel. The fiercely patriotic Welshman would make his way to Cardiff to help out his country, but there was little doubt where his true feelings lay. Jimmy Murphy's heart was with his lads as they prepared to take on the formidable Red Star Belgrade. After a short refuelling stop at Munich airport, the plane was back in the air and on its final leg of the journey to Belgrade. On board, the players passed the time away by playing cards and sleeping. The constant drone of the Elizabethan's huge engines hummed away endlessly in the background. Finally the message came from the cockpit for everyone to return to their seats as they were preparing to land at Belgrade airport. The streets of the Yugoslav capital whilst strewn with snow were brightened by bursts of sunshine, a sure sign that spring was just around the corner. Manchester United's hotel was on the banks of the Danube. Busby had taken no chances with his players' preparation. They were to be given only English-type food.

As for injuries, the only major doubt was Roger Byrne. The England defender was touch and go and if he was deemed unfit his place would go to Salford lad Geoff Bent. Bent had only been told the day before that he would be included in the trip. A more than useful full-back, he would easily have commanded a place in any other first division team. On the Tuesday before the game, United warmed up at Belgrade's training ground. It was there that Roger Byrne was given a thorough work-out by Busby and his trainers Bert Whalley and Tom Curry. Curry, after putting Byrne through a rigorous sprinting session, was overjoyed when the captain of his club gave him a thumbs-up. His would be a much-needed presence amidst what was sure to be an intimidating atmosphere at the Stadion Crvena Zvezda.

The day of the match dawned and the United players woke to a clear, crisp Belgrade morning. Their hotel foyer was filled to the brim with autograph hunters all intent on capturing the names of these famous English footballers. The coach taking the team to the ground was mobbed along the way by thousands of Red Star supporters screaming their support for the home side. If the Babes were going to go back to Manchester with a positive result it was clear they would need to be at their best. In warm sunshine and on a pitch soaking up the last remnants of melting snow, Manchester United and Red Star Belgrade lined up in full view of 52,000 fanatical Yugoslav supporters. The noise inside the stadium was deafening.

The previous season had seen Red Star's fierce local rivals Partizan Belgrade hammer three goals past the great Real Madrid only to lose narrowly on aggregate. Now, here in the Crvena Zvezda, the fans prayed that their heroes could beat that historic achievement and see off the Busby Babes. Within 90 seconds those hopes were fading as Dennis Viollet swooped like lightning onto a lax back pass and smashed United into the lead. The home side were stunned; and the Babes went for an early kill. As Red Star buckled under relentless pressure, Bobby Charlton fired in a second goal. Luckily for the Yugoslavs, and to the fury of United, the Austrian referee, Karl Kainer, blew for a very dubious offside decision. A clearly perturbed Red Star Belgrade were failing miserably to put any kind of decent move together; and with their supporters becoming increasingly irritated, Charlton dispossessed Kostic and let fly a screaming low drive that powered past a diving Beara. Two minutes later, with Belgrade aghast, Charlton incredibly scored again. Running through a muddle of Yugoslav defenders the United forward shot home with huge confidence to give his team an amazing 3–0 lead. Only 30 minutes gone and Manchester United looked home and dry. The semi-finals beckoned loudly for the Busby Babes. The half-time whistle was greeted with derision and jeers by the furious home supporters. Their pre-match hopes had been smashed to pieces by the Babes' magnificent display of attacking football. In the press box English reporters were staggered by the events which had unfurled in front of them. Although witnesses to many of United's finest showing, even the most hardened hack was impressed. This was something quite extraordinary.

Whatever was said or threatened in the home side dressing-room certainly had the desired effect. Red Star Belgrade began the second half transformed. It took them all of two minutes to grab back a much-needed goal when Kostic saw his effort scream past Harry Gregg, reducing the overall aggregate to 5–2. Sekularac was back on the scene too with vengeance in his heart and gold dust on his dancing feet. The little man's undoubted skill repeatedly cut the United defence to ribbons. It was he who was masterminding the Yugoslav all-out offensive on an increasingly embarrassed Manchester defence. United's cause was hardly helped by the shower of snowballs that rained down upon them at every opportunity. Gregg in the Manchester net was a particularly easy target, being forced to endure a constant barrage from behind his goal all through the second half. With United being pushed further and further back, Red Star were awarded an extremely dubious penalty when Tasic and Bill Foulkes clashed in the area. The referee pointed immediately to the spot, much to the dismay of the United players. For what had seemed an innocent collision Belgrade were given the chance to cut the deficit even further. Tasic stepped forward and unleashed a shot which just beat Harry Gregg's fingertips: 5–3 on aggregate.

The Babes were in big trouble. With Edwards reduced to nuisance value because of injury, and Harry Gregg lying hurt on the ground, Cotic missed an open goal from five yards out. It was bedlam in and around the English champions' goal as Red Star fought desperately to claw back the deficit. Cotic's miss caused a huge crush in the crowd as hordes of excited supporters surged down the terraces, only to come to a terrifying halt at a concrete wall. Dazed and staggering Yugoslavs, with their breath almost knocked out of them, were helped onto the running track surrounding the pitch by soldiers and policemen. As the clock ran down, Red Star's ability to find holes in the United defence increased rapidly. Roger Byrne had marshalled his team's rearguard action with huge heart and resolve. Alongside him Mark Jones, a tough no-nonsense Yorkshireman, had shown real grit as he battled to withstand a ferocious last effort from the Yugoslav champions. Two minutes remained on Herr Kainer's watch when Belgrade were awarded a free kick after Harry Gregg had slithered on the snow and ended up outside his own penalty area. With what looked like consummate ease, Kostic scored his second goal of the game by planting the ball over the United defensive wall and into the back of the net: 3–3. Red Star were rampant. With seconds remaining, a limping, bedraggled, ragged Manchester United were close to collapse. The Busby Babes were all but done. Requiring one more goal to take the quarter-final to a third game, the gypsy set off on one last foray into the Manchester half. With Mancunian hearts beating fast the referee ended the pain and blew the final whistle.

Manchester United were in the semi-final of the European Cup, but only after the shock of their young lives. The Red Star players dropped to their knees. They could not believe that their second-half revival had amounted to nothing. Despite a wonderfully courageous fightback the pride of Belgrade were out. It was a happy Matt Busby who celebrated into the early hours with his walking wounded at the post-match banquet. Laid on by Red Star, all hostilities on the field were forgotten as life-long friendships were struck up on both sides. Vast quantities of Belgrade's finest wine were downed as a merry time was had by all. Roger Byrne ended proceedings by leading his team in a moving rendition of a song which brought lumps to the throats of all present:

> *We'll meet again,*
> *Don't know where,*
> *Don't know when;*
> *But I know we'll meet again*
> *Some sunny day.*

When these lyrics were translated for their Yugoslav hosts applause broke out amongst them across the dining hall. Tears were mixed with laughter and joy, goodbyes were said and the memorable night drew to a close. Outside, the Belgrade sky was thick with snow falling like huge confetti onto the city. The date was 6 February 1958.

MUNICH DAWN

Next morning it was a sorry-looking, hung-over group of players, officials and reporters who boarded the plane that would take them back to Manchester. Bleary-eyed but happy, Matt Busby's Manchester United said a fond farewell to Belgrade and began the long journey home. Once on board they played cards or caught up with some shut-eye after their previous night's adventures. First port of call before the rainy city would be Munich whilst the aeroplane refuelled. Outside, a blizzard was sweeping across the airport as the huge Elizabethan prepared its descent onto the runway. Munich: the home of the famous beer kellers where Adolf Hitler had first met with his cronies. Munich: the home of elegant churches and world-renowned art galleries. Munich.

After a short spell in the departure lounge, when there was just time to buy a cup of tea and a sandwich, the call came for everybody to begin reboarding. At 2.30 p.m. the Elizabethan set off down the runway. Slowly gathering speed, it was suddenly brought to a shuddering halt with its engines still roaring at full power. After this aborted take-off, permission was granted by the control tower to try again. Once more she faltered and any idea of taking off was abandoned. After being told the hitch was due to a technical fault, the passengers returned to the departure lounge whilst repairs were made. After only a short time the call went out for everybody to head back across the tarmac and take their seats again.

At 3.03 p.m. flight G-ALZU A857 accelerated into the darkness of the Munich runway, reaching a speed of 117 m.p.h. Suddenly, Captain James Thain noticed a surge in the boost control. The air indicator dropped dramatically and, as the end of the runway hurtled ever closer, panic filled the cockpit. On board fear was etched on the faces of people who knew that something had gone badly wrong. Liam Whelan murmured quietly to himself that he was ready to meet his Maker. Others hid their terror through sheer bravado. As the slush and sleet from the wheels hurled against the portholes, the plane sped towards its tragic end. 'Christ, we are not going to make it!' screamed the voice of co-pilot Captain Ken Rayment as the aircrew fought a desperate battle to save their aeroplane from disaster. Back amongst the passengers many had their eyes shut, hoping and praying that the nightmare would have a happy ending.

Frantically Thain tried to retract the undercarriage, but the fuselage refused to lift. They were literally only seconds from disaster. From this moment on the aeroplane veered horribly out of control. It smashed through the runway perimeter fence, screeching and hurtling into a head-on collision with a nearby hut filled with oil and petrol reserves. By this time it had been literally ripped in two; a shocking, twisted mass of metal threatening at any moment to explode. On board, death had come to MUFC. Seven of the Busby Babes had been killed outright, their bodies scattered indiscriminately amidst the carnage. In the cockpit, Rayment lay trapped. Thain and Rodgers, the radio officer, had by some miracle survived. They clambered out of the flight deck and began work with fire extinguishers on the several small fires that were threatening at any second to lead to an inferno. What they saw as they doused the flames was akin to a scene from hell. Victims sat strapped to their seats, almost as if sleeping.

In the frightening darkness, the muffled cries of a baby were heard by United's surviving goalkeeper Harry Gregg. Gregg was in the act of scrambling clear of the carnage when he heard this heart-rending sound. Without any thought for his own safety, the big Irishman climbed back inside and after a short foray through the debris found the source of the crying. Quickly he grabbed the tot and headed for safety. Bill Foulkes was another who decided to stay in the plane and help others. He found Bobby Charlton and Dennis Viollet still strapped in their seats, both unconscious. At first

Foulkes had run clear of the wreckage, returning when it failed to explode. When the first ambulance arrived on the scene he helped lift a crucially injured Matt Busby inside and rode with him to the hospital. Within 20 minutes of the disaster all the injured had been transferred to the Rechts der Isar Hospital. The emergency procedure for such incidents had sprung quickly into action with typical German efficiency. Hovering between life and death, Matt Busby was twice given the last rites by a local priest. Busby's chest and foot had been crushed and one of his lungs had collapsed. There were grave doubts amongst the medical staff that he would survive.

Duncan Edwards had survived the crash but was now in a very serious state. His famous huge thighs lay smashed and, most importantly, his kidneys had been dreadfully punctured. There was little hope that he would pull through. These were the survivors. Back on that runway the dead were being carried out of the wreckage in mournful procession and placed in a line beneath blankets. In Manchester the news began to filter through in dribs and drabs. The BBC interrupted its afternoon programming to broadcast a newsflash. People listened to the words but few understood their true meaning. It was simply too terrible to take in.

Jimmy Murphy arrived back at Old Trafford from Cardiff clutching a bag of oranges. These had been presented to him by the Israelis following Wales's vital World Cup win. He was met by his tearful secretary, Alma George, who informed him of the dreadful events that had occurred in southern Germany. Murphy heard her words but said nothing. He simply walked into his office, shut the door behind him and opened a bottle of whisky. The following day Jimmy Murphy flew out to Munich and was stunned by what he saw. He was ushered in to see Matt Busby, who was being kept alive in an oxygen tent. Busby managed to utter a few words to his assistant. 'Keep the flag flying, Jimmy, till I get back.' Murphy broke down on seeing the state that Duncan Edwards had been reduced to. His former star pupil lying helpless before him was too much for the normally ferocious Welshman to bear.

A strange feeling of depression hung over Manchester. Everywhere people were in shock. The churches were packed with supporters offering silent prayers for the safe return of their heroes. Tragically the cost of life had been enormous. Twenty-three people in all had been killed, including the heart and soul of Manchester United Football Club: left-back Roger Byrne and his reserve, Geoff Bent; Eddie Colman, right-half; Mark Jones, centre-half; Bill Whelan, inside-right, the hero of Bilbao; Tommy Taylor, the 'smiling executioner', centre-forward; and David Pegg, outside-right.

For 21 days Duncan Edwards had fought and scrapped and battled as he had never done before. The German hospital tried desperately to keep him alive. A kidney machine was flown in from Stuttgart. A 24-hour watch was placed on the brave young Englishman as he steadfastly refused to bow to the inevitable. In Belgrade the news of the crash was greeted with horror. Sekularac spoke for all his team-mates and supporters when he declared: 'Edwards will not be beaten. He will win his fight for life.' Sadly the gypsy's magic did not amount to the power needed to grant such a wish. The hopes of all Red Star Belgrade were with Edwards and his manager as they lay wounded.

In his ailing state Edwards cried out for his much-valued gold watch presented to him by Real Madrid. Baffled, the hospital staff inquired as to its whereabouts. It turned out that the watch still lay amidst the burnt-out wreckage of the aeroplane. A special search was organised to see if it could be found. Luckily it turned up and was whisked off to the hospital to be reunited with its owner. Having his precious memento back seemed for a while to revive Duncan. Hopes soared amongst hospital staff and supporters for a miraculous recovery. But his injuries were too serious. Shortly after his watch had been returned Duncan Edwards finally lost his gallant fight for life. At 1.12 a.m. on 21 February 1958, the final whistle blew on the life of this heroic young man. He was 21 years old. The final word on Duncan Edwards must surely lie with the man more than any responsible for the harnessing of such a talent. Jimmy Murphy would often relate the tale of when he first heard Muhammad Ali proclaim himself the greatest. Murphy had smiled quietly to himself and said, 'No, son, you are not the greatest. You see, the greatest of them all was a young English footballer named Duncan Edwards.' It was a crying shame.

The dire news was kept from Matt Busby for six days. It was thought by the surgeon to whom he owed his life, Dr Georg Maurer, that Busby could not be informed of Edwards's passing for at least a month. The shock of such grim tidings might well have pushed the United manager past the point of recovery. Busby, however, sensed something had gone terribly wrong. It was a German Catholic priest who acceded to Busby's wishes to hear what had happened. Tears fell from the eyes of this quietly spoken Scotsman. It was to be a full two months before Matt Busby recovered sufficiently even to consider returning to England and his beloved United. Or what was left of it. The pain in his broken body was a constant reminder of the aircrash, but this in time would heal. It would be the scars on his soul that would linger. The loss of his Babes and especially big Duncan would haunt him till the day arrived for him to join them.

At first Busby wanted nothing more to do with football. He was adamant that he was through. But in time the thirst to rebuild his club returned and he did come back, filled with a burning desire to make his club the best in Europe and honour the memory of those who had perished. From the ashes of Munich Matt Busby and Jimmy Murphy dragged Manchester United back from the precipice to a dramatic European Cup final win ten years later.

6.

THE SECOND COMING

REAL MADRID V EINTRACHT FRANKFURT

1960 EUROPEAN CUP FINAL

he cynics and the doubters were all united in their opinion. The fairy tale was over. The Galloping Major had fought his last battle. Or so they claimed. In the summer of 1958 Ferenc Puskas boarded the aeroplane that was to take him to Madrid. He was pensive. Thirty-one years old and almost a stone overweight, Puskas had been handed the gift of redemption from a most exalted source. Ever since the revolution two years before, which had forced him into exile from his motherland, this most revered of the Magyars and his young family had been living out of a suitcase. The Communist Hungarian authorities took a grim view of this former hero of the homeland. Their decision to withhold his registration, allied to Puskas's continuing battle against his expanding waistline, made Europe's élite clubs wary of taking a chance on him. There was one man who looked beyond such minor problems. The president and self-proclaimed godfather of Real Madrid, Don Santiago Bernabeu, sensed the desire and genius that still burned within Ferenc Puskas. He sensed a soulmate; a man who like himself saw no boundaries. Bernabeu wanted the Hungarian to play alongside Alfredo di Stefano. Di Stefano had only recently led Real to their third European Cup triumph. Victory over AC Milan had been a hard-fought affair which had fiercely tested the Madrilenos.

The win was gained, however, under the shadow of the Munich air disaster. Manchester United, as close as any team to the great Real, had been wiped out in southern Germany. The reaction in Madrid to the disaster was one of total horror. Commemorative pendants issued by the club dedicated to the United players who perished were rapidly snapped up by Real supporters and the money raised sent over to England. However, their finest gesture of friendship came shortly after Madrid had defeated Milan in the 1959 European Cup final. Immediately following the game, the Spaniards offered the trophy to

Manchester. Despite being overwhelmed by the Madrilenos' magnificent gesture, United refused. It was ten long years before the red devils had recovered sufficiently to get their hands on the European Cup.

It was during Ferenc Puskas's early training sessions with his new team-mates that signs of a stand-off with di Stefano began to show. Two men who were masters of their trade quietly eyed each other. Like two heavyweight boxers fighting for the world title circling the ring, they waited to throw the first punch. Madrid was a large city but would it be big enough for these two characters? The former captain of the Magyars masterminded a plan.

Puskas reversed his traditional method of running out first. Instead he would make an equally dramatic entrance into the arena by appearing last. In no time at all Puskas was made to feel at home by his fellow Madrilenos, although di Stefano kept a respectful and much noticed distance. The Hungarian's wicked sense of humour had his team-mates appreciating him as more than just a brilliant footballer. Francisco Gento remembers Puskas juggling the soap in the showers with his legendary left peg, and his fellow players looking on in astonishment, while even di Stefano warmed to this likeable character. Slowly he fell under the Galloping Major's spell. During Real's pre-season training the weight fell off Puskas as he worked like a Trojan under the sweltering Spanish sun. When the time came round for the primera liga to begin the Major was ready to prove his worth. He so much wanted to repay the faith that Real and Bernabeu had shown in him. It was on 2 September 1959, against Oviedo in Madrid, in front of 100,000 people, that the fairy tale resumed. Real won 5–2, with Puskas himself grabbing a brace. Real's latest signing soon learned that he had to be at the peak of his game at all times. Whenever the Madrilenos attacked, whether di Stefano was on the prowl, or Gento and the great Frenchman Kopa were careering down the wing, Puskas had to be in or around the box waiting for the pass.

The early signs were promising. Despite not being a favourite of the coach, Carniglia, he quickly established himself as one of the deadliest hitmen in Spain. He and di Stefano were neck and neck in the goal-scoring charts all the way through that first season. In Spain there is huge prestige in finishing top scorer and for a man like di Stefano, whose huge ego forever needed massaging, prizes like this were essential. The wily Magyar could see a way in which his partnership with the legendary Argentinian could be sealed. If events went as planned it would prove to be a master stroke by Hungary's finest. It was during Real's last game of the season and the Madrilenos as ever were on the attack. Puskas had dribbled his way through the opponents' defence and found himself facing an open goal. Both he and di Stefano were on level pegging in the goal charts. With time running down this effort would have handed the trophy to Ferenc Puskas. However, with all of Madrid ready to hail their adopted Magyar as top scorer, Puskas noticed out of the corner of his eye Alfredo di Stefano charging into the penalty area. Knowing that if he scored, his number nine would never speak to him again, the Major rolled the ball sideways for his colleague to smash into the net. The Bernabeu erupted in joy! The White Arrow ran over to his new best friend and warmly embraced him in a bearhug. Ferenc Puskas had been granted the royal decree.

Di Stefano would finish with the glory, but it would be the Major who in time would prove to be the real winner. In that moment a truly formidable partnership was formed. Across Europe the clubs trying to hang onto Real Madrid's coat-tails felt the shudder. Such generosity of spirit boded well for the future of this sporting phenomenon. That season saw Madrid once more reach the European Cup final, whose trophy they had come to regard as their own. Puskas had more than played his part. It had been his deciding goal in the semi against fellow Madrid rivals Athletico that had seen Real through; this only after a third game had been needed to slice apart the teams. Their opponents in the final were to be the Frenchmen of Rheims, Madrid's first-ever opponents back in 1955. However, their Hungarian talisman would have no part to play in the final. Puskas's fiery relationship with Carniglia resulted in him being told by his coach that he would not be playing in the game. All this just an hour before kick-off. The excuse given by Carniglia when asked by Puskas was that 'you are injured'.

It was to make little difference to the result. On 3 June 1959, the fourth European Cup was Madrid's once more. Mateos and di Stefano scored the goals that had the Madrilenos roaring with delight in front of 60,000 people. Amidst the joyful celebrations one man found it hard to enter into the party spirit. Ferenc Puskas was unusually quiet during the after-match banquet. This was noticed by Santiago Bernabeu, who sat himself down next to Puskas and asked why he had not played. The Major smiled ruefully and said to Don Santiago that he should put the same question to Carniglia. Bernabeu puffed thoughtfully on one of his huge Cuban cigars, ringed of course with a Real Madrid wrapper. Something was not right behind the scenes. Carniglia was on borrowed time.

For the 1959–60 season, Real Madrid again dipped into the treasure chest. From South America came Didi; the Brazilian whose free kicks had the venom and swerve to send crowds behind the goal diving for safety arrived amongst huge pomp at Madrid airport. Stories that he had been brought in eventually to replace di Stefano caused ructions in the Real corridors of power. Di Stefano was not a happy man. Their first meeting was the heady stuff of football legends. Di Stefano was reported to have told his new team-mate in front of his fellow Madrilenos that he was 'neither good enough nor young enough' to take his place. Didi's was not to be a happy stay at the home of the European champions. Di Stefano's influence was clearly evident as Didi was passed over for game after game. A loan spell to Valencia followed before a return to Bofotago in Brazil ended an unhappy year for the shell-shocked Brazilian.

Back on home territory and his compensation from Real Madrid locked safely in his bank account, Didi revealed the story of his stay amongst the Madrilenos. He claimed that he had been the victim of a boycott; a determined campaign to destabilise his position in Madrid, led by di Stefano. Puskas would always claim that from his arrival at Real, Didi started gaining the weight that he himself had fought so hard to lose. The truth probably lies somewhere between the two stories. Basically, Didi had come to the dreadfully wrong conclusion that he had finally made it, not realising, as the Major had, that the hard work truly begins as the door of the plane is wrenched open at Madrid airport and the Spanish heat gushes wildly into your face. Puskas's own words seem to sum up the whole tragedy of Didi's short stay in the castle on the hill. The Major declared that the Brazilian became 'too fat and slow to play for the great Real Madrid'. Enough said.

With Carniglia deemed surplus to requirements, the next man through the door at Madrid was the experienced Paraguayan Fleitas Solich. Sadly for him he too fell foul of certain powerful individuals within the framework of the dressing-room. Solich would not see out the season. Instead, in a move based wholly to suit certain players (no names needed!), a familiar face was brought in. The former captain of Real Madrid, Miguel Munoz, became team coach. This was a decision that was hugely welcomed by the Real players. Munoz was a true Madrileno who understood the problems that came with pulling on that famous white shirt. Munoz had no problems in consulting his experienced players on matters that for him were difficult to resolve. He had no wish to experience the fate of the unfortunate Carniglia and Solich. For him, di Stefano and Ferenc Puskas were men who he clearly wished to have on his side. He had little to worry about. Both the Major and di Stefano were more than happy with Bernabeu's newest appointment.

One man who by this time had been sacrificed was Raymonde Kopa. Kopa had returned to France to pull on again the jersey of his former club Rheims. The reason was that Bernabeu had sent forth his treasurer Raimondo Saporta to South America to try for what would be, if successful, the most audacious coup of all. For Saporta, armed as ever with Spanish gold, was out to capture in his net a certain Edson Arantes of Nascimentes, known to millions around the world as Pele. If Saporta had succeeded in his mission the rest of Europe might as well have thrown in the towel. But it was not to be. Pele's club Santos, backed by the Brazilian government, refused to do business. Saporta, after repeatedly hitting brick walls in his negotiations, returned to Madrid a beaten man. Pele was not for sale at any price. Bernabeu simply had to take it on the chin. Despite being disappointed, the president of the Madrilenos knew well that his team could still prove more than a match for any club side in the world. Whilst the Madrilenos sat rather complacently on their heavenly perch, however, something was beginning to stir in Catalonia.

As Madrid conquered all before them on the European scene, events on home soil were proving more difficult. Their arch enemy, the Catalans of Barcelona, had acquired at a tremendous price the Argentinian-born master tactician Helenio Herrera. Herrera had gained a reputation as a worker of footballing miracles. Here was a man who possessed few equals when it came to motivating players to perform at their peak. Herrera's methods bordered at times on the bizarre. The Catalonian press were often baffled by his guru-like approach to management. However, even the most cynical hack could not argue with the positive effect which Herrera had on the team. The wily Argentinian, as soon as he arrived in Barcelona, set about ridding them of an inbuilt inferiority complex regarding General Franco's favourite football team. Herrera inherited a side overflowing with skill and attacking flair, undoubtedly the equal on its day of the Madrilenos themselves. However, there was a deep-rooted self-doubt which existed among the Catalans, amounting to paranoia. Referees were deemed totally biased in favour of di Stefano and his all stars. There were times when the Barca supporters had a point. Real were certainly the first love of the nation's leader, General Franco. With television in its infancy, decisions were made in Real's favour which at times beggared belief.

Herrera used all this to his advantage. It would be the Catalan nation against the world. Defend the honour of the Barca banner! Such talk worked wonders, but only on the players born within the boundaries of this proud region. Luckily for Herrera his defensive players were men who were born with Catalan blood pumping through their veins. He changed tack when rallying his international superstars. To them he simply talked money. Huge bonus schemes were set in place which almost immediately began to work wonders. World-class players such as Zoltan Czibor and Sandor Kocsis suddenly began to show their true worth. The Hungarian pair had underachieved badly before Herrera's arrival. Not any more.

There was also the case of Ladislao Kubala. Kubala was the idol of the Barcelona terraces. An attacking midfielder of immense subtlety and skill, this was a player on his day as good as any in the world, including what was on

offer in Madrid. Another Catalan idol was the slim figure of the elusive,
explosive Luis Suarez. This young Spaniard possessed the ability to rip teams
apart on his own. Later Suarez would transfer to Italy and Internazionale for
a then world record fee. With such talent at his disposal Herrera talked,
cajoled and bullied his Catalonian giant out of its slumber and self-doubt.
The Argentinian's impact on events was such that in his first season in charge
not only was the championship finally regained after a long and painful
struggle, but also the Spanish Cup was won to complete a wonderful double.
The Catalan nation celebrated like never before. This was one in the eye for
Franco and his army of Fascists and bully-boys.

Herrera was all but canonised by the Barca supporters. This strange
charismatic figure who had arrived amongst them after surviving a plane crash
had given them back their pride. At long last the Catalans could raise two
fingers at the hated aristocrats of Madrid. More importantly, Barcelona had
qualified for the European Cup. Here they would be given the chance to
attack the Madrilenos on the European front and take from them their most
cherished prize. Could they possibly loosen the champions' vice-like grip on
the trophy? It seemed almost inevitable that fate would decree a coming
together of these two great rivals. It happened at the semi-final stage, and
proved full of drama and controversy.

It was on the eve of the first leg in Madrid that the Catalans set about
cutting their own throats. Herrera had found himself entangled in a slanging
match with one of his star forwards, Kubala. The two men had never got on
and only tolerated each other for the good of the club. On this particular
occasion, however, the gloves came off and all hell was let loose. After hearing
rumours of what the Real players could earn in win bonuses for the upcoming
game, Kubala demanded that he and his team-mates be rewarded equally.
Along with the Hungarian Czibor he stood toe to toe with a furious Herrera
arguing their cause. With no one backing down, events threatened to turn
nasty. Finally a livid Herrera snapped and told the two desperados that he was
dropping them from the game. The decision had the desired effect. Both
Kubala and Czibor stood open-mouthed at Herrera. Surely he would not go
through with it? If events went wrong in the Bernabeu and Barcelona lost
without the services of arguably the two best players, Herrera would be
hanged, drawn and quartered back in Barcelona. Sadly for them they had
tangled with a man whose ego was equally as important to him as his bank
balance. Helenio Herrera was not for turning. Ladislao Kubala and Zoltan
Czibor were out. Barcelona would enter the territory of the old enemy sorely
weakened. It was to prove a ghastly mistake. The Madrilenos sharpened their
blades.

The following evening a Barca side still in shock from its vicious in-fighting were put to the sword by di Stefano and his electrifying white knights. With di Stefano running the show, Real ripped the Catalans to pieces. Their generalissimo helped himself to two whilst his loyal Major gleefully hammered home a third. The European champions at times toyed with the Barca side, much to the delight of the Bernabeu audience. Barcelona would escape with a 1–3 drubbing. Herrera had some serious explaining to do. The next day the Barca manager was mercilessly pilloried on his return to home territory. The Catalan newspapers swooped like a pack of wolves. From hero to villain in such a short time, Herrera clearly feared the worst.

The manager, nicknamed 'El Mago' (the magician), had one trick left up his sleeve. Both Czibor and Kubala were recalled for the second leg. Ninety-two thousand screaming Barca supporters crammed tight into the Nou Camp all desperate to cheer their heroes to a glorious comeback. Sadly for them it was not to be. In an atmosphere brimming with hatred and intimidation, Real Madrid breezed into Catalonia and blew away Helenio Herrera and Barcelona with some ease. It was a sumptuous performance by the Madrilenos. Two goals from Puskas and one from the jet-heeled Francisco Gento put paid to the home side's aspirations to European glory. The final moments of the contest saw Real play keep ball against their bedraggled opponents. It was quite clear that a fraught-looking Herrera on the touchline was a condemned man. Indeed, shortly after the final whistle Helenio Herrera was sacked by Barcelona president Miro-Sans. The night failed to improve for this fallen Catalan hero, for later in the evening he was set upon by a seething mob of Barca supporters who had waited impatiently to vent their wrath upon the man for whom only a few weeks earlier they would have laid down their lives.

Herrera could not get out of Barcelona fast enough. It was clearly time for the magician to do a vanishing act. The world had not heard the last of Helenio Herrera, though. He would soon reappear in the battleground and intrigue of Italian football with Inter Milan. Much to the exasperation of all Barca supporters he would lead them twice to glory in the European Cup. Incredibly, after Herrera's dramatic exit Barcelona regrouped, licked their wounds and pipped Real Madrid to a second consecutive primera championship. The Catalans snaked past the winning post in one of the closest finishes ever in the history of Spanish football. In the end only goal difference separated the two bitter duellists. Barca football club had regained some much-needed face after their terrible humiliation at the hands of Real in the European Cup. As for the Madrilenos: they had to recover from the disappointment of a second domestic loss and concentrate fully on the forthcoming European Champions Cup final.

Their opponents were German champions Eintracht Frankfurt. Eintracht had dismembered Glasgow Rangers over two legs in the semi-final. The final aggregate score of 12–4 was no fluke as the Germans overpowered the beleaguered Scottish champions. Their performance was such that many experts began to speak openly and loudly that they would be the team to put an end to Real Madrid's magnificent run. The critics had been saying for a while that Real were there for the taking but no side had yet managed the task, but such was the power and pace of this crack German outfit that many people expected the Madrilenos to face a most severe examination.

For one man the game could not come round quickly enough. Ferenc Puskas prepared to take part in his first major European final. A glittering career had seen the Major stumble at the last when it came to ultimate prizes. A heartbreaking defeat in the 1954 World Cup final against the West Germans still haunted Puskas. To have victory snatched from him in such dramatic and controversial circumstances made the bitter loss even harder to take. Now fast approaching the age of 34, time was running out for the Hungarian. Like lightning streaking through the night sky this very special footballer had illuminated the European game for a decade. Now the time had come for his reward. Along with his generalissimo di Stefano, the Major prepared to wage war.

The venue chosen to host Real Madrid's fifth foray into the European Cup final was Glasgow's Hampden Park. On 18 May 1960, 127,000 people paid the then massive sum of £55,000 for the privilege of witnessing an unforgettable evening; for on this warm, balmy Glasgow evening the Madrilenos took European football to another level. If what was being said at the time was true this was to be Real's swansong, the end of an era. Happily, nobody bothered to inform di Stefano and his galloping sidekick that they were over the hill.

Shortly before kick-off the atmosphere in the Madrid changing-room was one of quiet defiance. Jose Santamaria, the team's exquisite and outstanding centre-half, busied himself juggling a football. He felt the eyes of his compadres closely watching his every move, all happy to have something to concentrate on as they readied themselves for the signal to line up in the Hampden tunnel. Ferenc Puskas glanced around the room at his fellow Madrilenos: Gento, del Sol, Canario, Santamaria, di Stefano. Who in the world possessed such talent as this? The Magyar suddenly felt his stomach turn over with worry. That famous cockiness and confidence for once disappeared as Puskas for the first time felt his age. He began to remember old times: playing with Bozsik as a child – how he dearly missed his old friend – the slaughter of England; the battle with the Brazilians; the torment of the

Germans. It had been an unforgettable journey. The bell for the champions to head for the pitch shook Puskas out of his daydreaming. The time had arrived for this little fellow to carve his name along with his colleagues in footballing folklore.

The city of Glasgow found itself torn in two as to whom to support. The Protestant Rangers fans were firmly behind the Germans whilst Celtic's Catholics formed in procession behind the pride of the Spanish Church. Glasgow was in a world of its own when it came to sectarianism. It was sad that an occasion such as the European Cup final should have been dragged into the mire of religion and politics. Luckily Real Madrid were about to show that football can cross any barrier put in its path. Even the age-old problem of bigotry could not stand up to the magic of the Madrilenos.

Eintracht began the final in the same form that had demolished Rangers, a shot from their powerful Meier smashing violently against the Real crossbar. Quick and nippy in midfield, they broke fast on the wings and poured men forward when on the attack. It was clear that the champions had a real game on their hands. Del Sol produced a moment of magic for the Madrilenos, but his low shot failed to trouble Loy in the Frankfurt goal. The Scottish crowd watched enraptured as Eintracht tore into the Spanish aristocrats with a vengeance. On 22 minutes the Germans got the reward for their efforts when they took a well-deserved lead.

With Real struggling to gain a foothold in the game, the Frankfurt winger Stein accelerated to the by-line and crossed superbly for the waiting Kress to thump it past a despairing Dominguez from six yards. The Real Madrid players looked stunned. Santamaria appeared disgusted with himself at letting Kress get the better of him. Di Stefano gave him a look of disdain. It was time for the generalissimo to take control of the situation. Suddenly the white shirts began to make inroads on the Eintracht goal. It took them only six minutes to equalise. Canario swooped past the German defender and crossed for his leader di Stefano to shoot low past the Frankfurt keeper. The generalissimo had now scored in every European Cup final to date. The goal had a galvanising effect on the champions. Madrid tore into top gear and the Germans suddenly found themselves on the back foot. Three minutes later a fumble by Loy let in di Stefano to score again.

Real were now turning on the charm. To the annoyance of the Eintracht players the wizards of Madrid stroked the ball from Madrileno to Madrileno with pure nonchalance. Time and again Gento and Canario ripped like dervishes into the German area looking to feed the waiting Puskas. At the back Santamaria and Marquitos appeared to be winning the battle against the ever-dangerous Frankfurt forwards. But even amongst such majesty one man stood out. Di Stefano commanded centre stage as Real Madrid moved into full throttle. On the stroke of half-time Ferenc Puskas entered the spotlight as he let fly a thunderous strike which whistled past a besieged Loy. From what had looked an impossible angle the Galloping Major had found to perfection the right-hand side of the goal. The Glasgow audience roared their delight. It was rapidly turning into an exhibition by the European champions. Sadly, back in Puskas's homeland this momentous occasion was seen by hardly anyone as the Hungarian Communist government refused to allow the match to be screened on television. The reason was the inclusion of Puskas in the Real Madrid line-up. He had never been forgiven by the authorities for not returning home after the revolution. His decision to stay abroad along with Kocsis and Czibor had seen him condemned a traitor by the same people who once worshipped at his feet.

The determined Germans refused to throw in the towel, despite being turned almost into stooges. With huge pride Eintracht battled on. There would be no white flag raised by this team; indignant, harassed beyond all comprehension, slightly embarrassed but never ever bowing to the inevitable. Meanwhile the Real Madrid all-singing, all-dancing performance continued to grind them down. Nine minutes into the second half the Madrilenos wrapped up their fifth European Cup final. The shattering electric-heeled feet of Paco Gento flew past the flustered German defender Lutz and into the penalty area. Finally admitting defeat, Lutz nudged Gento and the referee blew for a penalty. Ferenc Puskas stepped up casually to convert number four. A little shimmy and the goalkeeper was dazzled.

A dumbstruck Hampden crowd watched the almost surreal goings-on in their famous old stadium. Real had begun to show off. A whirling haze of white shirts moved across the turf torturing the bewildered Germans. The ball never seemed to be kicked. It was caressed, cajoled, flicked and stroked. The Scottish crowd had fallen in love with Real Madrid. On the hour Gento, with a weary Lutz in pursuit, soared once more into Eintracht's penalty area. The little winger crossed superbly for his friend Puskas to gleefully complete his hat trick. By now it was nothing less than a massacre. Instigated by di Stefano, Real continued to go for the German throats. On 70 minutes Puskas, as if by magic, killed the ball dead in the penalty area and smashed in his fourth goal and Real's sixth of the evening. This brought an astonishing reaction from the Hampden Park crowd, who all stood and roared approval of this wonderful goal from a truly magnificent player.

Two minutes later Eintracht pulled one back. Stein shot past Dominguez and lowered the humiliating scoreline to 6–2. The crowd responded with loud applause for the Germans' efforts. It was almost cruel that any team had to endure the kind of beating that Real handed out to them. The Germans were a fine side. The slaughter of Rangers in the semi-final had been a prime example of what they were capable of. It just so happened that the team they were now up against was from another planet.

Enter stage right Alfredo di Stefano. Inevitably it would be the generalissimo who would deliver the *coup de grâce*. The man who had orchestrated this bloody if beautiful massacre would seal his command performance with yet another marvellous goal. Playing any number of intricate one-twos the White Arrow glided through midfield and strode majestically towards the German goal. On reaching the edge of the box di Stefano let loose a strike which screamed low into the Frankfurt net. It was a cameo of all that was so special about the great Real Madrid: bewildering skills, fantastic pace, stunning finishing.

A lone klaxon sounded in sheer defiance as 15 minutes from time the Germans scored a third. The ever-dangerous Stein stole a back pass off a too-cocky Vidal to lower the deficit. Real Madrid 7, Eintracht 3. There were to be no more goals. The final whistle saw di Stefano and Puskas passing the ball between themselves, both intent on having the last touch, thus gaining the match ball. When the referee, Mr Jack Mowatt, finally ended proceedings, it was the Major who had won the fascinating little duel, but in a nice twist one of the German players pleaded with Puskas to be allowed the ball for a memento. After what he and his fellow Madrilenos had just done to his side how could the little Hungarian refuse him? Puskas shook his hand and joined his compadres in their moment of triumph.

The Scottish spectators rose en masse to acclaim the Spanish masters. This grand old stadium of Scottish football rocked and swayed as the roar from the terraces swept down onto the Real players. A friendly pitch invasion followed as the Madrilenos tried to set off on what would be the first of many laps of honour. Commentating for the BBC that night was Kenneth Wolstenholme. He described Real's performance as like '*Swan Lake* on turf'. The Frankfurt players themselves stayed behind to form a guard of honour as the Madrid players made it off the field. They would return to Germany well beaten but with their honour intact.

The crowd refused to leave the stadium. Almost an hour after the game had ended over 40,000 people remained on the terraces, many simply unable to comprehend what they had witnessed. Long after the Real players had disappeared to the dressing-room, the Scots stood gazing quietly out onto the empty Hampden turf.

The Madrilenos weren't going anywhere either. Glasgow's heart belonged to them as the Scots celebrated their magnificent triumph almost as if it was their own. The next day the players were paraded on an open-topped bus around the city as thousands turned out to honour them. After a civic reception at the town hall, where the European Cup had pride of place, the Real party moved onto the relative peace of Glasgow airport. Or so they thought! If Madrid thought that their hosts would let them go without saying a final goodbye they were badly mistaken. Waiting inside the airport were hundreds of supporters all intent on catching a final glimpse of their new heroes. Finally the plane taking the European champions home soared high off the runway and headed back to Madrid. And so Ferenc Puskas had his medal. The man the so-called critics had claimed was washed up on his arrival in Madrid had proved them all wrong. Puskas had shown that he had the heart to go with his undoubted skill. At the age of 33 the Major was playing better than at any time in his career. Maybe the gallop had eased into more of a trot but his star still shone bright. Ferenc Puskas had exploded like a supernova back on the world scene. It had indeed been a second coming.

7.

SUNSET OVER GUADAMARRA

BARCELONA V REAL MADRID

1961 EUROPEAN CUP

I t was on 6 August 1936, with the sun setting low over the peaks of the Guadamarra mountains in northern Spain, that the president of FC Barcelona, Josep Sunyol, was led out into an army courtyard. A blindfold was placed over his eyes as a priest administered to him the last rites. Sunyol stood deathly still. He awaited his fate with great courage. Seconds later militia men loyal to General Franco took careful aim and shot him dead. Sunyol's crime had been to drive accidentally into Fascist territory. After being taken prisoner by Franco's troops, he was tried, condemned as a traitor to his country, and made to pay the ultimate price. A hail of bullets through his Catalan heart.

Twenty-four years later came the momentous events of 25 November 1960. It would be then that Sunyol's memory could be suitably honoured by his fellow Catalans, for as they rejoiced in knocking out Real Madrid in the European Cup, revenge had also been gained for the murder of their president. Honour was finally seen to have been restored. Throughout Europe the press wires blazed with this dramatic and poignant news. Real Madrid's six-year reign as European champions had that evening been brought to a shattering end. One hundred and twelve thousand Catalans roared their delight at seeing their heroes dethrone the arch enemy. The walls to the castle on the hill had finally been breached, but the Madrilenos had certainly gone down fighting.

After Helenio Herrera's traumatic departure, Barcelona recovered sufficiently to gain entry back into the European Cup by hanging onto their league title by the slightest of margins. Herrera's replacement was an unlikely choice. The Yugoslavian coach Brocic was chosen to lead the Catalans in their eternal crusade against Real Madrid. Brocic inherited a magnificent squad. He strengthened it even more by acquiring the services of the great Jesus Garay from Athletico Bilbao, the man whose epic duels with Tommy Taylor had become the stuff of legends in both Spain and England. Barca had unfinished business with Real in the European Cup. The previous season had seen them ravaged by the Madrilenos at the semi-final stage. Both home and away di Stefano, Puskas and Gento had twisted the knife deep. These results had caused Herrera to make a swift exit from Catalonia before the Barca supporters hanged him from the highest tree. His decision not to play Kubala and Czibor in the first leg rebounded horribly upon him and Barcelona. Now an early chance of redemption had appeared, for in the second round of the 1961 European Cup, fate intervened to throw them together once more. All of Spain held its breath. The new manager Brocic had the opportunity to finish off a legend, and in doing so make himself an instant hero.

The animosity between the two clubs did not always extend to the players. The Hungarian contingents in both camps kept in regular contact during their time in Spain. Whenever the teams played in Barcelona, Ferenc Puskas would arrange to meet up with his countrymen Zoltan Czibor and Sandor Kocsis to talk of times gone by. Sadly, such was the bitterness between the sides, this was never possible in Puskas's home city of Madrid. Barca were not prepared to sip champagne in the hospitality suite of Don Santiago Bernabeu. The memory of Stuka dive bombers screaming low over Barcelona and slaughtering innocent civilians was still fresh in the mind. Besides, General Franco was still residing in Madrid. To say that the Catalans never hung around long at the Bernabeu after a game would be an understatement, but this rivalry never interfered in the friendship between the former Magyars. Whilst Puskas was enjoying success in Europe, Czibor and Kocsis enjoyed successive Spanish championships. This was not lost on the Barca pair. They would constantly remind their fellow Hungarian in Madrid of this fact. Puskas would receive endless phone calls from Catalonia gleefully asking if he knew who the reigning champions of Spain were at that moment. However, when the draw was made to pair them in the European Cup campaign of 1961 the laughing temporarily stopped.

This was serious. Even the affable Hungarian trio realised what this tie meant to both clubs. Whilst the friendships off the pitch remained strong, all three Magyars would happily throttle each other in the torrid atmosphere of these intense encounters. Events in the forthcoming games would test their bond of unity to its extreme. This was war.

Madrid was to host the first leg. For days leading up to the game the atmosphere in the city was tense. The Madrilenos waited eagerly for the arrival of the wretched Catalans. If the folk of Barca had little time for the people of the capital, then the feeling was completely mutual. They considered their rivals the lowest of the low. Their ultimate desire to rid themselves of Spain and declare their own independence infuriated the Madrid supporters. The Madrilenos' confidence had been rocked slightly by an injury to their powerful Uruguayan centre-half Jose Santamaria, but with home advantage they remained convinced that their generalissimo di Stefano would marshal his troops sufficiently to put these arrogant sons of bitches in their place. Barcelona arrived in Madrid at the latest possible hour. Enough to say they kept themselves to themselves.

Come 9 November and the Santiago Bernabeu stadium was awash with tension and excitement. A sea of white flags flew the crest of the European champions with pride. Well before kick-off there wasn't a spare seat in the ground. Rockets exploded in the night-time sky as the crowd waited impatiently for their heroes to take to the pitch. Suddenly the noise level increased as the teams came out of the tunnel and into view. The baying hordes of Madrid roared for their boys, whilst insults of the lowest kind were hurled in the direction of the Barcelona players.

Real could not have had a better start. After only two minutes, Mateos swooped to lash the ball into the Barca net. Only recently restored to the line-up, he received the acclaim of his team-mates and supporters, disappearing under a flurry of white shirts. Barca found themselves rocked back on their heels. For them it was the worst possible situation. With Real boosted by the early goal they roared forward against their hated foe. The Catalans held firm. Amidst a truly intimidating atmosphere they fought and battled and scrapped for every ball. Their just reward arrived when a Luis Suarez free kick totally deceived the new Madrid goalkeeper Vicente and soared into the goal. A silence descended upon the Bernabeu. The celebrating Barca players gestured to their bench. No words were needed to show how much the goal meant to the Catalans. The home side was struggling. Di Stefano tried in vain to raise his compadres but it was to little avail. However, just when it seemed Barcelona would reach half-time on level terms, Francisco Gento ran like the wind to latch onto a loose pass and shoot his side back in front. The home supporters celebrated more in relief than joy. The massacre they had expected after Mateos's early strike had failed to materialise. The white hordes had been nervous. Now with Paco's typical lightning break surely they could relax and get on with slaughtering these Catalan vermin?

As the minutes ticked away, the closely fought out contest looked like a narrow win by the Madrilenos. Even though they had hardly distinguished themselves they had held onto their slender lead. Barca looked quite satisfied with events, seemingly content to defend what they had and bring di Stefano and his circus of performing clowns back to Catalonia and finish them off. It was perhaps to be expected that this encounter would have a sting in its tale.

With time running out, the Barcelona midfielder Evaristo split Real's defence and sent Sandor Kocsis clear through on goal. The Madrid defenders, appealing desperately for offside, were relieved when the linesman agreed with them and put up his flag, but English referee Arthur Ellis refuted his assistant's claim and waved play on. Kocsis roared onwards and was finally sent sprawling just inside the box. To the disgust of the home team Ellis pointed towards the penalty spot. The linesman found himself surrounded by infuriated Madrilenos screaming at him to intervene with the referee.

The controversy raged on. Did he flag for the offside or the penalty kick? It had also seemed a dive by Kocsis, which only infuriated the Real players more. Finally, order was restored and Arthur Ellis's initial decision stood. Barcelona had been given the chance of an equaliser. Back in Catalonia they held their breath. It would be down to one of their favourite sons, Luis Suarez, to take the kick. To a barrage of whistling, booing and insults, Suarez quite nonchalantly stepped up and smashed his penalty cleanly into the Real net. Again a deafening silence gripped the Bernabeu. The terrible possibility of losing their cherished European Cup to the infidels of Barca had suddenly become more real. Far away in the hills of Catalonia they had begun dancing in the streets. The final whistle sounded. For the first time Real Madrid had failed to win at home in the European Cup. With heads bowed, the champions vacated the stage. The fans were stunned. The Madrileno supporters knew well that their hold on the trophy could not last forever; but why, oh why, of all the teams in Europe did the sword of defeat have to be plunged into them by the hated hordes of Catalonia?

A pent-up Ferenc Puskas manhandled Sandor Kocsis in the tunnel and accused him of diving for the penalty. Kocsis could not look his old friend in the eye. He disappeared quickly in the direction of the celebrating Barca changing-room. Real Madrid, champions of Europe since the competition had begun, now faced their most difficult challenge. They would have to travel to the lion's den. In two weeks' time the Madrilenos would find themselves battling for their lives.

'Good evening and welcome to Barcelona. And this is the game of all time to decide who goes into the quarter-finals. Everybody here believes that whoever wins tonight will win the European Cup. And Real Madrid, who have won the European Cup ever since it was introduced five years ago, are in big trouble. They were held on their own ground to a 2–2 draw. So they are really up against it tonight here in Barcelona.' These were the words of Kenneth Wolstenholme welcoming BBC viewers to late-night highlights of the epitaph to Real Madrid's European fairy tale. It was indeed to be the end for the Madrilenos, but they would not bow out without one hell of a scrap.

With a full house inside the Nou Camp screaming for their blood, Real Madrid appeared in full view of the enemy. They were greeted by deafening abuse. The venom that rained down from the Nou Camp's vast terracing came laced with memories of this proud region's recent history. The Barca supporters had a saying: '*Més que un club*'. Translated into English this means 'more than just a club'. Never was this more obvious than on the evening of 25 November 1960. Barca delayed their own entrance into the arena to allow the Madrilenos to feel the effect of their crowd's welcome. But now it was time for them to enter the stage. The Nou Camp erupted with joy. A mass of firecrackers exploded around this magnificent cathedral of football. Flashbulbs glittered like millions of fireflies as photographers fought and jostled to capture the unfolding scene.

It was another Englishman who had been given the dubious honour of handling this intense and inflammatory contest. Reg Leafe found himself heavily criticised for inept refereeing throughout the game. Both teams had goals disallowed in controversial circumstances before a breakthrough finally occurred. Once again it was Sandor Kocsis who proved a pointed thorn in Real's side. His whipped-in cross found Vegas, whose shot was badly deflected by the Madrid defender Pachin. Vicente, in the Madrileno goal, looked on helplessly as the ball bobbled over the goal-line. Kocsis leapt up in delight. For the first time ever in the history of these two clubs in the competition Barca had the aggregate lead. Real launched themselves at the Catalan rearguard in a desperate effort to pull level. Twice more they would have the ball in the net only to see both disallowed by a clearly perturbed and floundering Leafe. Di Stefano was dreadfully unlucky when his whiplash effort sped past the Barcelona goalkeeper Ramallets, only to hammer against the side of the post and rebound to safety. It appeared that the script had already been written for this particular occasion. Puskas was becoming increasingly frustrated. The white shirts of Real surged forward in search of redemption, but they were running into a red and blue brick wall. Barca were unyielding. Nine minutes from time Real Madrid were dead and buried.

A lightning counter-strike by Barcelona caught Real struggling to get men back in defence. Away sped the Catalans on a mad dash into the Madrid penalty area. Finally, a cross was put into the box and there waiting was the Brazilian Evaristo to sweep his header past a diving Vicente. The Nou Camp erupted in a mad frenzy. The Madrilenos fell to their knees. Two goals down – a miracle was now needed to keep them in the European Cup. Di Stefano rallied his shaken troops. In a last-gasp cavalry charge Real stormed at the Catalans. The ball was played into the Barcelona box. Suddenly, from nowhere, Canario stabbed out a foot and the ball flew past Ramallets and into the net. A dreadful silence enveloped the Nou Camp. With six minutes remaining it was not yet over. Barcelona began to panic. A feeling of dread cut through the Barca masses. Again the ball sped in the direction of their goal. There was no more time for fancy skills and conjuring tricks. With Madrid throwing everything they had left at Barca they were handed a final chance to save themselves. With the crowd pleading for the referee to end their torment, the Real defender Marquitos came steaming through and, from just 12 yards out with only Ramallets to beat, he shot despairingly over the bar. His team-mates could only look on in horror. With di Stefano trying to orchestrate one final attack, Reg Leafe ended the contest and sent the whole of Catalonia soaring into fiesta mood.

Leafe had to be smuggled out of the Nou Camp side exit as rumours abounded that several of the Madrilenos were seeking serious retribution. He was put into a waiting taxi by an English journalist and driven away into the Catalan night, leaving his lynch mob searching high and low to throw a noose round his English neck. Puskas and di Stefano amongst others were finally calmed down by their president, who told them to behave with some dignity. Bernabeu himself was no lover of Barcelona. During the civil war he had been a senior officer in Franco's army. He had once memorably declared that 'the only thing wrong with Catalonia is the Catalans!' Real Madrid returned to the capital licking their wounds and sick to the stomach with defeat.

Barcelona now viewed themselves as the club most likely to take over Real's mantle. But despite reaching the final that year the Catalans slumped to a shock 2–3 defeat against the emerging Portuguese team of Benfica. The final was staged at the Wankdorf stadium in Berne, Switzerland, the scene of Hungary's staggering collapse against the Germans in the 1954 World Cup. Before the game, Barca's two former Magyars, Kocsis and Czibor, experienced weird premonitions of defeat. They were proved correct, for despite Barcelona swamping Benfica for large periods of the match and hitting the woodwork on countless occasions, they were to finish empty handed. Both Hungarians finished the game in tears. Czibor was inconsolable. Lightning had incredibly struck twice. It was scant consolation that the Barca midfielder scored a goal that would rank among the best ever scored in the European Cup, a rasping, snarling drive from 30 yards that thundered past the Benfica goalkeeper.

On hearing of his fellow countrymen's heartache Ferenc Puskas found it hard not to raise a wry smile. 'I heard they were on a massive win bonus,' quipped the Major. 'Maybe that is what brought tears to their eyes.' How cruel! It was to be 30 years before the Catalans finally got to lift the European Cup on high. In 1992, on a warm summer's Wembley evening, Ronald Koeman crashed home a superb free kick which ended Barca's quest for the holy grail. Under the astute leadership of Johan Cruyff, Barcelona's 1–0 win over Sampdoria gave the Catalans what they had always craved. However, for a club of Barca's size and stature one win in Europe's premier competition doesn't do them justice – a situation that their close friends in Madrid have never been slow to remind them of.

Real Madrid were shaken by their defeat at the hands of their arch rivals but they were by no means spent. Just a short time after having their hearts ripped open by the Catalans they returned to the scene of the crime and thrashed Barca 5–3 in a vital league game. One man in particular was magnificent during that match. Alfredo di Stefano had been the victim of tremendous criticism after Real's exit from Europe. Playing with a point to prove, the White Arrow destroyed the home team with a bravura performance. How dare they question the great man! Come the end of the season, the Madrilenos had won back the Spanish title and were preparing once more to re-enter the upper echelons of the European Cup and win back their crown. Sadly, events would prove that di Stefano and Puskas were now up against an opponent whom even they would find impossible to overcome . . . Time.

8.

THE PANTHER AND THE GYPSY CURSE

BENFICA V REAL MADRID

1962 EUROPEAN CUP FINAL

ike an aged movie queen who refutes steadfastly the onset of old age, so Real Madrid refused to go gently into the night. Their love of the big stage was just too strong and in 1962 the white knights of the Bernabeu once more reached the European Cup final. Real's two brightest lights showed little sign of dimming. Alfredo di Stefano and Ferenc Puskas had both reached the ripe old age of 36, but the magic and desire still burned as fierce as ever. The generalissimo and his Major were basking in the glorious twilight of what had been a wonderful partnership. What finer way to bow out than to reclaim that most illustrious of prizes. However, elsewhere times were changing. Not too far away in the Portuguese capital of Lisbon, Benfica's Estadio da Luz (Stadium of Light) proudly flew the banner of European champions. Their spectacular victory over the Catalans of Barcelona the previous season had catapulted the team (nicknamed the 'Eagles') to previously unheard-of heights. Despite riding their luck against Barca, Benfica were more than worthy successors to the Madrilenos' crown. As if the footballing gods were not already smiling enough on the Portuguese, there was straining on the leash a young colt who was screaming to be given just one chance. From the back alleys of a small shanty town in Mozambique the Black Panther suddenly sprang on an incredulous world. Eusebio da Silva Ferreira was one of eight children raised by his widowed mother. As a child Eusebio would play football with his brothers from dawn to dusk. As a ball they would use old ragged cloth tied together in a bundle. As night fell and the stars appeared in the dark Mozambique sky above his ramshackle home, this special boy would gaze above with longing eyes and dream. Never realising that he had already been selected to live his life amongst that glittering array of faraway lights.

It began in a barber's shop. The Benfica manager, Bela Guttman, sat comfortably being attended to in his favourite chair, his mind for once not racing with the problems of running a club such as his. Guttman was happily daydreaming when his peaceful little world was shattered by the sound of the door springing open. An old player of his, Carlos Bauer, stood staring breathlessly into his face. 'Bela!' exclaimed this excited individual. 'Bela, my dear friend, you are not going to believe what I have just seen!' Bauer had only just returned from a coaching trip to the Portuguese African colonies where his mission had been to seek out talent for Benfica. After what had been a fruitless journey, Mozambique had been the source of redemption. It was there that Bauer had witnessed a player who was to have a profound effect on himself and his beloved Eagles. He could not return to Portugal quickly enough to tell of his exciting discovery. Guttman was not a man to become too excited. This 62-year-old Hungarian Jew had seen the best and the worst that this world could offer; but such was the excitement in his friend's voice that something made him sit up, wipe his face clear of shaving foam and inquire just what was so bloody interesting! So he heard about a young Mozambique footballer whose growing reputation in the colonies was already beginning to attract interest from around the world. Guttman listened intently as Bauer talked of having had an almost religious experience at the hands of this young African. 'We have to have him for Benfica, Bela,' implored the messenger. 'He is not of this world. I swear to God he is not of this world!' After hearing similar reports from others whose faith he trusted implicitly, Guttman made up his mind that Eusebio must be brought to Portugal to fly with the Eagles.

There was, however, a major obstacle that would first have to be overcome. Eusebio played his football for one of Sporting Lisbon's junior teams. Sporting were Benfica's deadliest rivals. The city of Lisbon was home to huge clubs who frankly hated each other's guts. Sporting would resist with every breath Benfica's attempts to steal their most precious gem. They knew well the detested Eagles' interest in Eusebio. No effort would be spared to keep them well at bay. Unluckily for them, when it came to Bela Guttman they would be up against a wily old gypsy who knew and had probably invented every trick in the proverbial book. To snare the Black Panther he would concentrate on the source. Guttman had done his homework on Eusebio's family background and the plan he finally conceived was simple but brilliant. Benfica offered Eusebio's mother the princely sum of $20,000 for her son's services. Guttman knew well that she could not ignore such a figure. When there are little mouths to feed there is simply no argument. Mother's message to her doting son was that there was no way on earth she could turn down this fortune. Like any good son Eusebio did as he was told. Benfica had their man. It was daylight robbery. But this was only the first stage of the plan.

Eusebio now had to be sneaked out of Mozambique and into the wings of the waiting Eagles. In a cloak and dagger operation he was given a disguise and placed very discreetly on a plane to Lisbon. Unbeknown to Benfica, Sporting had got wind of their scheme and had appropriate people waiting to meet Eusebio when he eventually landed on the Iberian peninsula. These were men who had strict instructions to hold on tight to Sporting Lisbon's Black Panther. Guttman, however, had planned for exactly such a situation. On landing, Eusebio was whisked straight off the runway to a waiting car and taken to a hideaway. All this while Sporting's welcome committee stood around impatiently in the airport lobby, wondering where on earth their man had vanished to.

Once Eusebio's kidnapping had been made legal, Benfica felt confident enough to allow their new star to join his fellow Eagles in a training session. Bela Guttman could not believe his own eyes. 'Oh, my God,' muttered Guttman to himself. 'Gold, gold, gold!' Never in his whole life had he witnessed such wealth of genius in one so young. This was a man who had travelled the world in his footballing career; a man who had suffered and survived the horrors of a Nazi death camp; a man who was resigned to thinking that nothing in this life could ever surprise him again. He was wrong. Eusebio was unique; a forward who had everything – blinding pace, wonderful skill, strength, and a right-foot shot that possessed the power of a rocket launcher. His nickname of 'The Panther' was well deserved. This was a predator, a player to rival any elsewhere in the world, even the great Brazilian Pele. Benfica could not believe their luck.

There was an early chance to compare the two when the week following their European Cup triumph over Barcelona, the Eagles took on Pele's club Santos in a challenge match played in Paris. For an hour of the contest the newly crowned European champions were absolutely humiliated by a Santos team playing football of another level. With Pele running riot the Brazilians had run up a 5–0 scoreline and looked good for many more. Guttman, watching in horror, decided to let loose his secret weapon. Turning to the raw recruit from the back streets of Africa his advice was simple. Bela Guttman whispered in Eusebio's ear, 'Show me what you can do.' Within moments of entering the game, Eusebio played as he had as a child. With a sense of enjoyment and relief in finally being let off the reins he tore into his opponents. By the game's finish Benfica's honour if not the match had been saved. Despite a 6–3 scoreline in favour of Santos, Guttman was not downhearted, for he had found himself a golden nugget.

In 1962, with the Panther running riot in his first full season, Benfica advanced into the semi-finals of the European Cup. After a massacre of the

German champions Nuremburg in the previous round, the holders were drawn against England's finest, Tottenham Hotspur. The Spurs were arguably at that time the best team to emerge from the British Isles since the end of the Second World War. Along with the tragically short-lived Busby Babes, Tottenham played the game as it should be played. Their first-time crisp passing cut an impressive swathe through English first division defences. Playing in an all-white strip the Spurs saw themselves as a British version of Real Madrid. The manager, Bill Nicholson, was quietly confident that his team could win the European Cup. If Benfica could be overcome then only a rapidly ageing Real stood between them and glory. The Madrilenos were approaching the point of no return and were ripe for the taking. With players such as Dave Mackay, Danny Blanchflower and the explosive genius of Jimmy Greaves in their midst, Spurs had good reason to be confident. First, however, they would be faced with the formidable task of bringing the flying Eagles down to earth.

The first leg of this memorable semi-final took place in Lisbon. Guttman had stressed to his players the importance of a good lead to take over to London. They must surely have been listening to him, for in the first 20 minutes Benfica ripped into the English champions with a vengeance to take a 2–0 lead. The Stadium of Light was awash with noise and excitement as the Eagles came roaring out of the traps. With Eusebio and the stirring Coluna rampaging forward, the North London club looked set for a mauling; but this was a team that had huge heart as well as skill. Slowly Spurs stemmed Benfica's fire and shortly into the second half scored themselves through their centre-forward Bobby Smith. Soon after, Tottenham thought they had an equaliser, only to see it very dubiously ruled out by the referee. With Nicholson shaking his head in disgust on the touchline, Spurs again had the ball in the net, only once more to see it disallowed by an over-zealous official. Benfica swooped upfield for Augusto to seal the match with a flying header. The final whistle saw Benfica players celebrating the victory almost as if it was the final itself. There still remained a second leg to be played. The English travelled home bemoaning their bad luck and grumbling about the standard of refereeing. They were determined that come a fortnight's time White Hart Lane would be the end of the line for the European champions. Dave Mackay and his men would go hell for leather to pull back the two-goal deficit. Many believed that this semi-final was far from over.

Two weeks later Bela Guttman brought his team to London to defend their coveted trophy. The English newspapers were fascinated by Benfica, most especially by Eusebio. This mysterious, magnificent-looking athlete from Africa was perfect copy for editors looking for a good story. Not since the

Magyars all those years ago had a continental side attracted such interest. The whole country waited eagerly to see if Spurs could come back from the dead. Sixty-five thousand supporters packed White Hart Lane and more than played their part in what turned out to be an unforgettable evening. In the end Spurs won a magnificent contest 2–1, but that in no way tells the story of a wonderful effort by the home side. With their fans screaming themselves hoarse, Tottenham threw everything they had at the Eagles in a courageous attempt to get back into the match. Spurs constantly left themselves wide open and Benfica's lethal forwards caused heart attacks amongst the crowd with their blistering, frightening counter-attacks. On 15 minutes Simoes sliced through the home defence to give the Portuguese a 4–1 lead on aggregate. Surely this would finish the English champions? Nothing could have been further from the truth. Inspired by Dave Mackay, Tottenham Hotspur Football Club stormed forward and went straight for Benfica's throat. To the disgust of the crowd yet another Spurs goal was disallowed, but instead of being deflated this only served further to drive them on. Seven minutes before half-time they finally managed a much deserved equaliser, Bobby Smith again on hand to shoot powerfully past Costa Pereira in the Benfica goal. Three times Tottenham players struck the woodwork as the European champions' goal led a charmed existence. But still they hit out devilishly on the break. Right on half-time Aguas shot violently against the Spurs bar, causing gasps from the crowd who could barely stand to watch. The referee's whistle was as big a relief to the home supporters as it was to the Benfica players.

Whereas before the game the European champions were booed out onto the field, as they re-entered the arena they were very politely clapped. This respect had been well earned. Benfica were defending their crown with great passion and skill. Shortly into the second half Tottenham were awarded a penalty. As cool as a cucumber, Danny Blanchflower stepped forward and calmly placed his kick past Costa Pereira, sending White Hart Lane into a frenzy of excitement. This famous old ground rocked and swayed as suddenly a miracle looked on the cards. For the remainder of the game it was wave after wave of Spurs attacks. Frantic goal-line clearances and inspired defending somehow kept the Portuguese in an aggregate lead. Finally the contest ended and the crowd rose as one to applaud two marvellous teams. Tottenham had bowed out but could hold their heads high. Theirs had been a performance to remember with huge pride. But it would be Benfica who would go forth to contest their second European Cup final. Bela Guttman had again waved his magic wand. Waiting in the final for them would be a side who possessed a few magicians of their own. For Real Madrid had risen like a phoenix from the ashes. In Amsterdam on 2 May 1962, Benfica would find themselves facing more than just another football team, they would be facing a living legend. Then again, even legends do not go on forever.

LAST ORDERS

A shooting star is at its brightest as it soars high in the night sky. So Real Madrid will always be remembered. Their reign as European champions remains a golden period in the history of the European Cup. Like a punch-drunk boxer who cannot live without the sound of the bell and the smell of battle the Madrilenos gathered for what would be their last stand. They would go out in true show business style.

The Madrilenos' march to their seventh European final was nothing if not dramatic. The quarter-finals stage saw a tremendous struggle with Juventus of Italy. A goal from di Stefano saw Real clinch a fine victory in Turin. The game will forever be remembered by both sets of supporters for a tumultuous battle between Juve's Welsh giant John Charles and Real Madrid's magnificent Uruguayan defender Jose Santamaria. The tussle continued long after the final whistle had blown, carrying on in the tunnel and only being brought to an end by Real's Ferenc Puskas, who grabbed Santamaria and pushed him into the relative safety of the Real changing-room. If Real Madrid thought the tie was won they were in for a dreadful shock back on home ground. For Juventus, against all the odds, ended Real's unbeaten home record with a 1–0 victory, sending the tie into a third match play-off in Paris. The myth of the Madrilenos' home invincibility disappeared forever when Juve's scheming little Argentinian Omar Sivori shot home the Italians' winner in the Bernabeu. The final whistle was the signal for poignant scenes amongst the Spanish players and supporters. Suddenly, after all those years of superiority, the Real players looked human, di Stefano and Ferenc Puskas finally succumbing to the harsh realities of their rapidly advancing years. Still, however, the swansong was put on hold. In the play-off Real had enough left to put Juventus in their place with a 3–1 victory. Sadly the win was tarnished by the continuing feud between John Charles and Santamaria. Charles found himself the victim of a Real defence determined it seemed at times to put him in an early grave. The financial incentives given to players were finally becoming more important than sportsmanship.

A semi-final was followed by a 2–0 win in the Low Countries over Belgian side Standard Liege, del Sol and Puskas putting the Madrilenos out of harm's way. Amsterdam and Benfica beckoned loudly for this team who refused to retire quietly. The movie queen may have put on too much make-up to cover the ever-increasing wrinkles, but one thing was certain, Real Madrid had one last great performance left in their repertoire. Would it be enough to snare the Panther?

On the eve of the final, Bela Guttman left his team's hotel and took himself off for a midnight stroll along the banks of Amsterdam's winding canals. This was not a man at peace with the world. That same evening he had found himself involved in a bitter argument with his club's directors over money he felt was due to him. The Benfica hierarchy were adamant that his pay was sufficient and they refused point blank to meet his demands. His pride hurt, the indignant Guttman threatened to walk out and quit the Eagles. Considering this mere bravado, the directors dismissed him out of hand. It was to prove the biggest mistake in the proud history of this great club. For the old fox had never been more serious. Guttman no longer felt loyalty to his employers, but his players – well, that was different. They knew nothing of what had unfolded between their manager and the boardroom. Guttman made sure the situation would remain like that until the final was over. He owed them that much. To walk away from such genius would indeed be a terrible wrench, but he was prepared to do it.

Whilst his manager ambled along the canal banks pondering his future, Eusebio was having trouble sleeping. His mind was racing. Tomorrow he would be on the same pitch as his boyhood idol Alfredo di Stefano. The times when he used to play football with his brothers now seemed a lifetime away. Unable to close his eyes Eusebio rose from his bed and stared out of his hotel window. Staring up at the stars he wondered if they were the same ones that he had gazed upon when he was a child. Was this really happening to him or was it all just a dream? Maybe he would wake up in the morning and he would find himself back home in his old bed. The kid from the back alleys of Lourenco had come a long way.

The seventh European Cup final turned out to be a classic encounter. The first half was a marvellous epitaph for Real Madrid. The Madrilenos gave their all in a performance that defied the critics. For 35 minutes di Stefano and Puskas rolled back the years with touches of rare genius. With the generalissimo and del Sol in support, Real supplied the ammunition for Ferenc Puskas to score a wonderful hat trick. Benfica, however, held onto their coat-tails by scoring twice themselves. Ferenc Puskas had become the first player to score two hat tricks in European Cup finals. The Major had taken all his goals quite majestically. If the baton was going to be passed on it would be with great reluctance.

His first was a cameo of years gone by. Di Stefano's deft first-time pass put the Major clear to finish with huge poise past Costa Pereira in the Benfica goal. The second was equally well finished. A typically left-foot finish drilled low into the net. For his third and final goal Puskas side-stepped two Portuguese defenders and smashed his shot with great aplomb past a well-beaten Costa Pereira. No wonder the little Hungarian was mobbed by his coaching staff as he left the pitch at half-time. In a rousing first 45 minutes, Benfica struggled at times to live with Madrid's mercurial football. It was only through sheer grit and determination that they had managed to keep the Madrilenos in sight. Goals from Aguas and Cavem gave the European champions a more than fighting chance to hold onto their hard-earned trophy. The referee's whistle saw Bela Guttman glad to be given the opportunity to remarshal his forces, for Guttman noticed that Real were becoming tired. Di Stefano, as half-time approached, had begun to feel the pace of the contest. No longer prowling the length of the pitch, the generalissimo had begun to sit deep. The Benfica manager told his scoring midfielder Cavem to man-mark him. Cavem was told to 'follow that man to the ends of the earth'. Guttman was more than confident that his team had enough left in reserve to prevail. Eusebio had experienced a relatively quiet first half, seemingly overawed at being on the same pitch as his childhood heroes. But all this would soon change. As the second half began Benfica almost immediately began to turn the screw tight against the challengers to their crown. The speed and movement of their forwards and attacking midfielders saw the Madrilenos being pushed back relentlessly. Up front Puskas had become increasingly isolated with Cavem's man-marking of di Stefano. The generalissimo no longer had the electric pace to outrun such ferocious attention.

Frustrated by his lack of service, the Major dropped back to see more of the action. It was to prove a terrible misjudgement. Carelessly losing possession, he allowed the barnstorming Coluna, the towering Angolan for so long the heart and soul of Benfica, to sweep forward and smash his shot into the Madrid goal: 3–3. The Portuguese swarmed over their wonderful midfield talisman in delight. It seemed now only a matter of time. Inspired by Coluna's equaliser, the champions had the whiff of Spanish blood in their nostrils. Real Madrid now stood wearily on the brink of being vanquished. Eusebio was on fire. Time and again he would roar through gaping holes in the wilting opposition rearguard. The Panther was causing heart attacks amongst the Real aristocrats as he teased and tormented and effortlessly ripped them to pieces. It was on one of these many occasions that the Madrid defender Pachin was panicked into giving away a penalty. Eusebio, picking the ball up on the touchline, streaking like a runaway train past an exhausted di Stefano, had his legs taken away from him by Pachin. The famous Dutch referee Leo Horn could have had little doubt. Dusting himself down, Eusebio da Silva Ferreira gathered his thoughts. Walking past his idol di Stefano, Eusebio could feel the eyes of the Argentinian master upon him. Would his nerve hold out? With great calm the young maestro stepped up to the ball and placed a fine shot into the back of the net. The heads of the Real players dropped. They appeared a beaten side. Benfica led for the first time in the contest. There was to be no let-up for the Spanish. With great venom the Portuguese lashed at the Madrilenos' defence until almost inevitably they cracked again. Eusebio robbed a flagging Santamaria of the ball before seeing his deflected shot sneak in and seal the match for the Eagles: 5–3. The European Cup would remain for another glorious 12 months in pride of place in the Benfica trophy room. Jubilant supporters ran onto the field to lift their heroes high. Guttman was hoisted, so was Coluna and so was Aguas. But by far the main target of their affections was Eusebio. Despite his moment of glory, Eusebio was a worried young man. Before the game began he had pleaded with a smiling Mario Coluna to ask di Stefano for his shirt at the end of the game.

To Eusebio's delight the generalissimo had agreed to his request. Viewing such an action as a compliment, di Stefano knew deep down that his time was near an end. Eusebio was most likely to emerge as his heir. His mantle would be in safe hands. Touched by the humility of this special talent, Alfredo di Stefano, never the best of losers, did as he had promised. As soon as the referee blew for full-time Eusebio ran over to his idol. A weary di Stefano embraced his young tormentor and handed over his shirt. Eusebio now found himself mobbed by his adoring supporters. Fighting desperately to hold onto his most treasured memento, he just kept his modesty as the Benfica fans stripped him bare of all his football kit. In a mad dash for safety he finally, with the aid of a Dutch police escort, rejoined the ecstatic footballers of Benfica. The shirt was safe. While his team-mates cavorted gleefully in the dressing-room the young man from Mozambique sat quietly. Suddenly he began to cry. The tears quickly turned into a waterfall as the stunning reality of his situation hit home. It was only later that he joined in with his fellow Eagles in celebrating a magnificent victory. Amidst the joyful scenes Bela Guttman struggled to hide his true feelings. Inside he was heartbroken, for he had decided that once more it was time for pastures new. His disgust at the way he had been treated by Benfica's hierarchy had left a bitter taste in his mouth. He had no wish to help such people to further success. It was time for the gypsy to hit the footballing high road. Guttman announced his fateful decision at the winners' banquet. It was greeted with a stunned silence by all the Benfica party. Led by Mario Coluna and a tearful Eusebio they pleaded with the old man to stay. The directors looked on embarrassed. The cigars and the wine had suddenly

turned a little sour. It was all to little avail. Bela Guttman was not a man for
turning. He bade a sad farewell and headed off to South America.

Real Madrid were devastated by the result. They returned to Spain refusing
to believe that their loss would signal the end of the road for them. It was
surely a mere blip. Puskas had had a run-in with the referee Leo Horn. He
informed him shortly after the game had ended that he could 'positively feel
his friendship with Guttman during the game'. Such spiteful remarks were
totally uncalled for. The true facts were that in the second half Benfica had
with some ease put Real in their place. The winds of change had blown open
the doors to the Bernabeu. The best team had won. To rub salt further into
the Madrilenos' wounds, the next season saw them humiliatingly knocked out
in the first round. A 3–3 draw at home to Anderlecht meant they travelled to
Belgium under tremendous pressure. It proved to be a disastrous trip as the
Belgian champions beat them 1–0. What was most upsetting was that the
result was no great surprise. The old lady had been unmasked. The show was
over.

For Benfica also it was the end of an era, for despite reaching the final
several times more, they failed to recapture the trophy. Strange stories began
to emerge from Lisbon of a curse placed on them by Bela Guttman on his
departure. Scoffed at by many, as the years went by and still the Eagles failed
miserably, some began to have second thoughts. Indeed, on Guttman's
passing, legend has it that Eusebio visited his old mentor's grave and placed a
rose upon it, secretly praying that the curse would be lifted. An old man's
curse or just plain bad luck? We will never know. But what is known is that
the Eagles have failed since then to soar to previous heights. In the case of
Benfica, the old warning never to cross a Romany traveller may well have
proved true.

9.

THE SUMMER OF '66

ENGLAND V WEST GERMANY

1966 WORLD CUP FINAL

It had been 13 long, lean years since Ferenc Puskas and his exalted red-shirted Magyars waltzed around Wembley making a mockery of so-called English invincibility; a decade and more in which the three lions failed miserably to make the slightest impression on World Cup competition. For a nation renowned worldwide as the home of football this was deemed unacceptable. In 1962, the former RAF wing commander Walter Winterbottom called time on his 17 years at the helm. Step forward, Alf Ramsey. Ramsey, the Ipswich Town manager, had led this rural, unfashionable team to the league championship. In doing so he had proved adept at turning journeyman players into a hugely efficient outfit. A no-nonsense character, he insisted if he took the job he must be allowed to pick the team, and not be forced to doff his cap at some inane bunch of carpet-slipper-wearing, whisky-sodden, octogenarian FA officials. Promised a free hand he gladly accepted. Ramsey had played in the infamous 6–3 mauling by the Hungarians. This was a daunting experience which had a profound effect on him. After being tortured by the beguiling movement and pace of Puskas, Bozsik, Czibor and Hidegkuti, Ramsey realised that if success were to be had on a world level, his England team must be tactically if not technically of a level akin to their opponents. In declaring early in his reign that England would win the World Cup during his time, he upped the stakes for himself and his team. The Fleet Street hacks made mocking if rather ignorant noises. However, following the opening game in the Nations' Cup, a 5–2 thrashing by an exuberant French side in Paris, the manager's outlandish claim began to sound like the rantings of an eccentric.

But Ramsey refused to panic. Slowly, if at times rather painfully, a team was assembled which would give England a fighting chance on the world stage. Players whom many considered ordinary suddenly became cornerstones of

Ramsey's set-up. Remaining focused on the job in hand, this strangely remote man went about his job briskly and with great intelligence and determination. Alf had a plan! On home soil, in front of his own people, he prepared to bring it to fruition. Come 1966, England would be ready to do battle for the greatest prize on earth.

After a steady if unspectacular start to their World Cup campaign, England had advanced into the quarter-finals. A drab opening goalless draw against Uruguay was followed by a brace of victories against Mexico and France, the highlight by far being a rasping long-range rocket hit by Bobby Charlton against the Mexicans. However, huge doubts still remained as to whether they possessed the necessary guile to go much further. For waiting impatiently to break English hearts – and if necessary legs – in the next phase were Argentina; Antonio Rattin and all.

The manager of Argentina, Juan Lorenzo, was a man driven by a burning desire to derail the host nation's dream of glory. He had instructed his leader on the pitch, the magnificent Antonio Rattin, that victory had to be achieved at any price. There were to be no prisoners. If a goal could be had on the break then so be it. If not, they would play for a draw and rely on the whim of the gods with the toss of a coin. Such an attitude defied belief, for the South Americans had in their ranks players of immense skill and technique, none more so than Rattin. A wonderful touch allied with an eye for the killer pass made him amongst the best footballers on the South American continent. Sadly this tall, impressive figure was to be immortalised in World Cup folklore for entirely different reasons. For Rattin would, more than any other, embrace with relish the spirit of cynicism and foul play called for by his manager as they prepared to slay the English bulldog.

Alf Ramsey had problems. The mercurial goal-poaching talents of Jimmy Greaves had been lost to him as the player had a badly gashed knee. To replace him Ramsey turned to West Ham United's Geoff Hurst. Hurst had only made his international début the previous February. He was hard working and powerful but by no stretch of imagination was he in Greaves's class. Also winning a place back in the line-up was Alan Ball. The young Blackpool star had found himself dropped after a poor display against the Uruguayans. But Ramsey had huge faith in this young lad who played football with his heart firmly lodged on his sleeve. Such character would be badly needed against a side as difficult to overcome as Argentina. Shortly before kick-off, in the English dressing-room, their manager called his players together, 'Well, gentlemen, I am sure you are aware of the kind of game you have on your hands this afternoon.' He implored his team not to retaliate, whatever the provocation.

In front of a packed house of 90,000 the two teams stepped out of the Wembley tunnel and into full view of a watching world. Scenes of hysteria greeted them on the terraces. England in all-white and Argentina in their traditional blue-and-white hoops with black shorts took their place for the national anthems. With the pleasantries completed both teams broke away for a brief warm-up. Then it began. The German referee, Herr Kreitlein, blew his whistle and all hell was let loose in this famous old ground. Crashing tackles flew in from both sides as the early skirmishes threatened at any moment to ignite into open conflict. Rattin was booked within minutes for a nothing foul on Bobby Charlton. But this England side was no bunch of shrinking violets. Players such as Nobby Stiles and Jack Charlton gave as good as they got. Kreitlein was diving into his notebook with an enthusiasm bordering on manic. Five South Americans were cautioned in the first half-hour. It appeared it would only be a matter of time before one was asked to leave the field.

When not berating the referee, Rattin, when focused, cut holes through the English midfield with his astute passing. Sadly, the urge to revert to his darker side proved overwhelming in his undisguised attempt to do Herr Kreitlein's job. Any decision that went against his team (and there was many) saw the Argentinian captain full in the German's face. It could not go on. After 36 minutes Rattin pushed his luck too far. Spitting openly in contempt of yet another booking for one of his compadres Kreitlein finally snapped and ordered the South American off the pitch. And what followed defied logic. A rampaging horde of infuriated Argentinians surrounded Kreitlein demanding that he reverse his decision. But this was not a man to be bullied. Rattin meanwhile inflamed events by refusing to leave the field. By this time Argentinian officials had come on in an inane attempt to join in the fracas. Bedlam reigned in Wembley stadium! This World Cup quarter-final had been reduced to a farce. The crowd chanted, 'Why are we waiting?' World Cup officials entered the fray and explained in no uncertain terms to Rattin that unless he vacated the stage Argentina would be thrown out of the tournament. On hearing such a threat the captain appeared to see reason and admit defeat. And so began his long walk into footballing infamy. Accompanied by two gentlemen of the London constabulary, Antonio Rattin allowed himself to be escorted along the running track, swapping insults with the Wembley crowd as he went, stopping only for a moment to wipe his hands on the Union Jack corner flag. The scoundrel! Chants of 'Cheerio' and 'Dago' were hurled down upon Rattin's head as he headed for the tunnel. For years Antonio Rattin would be immortalised in the English press as 'the rat'. Hardly a fitting epitaph for a supreme footballer. Argentina would hold on for the final nine minutes of that first half. To a crescendo of catcalls and derision, the South Americans again launched into Herr Kreitlein as he attempted to escape their wrath. Only the intervention of two London bobbies saved him from a possible lynching. As the mayhem raged, Ramsey ushered his team swiftly into the sanctity of their dressing-room. There, away from the chaos, he told them to remain calm: keep their discipline. If they did, he said, then the game would be theirs. The three lions of England would never have a better chance of making the semi-finals.

The second half began with the English laying siege to the Argentinian goal. After fine approach work from Bobby Moore and Ray Wilson, Hurst brought out a breathtaking save from goalkeeper Roma. This apart, though, clear-cut opportunities were denied them. Even without their inspirational captain, Argentina were unyielding. England began to struggle intolerably against such a ferocious and ruthless blue-and-white rearguard. As the game entered its final quarter, the massive expectation which had gripped the crowd at the beginning of the second half had melted away. Now all that remained were nervous whispers, mixed with groans whenever a white shirt lost possession. The Argentinians were defending for their lives. As a full house sweated profusely, the Wembley clock continued to tick down ominously. England were up against a team who were prepared to maul, kick, punch and spit in defence of their goal – Jack Charlton being one victim as he was set upon and literally mugged! The first-half expulsion of captain Rattin only increased Argentina's determination to hold on. England, as time ran down, appeared to be running out of ideas, seemingly content to match their opponents blow for blow as the contest simmered violently off the ball. As the sun beat down to drench Wembley's wide-open spaces in dark, looping shadows, there was at last a ray of light for the home side. The West Ham duo of Martin Peters and Geoff Hurst finally combined to break South American hearts. Peters's wonderfully floated cross was met decisively by Hurst, who arched his header high over the Argentinian goalkeeper Roma to send 90,000 English supporters delirious. Hurst, who was only in as a replacement for the injured Jimmy Greaves, had saved his country from the nerve-jangling scenario of extra time and – God forbid – the toss of a coin. A feeling of relief flooded across the massed terraces of this famous old stadium. Argentina's brave if dubious stand had finally been broken. A young boy ran from the terraces to join in with the celebrations of the English players. As he sprinted past the Argentinians, one of their defenders, Mas, clipped him across the ear, thus inciting the crowd to aim further torrents of abuse in the direction of these sulky and surly foreigners. This was to prove the winning goal.

The fun and games continued long after the final whistle. Enraged with the

antics of his opponents, Alf Ramsey labelled them 'animals', a remark which
cut deep and to this day helps to fuel the animosities that exist between the
two nations on a football pitch. However, the madness spread to the tunnel
and a chair was hurled through a glass door. Ramsey had good reason to feel
justified with his comments, especially when several of the Argentinians
urinated openly against the tunnel wall and banged on the Englishmen's
changing-room door to demand they come out and fight! Luckily for them
the offer was not taken up and a livid Jack Charlton was left to seethe quietly
in a corner. Ramsey had even ordered his players not to swap shirts with the
South Americans, such was his disgust with their performance. As the war
raged at Wembley, news filtered through of who England's opponents would
be in the semi-final. It was to be the red shirts of Portugal and, more
importantly, the boy born under the Mozambique stars – Eusebio.

With Eusebio inspired beyond even his exceptional standards, the
Portuguese advanced upon Wembley with all the force of a forest fire at their
backs. The player nicknamed the 'Black Panther' had proved almost
unplayable at times as Portugal blew away all in their path, including the
world champions Brazil. The Brazilians were unable to cope with the pace and
skill of the Portuguese number nine as he ran amok amongst them. Eusebio's
incredible four-goal haul against the diddy men of North Korea in the
quarter-finals only helped to fuel the debate that it was he, and not Pele, who
was the world's best. If the Portuguese could overcome England on home soil
and take the trophy then such an argument would be almost complete. With
Pele back out of sight, far inland from the Copacabana and already talking of
retirement, the mantle was ready to be passed on. 'The king is dead,' screamed
the critics, 'long live the king!' However, no one had counted on a toothless,
shortsighted, squat little battler from the back streets of Manchester ruining
the coronation.

It can be said that if ever such a football royal crowning took place, Norbert
'Nobby' Stiles would not have been allowed to watch it on television, never
mind receive an invite, such was his man-marking capacity and his ability to
nullify opposing star forwards. Nobby himself would always admit that he
never possessed the class and skills of his team-mates at Manchester United or
England. But few had more heart or thirst for a fight than Stiles. Like Matt
Busby at United, Alf Ramsey understood that players such as he were essential
in a team make-up. Somebody had to win the ball to give it to a Charlton or
a Peters. Controversy erupted in the first round when Stiles launched what
can only be described as an over-the-top tackle on the French play-maker
Simon. Such was the severity of the challenge, senior members of the FA
hierarchy insisted to the England manager that the United man be dropped

from the team. Not surprisingly, Ramsey told them that if they attempted to play God with his team selection they would very quickly find themselves in need of a new manager. Not surprisingly, such talk very swiftly caused a rapid change of mind and Nobby was back in. Ramsey realised that if the dream were to be had he needed such men with fire raging in their belly. The previous season had witnessed Manchester United achieve a staggering victory over Benfica in their own fortress, the Stadium of Light, by a lavish five goals to one. Busby had asked Stiles to perform a marking role on Eusebio. This he did with great effect, and to such an extent that the great man practically waved the white flag in the second half. This match was prevalent in Ramsey's mind as he planned his tactics. Eusebio was, if given the chance, capable of destroying England with heartless ease. Alf did not have to think too hard, for this lad – born and raised in Collyhurst, Manchester, a breeding ground for footballers, crooks, philosophers, and giant hearts – was handed the task of pulling in the reins of the 'Black Panther'. In such a plan lay the possible destination of the Jules Rimet trophy itself.

On the 26 July 1966, only three days after the Argentinian débâcle, England and Portugal stepped out onto Wembley's hallowed turf to contest the right for a place in the World Cup final. Led by the two captains, Bobby Moore and Mario Coluna, both sides looked around in astonishment at the sea of Union Jacks that surrounded them. A look of bewilderment crossed the faces of several of the Portuguese players, suddenly realising the size of the task that lay before them. For not only were they up against a formidable team, they would have to overcome the passion and desire of an entire nation. Ramsey had once more plumped for Geoff Hurst over an unfit Jimmy Greaves, but this apart the team would pick itself. And so it began. Unlike Argentina, Portugal were here to play football. Not for them the sly, intimidatory style of the South Americans, although it has to be said, if they were in the mood they could dish the dirt as much as any other. Their crippling of Pele in the early rounds was a prime example: a double assault by defenders Vicente and Morais, which caused the Brazilian to announce his retirement from World Cup football to escape the wrath of the assassins. In the game against England both these players had been left out. It showed, for in the first 20 minutes not a single foul was committed by either side. The English defenders were backing off, watching their tackles. Stiles was never more than a hair's breadth away from Eusebio, watching, hassling, always aware that at any moment the Panther could spring free. England were playing as well as at any time in the competition, their football freewheeling and flowing. On the half-hour they took a deserved lead, Bobby Charlton following in after the Portuguese goalkeeper Pereira could only half block

Roger Hunt's effort. Half-time arrived with the home team in front. However, as the second period began, Portugal had stepped up several gears and were forcing the English back. There was many a nervous moment as England were forced into fighting a rearguard action. Throughout this, Bobby Moore calmed, cajoled and organised his troops, as Portugal, led by their leader Coluna, tried in vain to bypass them. As time drew on and the London sky turned black, the realisation began to seep in amongst the home supporters that a famous victory was almost upon them. The tension mounted, and 11 minutes remained when Bobby Charlton, in possibly his best-ever match for his country, calmly shot home a low-hit drive from the edge of the area. Wembley stadium erupted in jubilation, and at last the nerves eased. Charlton's cool finish was equally appreciated by his opponents, as every Portuguese player he ran past back to the halfway line took time to shake his hand. It was a wonderful show of sportsmanship by a team obviously sick to the stomach at the knowledge they were out of the competition.

The final ten minutes saw Portugal throw caution to the wind in a desperate, last mad gamble. The Benfica winger Simoes, for once cut free from George Cohen, lashed in a cross for the head of the giant Torres, whose storming goal-bound header struck Jackie Charlton on the arm. It was a penalty to Portugal. Eusebio stepped forward. Gordon Banks had already made up his mind on which way he was going to dive. He had studied his opponent's past record of spot kicks and was convinced he knew where Eusebio was going to hit it. But just at the last moment Coluna walked over to his team-mate and whispered into his ear. Thinking he been second-guessed, Banks decided to go against his original plan and dive the other way. As cool as ice the Panther strode forward and stroked the ball into his usual corner. The England goalkeeper was livid, convinced that Coluna had hoodwinked him. Game on.

Portugal roared and raged, only a last-ditch tackle by Nobby Stiles thwarted the darting Simoes. Maddened by his fellow defenders' lack of cover, Stiles turned with a vengeance and let rip a torrent of abuse at his colleagues. England were so close, it would be a crime to blow it now. But still the Portuguese came. Mario Coluna sidestepped a desperate lunge and let fly only to see Banks tip his fine effort over the bar. Wembley stadium held its breath, a hail of whistles pleaded for the referee to end the torment. Then the final whistle came; tears for the brave Portuguese, elation for England. Eusebio sobbed bitterly in the centre circle, wiping his eyes on his sleeve. This had been the chance for immortality, but it was not to be. Nobby had done his job to perfection. The lad from Collyhurst had slain the snarling threat of the Black Panther. Alf Ramsey watched with huge satisfaction as his players celebrated, but he knew well that their greatest test was still ahead. For it was true that a World Cup final beckoned. But was it not also true that their opponents were to be the Germans? A nation held its breath. The mist that had engulfed Wembley stadium all those years ago as the Magyars ran amok was close to being lifted. England, after so many false dawns, could at last glimpse the light of day. They had come too far to lose it now, surely?

THE 1966 WORLD CUP FINAL

On 30 July 1966, West Germany and England clashed in arguably the most dramatic World Cup final of all time. The Germans, under the astute control of Helmet Schoen, mirrored Ramsey's England in the way they played both in attitude and tactics. Schoen had spent his apprenticeship under the guiding hand of the great tactician Sepp Herberger, the man who had schemed the downfall of the Magyars back in '54. Schoen would be leading his men into the lions' den in their attempt to prise the trophy away from an expectant host. History screamed out that they would not succeed. For the Germans had never beaten the English in 65 years of competitive matches. And yet such was the quality and competitive nature of their players that if anyone was going to strangle the English bulldog in his crowning moment of glory, it could well be the dogged, resilient Germans. As for team selection there really was no choice for the English. Ramsey would persevere with Geoff Hurst and the inestimable talent of the now-fit Jimmy Greaves would be left to ponder the eternally frustrating 'what if?'. The subsequent tragic demise of Greaves into a haze of booze can in no way be blamed on Ramsey, but it is clear from listening to the player himself that his omission from the England team for this final set off a cycle of events which would lead him to purgatory. That he recovered so well speaks more for his character as a man than for anything he could ever have achieved on a mere football field. But for Ramsey, in 1966, the decision was one which had to be taken, even if it was difficult. Greaves was out; Geoff Hurst was in.

The band of the Royal Marines, splendid in their white helmets and black uniforms, all polished buttons and red braid, was providing superb entertainment for the expectant Wembley audience. But as kick-off drew near all thoughts turned towards the forthcoming 90 minutes. To a rising crescendo both teams appeared from the tunnel. A whirling tide of red, white and blue covered the terraces, sprinkled with a heady dose of German tricolours. England played in red; West Germany in white shirts and black shorts. Both teams strode across to take up their positions for the national anthems. Happily there was little mention in the pre-match build-up of events only 25 years before. (The fact that Gordon Banks was married to a German girl saw such talk kept to a minimum amongst the England set up.) Swiss referee Herr Dienst called the two captains into the centre circle for the toss. Bobby Moore shook the hand of his opposing number, Uwe Seeler. Moore handed Seeler a plaque, and received in return a decorative pendant. A final shake of the hands, and it was time to begin the contest. Both countries held their breath. The final act in the eighth World Cup was under way.

Schoen had gambled in handing his most precious prodigy, Franz Beckenbauer, the ominous task of manmarking Bobby Charlton. In doing so he sacrificed Beckenbauer's immense ability to attack from the middle of the park. But Schoen felt this would be a risk worth taking. For with Charlton shackled England's threat would be considerably weakened. The game began with the Germans having the best of the early stages. In midfield Beckenbauer and Overath appeared to have the edge, England time and again giving away easy possession. After 13 minutes disaster struck. From out on the far left Siggi Held crossed deep into the English penalty area. The ever-reliable full-back Ray Wilson misheard his keeper's instructions to leave the cross and instead could only manage to head weakly down into the path of the prowling West German forward Helmut Haller. Wasting no time, Haller forced a whiplash effort low past a grasping Banks and into the back of the net. Around the stadium thousands of German supporters, easily identifiable in pockets of red, yellow and black, danced with joy at their team's early breakthrough. The massed English who surrounded them looked on gloomily as their team prepared to restart. For the first time in the competition England would have to come from behind. The next five minutes saw the host nation dance precariously on the edge of disaster. For as they struggled to gain a foothold in the match, the white shirts of the Germans were threatening to run riot. In a rare foray upfield, Booby Moore found himself fouled by Wolfgang Overath. With typical quick thinking Moore launched his free kick straight onto the head of Geoff Hurst who, unmarked, headed low past the German keeper Tilkowski. It was 1–1. It had taken only six minutes for the English to equalise.

Back on level terms, England began to settle. Half chances appeared for both sides as the first period wore on. Seeler twice tested the awesome Banks. Bobby Charlton for once escaped the clutches of the young Beckenbauer, only to see his shot saved comfortably by Tilkowski. The Germans hit back. Overath found time and space inside the English penalty box to let fly a wicked half-volley which was blocked by Banks. Following up was the towering Emmerich, whose close-range blast was again saved by the England keeper. The three lions roared and Ray Wilson's cross was met by Hurst, whose knockdown fell to Roger Hunt. With all of Wembley holding their breath Hunt failed to guide the ball past a flailing Tilkowski.

Half-time came and once more the Royal Marines appeared to soothe nerves and offer a brief respite from the tension. Overall it had been an even contest so far. With England improving after a nervy beginning, a war of attrition appeared to be developing. A slight dash of sunlight was threatening to break through the London sky and envelop all in its rays, hopefully kissing farewell to the incessant rain, which had so far dampened this sumptuous occasion. The teams once more appeared from the bowels of Wembley to resume their positions. The summer of '66 was reaching its rainbow's end.

The second half swiftly became a bit of a stand-off. Both sides, while not sitting back, appeared unwilling to go all out for victory. Of the two, though, England were the more adventurous. The little red-haired firebrand Alan Ball was running the legs off the German defender Schnellinger. Occasionally an opportunity would show itself, but as the clock ticked down extra time was becoming an ever-increasing option. Only 13 minutes remained when Ball once more flew at the German rearguard and earned a corner for his team. The incoming cross was initially cleared by the Germans, only to then fall at the feet of Geoff Hurst. Hurst's attempted shot looped off Hottages, spun wildly into the air, to drop invitingly for the ghosting figure of Martin Peters to volley home past Tilkowski. At six yards out, it was nothing more than a gift from the heavens for Peters.

Wembley stadium once more erupted as supporters and players alike celebrated. West Germany regrouped. Abandoning their rigid defensive they went for broke. A Schnellinger shot was easily held by Banks, while Weber could only head weakly past the post. With four minutes left to play England should have wrapped it up. With the Germans almost wasted and committed to all-out attack, they flew away on the break. Ball's slicing pass put Roger Hunt clear. Hunt had only to look up and give the ball to Bobby Charlton for him to have a clear run on goal. Sadly, Hunt delayed and the chance was lost. For this, England were to pay a price beyond their worse nightmares.

There was less than a minute remaining when Jack Charlton was alleged to have fouled Siggi Held some 30 yards from Gordon Bank's goal. With the crowd baying for Herr Dienst to call time, the desperate Germans rushed to take the free kick. Wembley was aghast with nerves; many could hardly bear to watch as Emmerich's pot-shot deflected wildly, only to be sent by Held across the face of England's goal. Missed by Wilson and a groping Banks, Weber came roaring in to break English hearts and save his country's neck. At 2–2, extra time was called.

Ramsey came onto the pitch to rally his troops. 'You have won it once,' he declared, 'now go out and win it again.' The first period of extra time saw England heed their manager's words as they found extra reserves of strength and energy from somewhere. Alan Ball was torturing the German defence with his boundless enthusiasm and pace. A rasping drive by the boy from Blackpool forced Tilkowski to tip the ball over his crossbar. Bobby Charlton also found a new lease of life, his scorching left-foot shot striking the German post. Ten minutes in and it was Ball again outpacing Schnellinger to cross in low for Geoff Hurst. Hurst, with his back to goal, turned and hit a ferocious effort which crashed against the crossbar, bounced down and appeared to cross the line. In the ensuing mêlée, Weber headed the ball clear of danger. Herr Dienst was unsure. Roger Hunt had been only inches away. His initial reaction to not follow in, but instead to raise his arms in salute of a goal, convinced every Englishman alive that it had crossed over. The Germans were adamant, though, that it had not done so. Dienst found himself besieged by players of both sides. Across he strode to the Russian linesman who appeared to be flagging in England's favour. Tofik Brahmakov was about to enter World Cup folklore. For a moment time stood still as the two officials made their decision. The goal, it was settled, would stand! Herr Dienst pointed to the centre circle and England once more had the lead. Brahmakov waved his flag excitedly towards the halfway line. The Germans looked at him in disgust. (A penny for their thoughts?)

Seemingly shocked by the injustice meted out to them, Schoen's side appeared spent. The first period ended with Wembley stadium ablaze with excitement. So close, and yet . . . In a last hurrah West Germany tried desperately for redemption. But as the excitement mounted and the crowd reached even higher levels of euphoria, it appeared that for the Germans the day was lost. Seconds remained when Bobby Moore's long, searching pass fell invitingly for Geoff Hurst to run onto, and blast a stupendous effort high past Tilkowski – and win for himself and his country the Jules Rimet trophy. It was a glorious hat trick for the West Ham man, providing a perfect ending for the greatest day in English football. The final whistle saw wonderful scenes of tear-stained joy. Jack Charlton collapsed to his knees; Nobby Stiles performed an Irish jig; Alan Ball suddenly looked his age. And of course there was the crowning moment: a smiling Bobby Moore receiving the World Cup trophy from the Queen. Across the country riotous celebrations ensued. Street parties which had at times during the afternoon come precariously close to being turned into funeral wakes now launched into full flow. And for the man who made it all possible, Alf Ramsey bore the look of a man satisfied with a job well done. Nothing more, nothing less. As for the beaten Germans, the opportunity for revenge would rear its head many times over the coming years. And how they would take it . . . England would be made to pay with interest for the hurt they handed out to West Germany in that long, fair summer of '66.

10.

CELTIC NIGHTS

CELTIC V INTER MILAN

1967 EUROPEAN CUP FINAL

The white knights of Real Madrid had been slain, their reign as European champions resigned to the fading pages of history books. Benfica's reign, albeit enchanting, had shown itself to be but a mere fling. A competition which was once a lavish, red-veiled theatre stage for such stupendous performers as di Stefano, Puskas and Eusebio, had by the mid-'60s found itself compromised and sullied by the dark and dreary defensive system of catenaccio. An unhealthy wind of change had sadly turned into a hurricane, blowing away all the glamour and excitement of those early years. For now the European Cup had become almost the sole property of the rich, aristocratic Italians of Milan. The manager, Helenio Herrera, was a man who embraced such ideals with frightful relish. Herrera, a much travelled mercenary with a suitcase o'erflowing with memories of trophies, and echoing stories of battles past, appeared blessed with the Midas touch. So much so that the president of Inter, the oil millionaire Angelo Moratti, was alleged to have asked him to name his price. A smiling Herrera, plucking a figure out of the air, replied, '£30,000 a year.' Truly a king's ransom for the time. But Moratti was determined to acquire the unique talents of this footballing guru. It was a gamble worth the risk. A deal was struck and the 'Black Prince' pitched his tent in one of the most fashionable suburbs of Milan. It was to prove for Moratti an excellent piece of business. So much so that, come 1967, Inter Milan had reached their third final in four years. Many worried that another victory for such negative tactics would do untold damage to a game already fighting to preserve its soul. The cynics declared that romance was out, Helenio Herrera had succeeded in caging football's very soul. There was but one last hope. Their opponents in the final were to be a team who still played football from the heart. For heading to Lisbon, o'er land, sea and air, were the rampaging green-and-white hordes of Jock Stein's Celtic FC.

It was on 6 November 1887 that Brother Wilfrid had a splendid idea. In order to fund Catholic charities, and to help the poverty-stricken Irish immigrants of East Glasgow, he formed a football team. Wilfrid wanted a name to galvanise support amongst the masses. He opted for Celtic Football and Athletic Club, and so a legend was born. For unbeknown to Brother Wilfrid, his good deed was to spark the creation of a footballing institution.

Ninety years on and Celtic Football Club stood on the brink of their greatest hour: a glorious season in which a domestic treble already achieved was set to be crowned with an appearance in the European Cup final. Three weeks previously, Helenio Herrera had flown over from Milan to watch Celtic clinch the league championship with a 2–2 draw against eternal rivals Rangers. Played in an atmosphere tinged with hatred, amongst flags and songs of ancient wrongs and victories, Herrera watched in disbelief. The pace and stamina which Celtic possessed disturbed him. Here was a side that attacked at great speed, but also with perception and skill. Each player performed with a passion and commitment that could come from only one man.

Jock Stein arrived at Celtic in the early months of 1965. His appointment caused controversy for two reasons. Firstly because of the statement of chairman Bob Kelly saying that the new man would have total control over team affairs. Celtic at the time was notorious for its directors meddling with player selection. It was obvious that Stein had insisted if he took the job that was to cease. Secondly, Stein was a Protestant. This was a brave and unprecedented move by the Celtic board. For once the religious bigotry and fear which stalked the rivalries between Glasgow's two warring clans had been put aside to aid the club to simply appoint the best man for the job. Catholic, Protestant, Jew or Muslim – to big Jock it mattered little. For him football was the only true religion.

It was an invasion steeped in an abundance of fun and goodwill. Twelve thousand Celtic supporters poured into Lisbon by car, bus, train, plane and ship. In the days leading up to the final the bars and clubs of the Portuguese capital were immersed in a green and white tidal wave, all intent on drowning in a sea of whisky and local wine. And yet, such was the good-natured humour shown by the Celts, events never even hinted at getting out of hand. Indeed, many Portuguese joined in with the partying. Many a smiling senorita found herself being serenaded by a drunken, unmelodic Scotsman! There was, though, a much higher force which benefited from the generosity and affability of this motley army of peaceful marauders. For the Catholic churches of Lisbon saw their gates boosted enormously by Celtic fans eager to advance their chances of victory by calling on the

Almighty to deliver Milan a horrendous injury crisis. Was it really asking too much to grant the great Sandro Mazzola a temporary bout of chicken pox? Jock Stein himself joked about the crowds of Celtic supporters packing into the city's places of worship. 'They are getting some gates since we came,' he joked. 'The nine o'clock and ten o'clock were all ticket. They have had to get extra plates!' The Italians, who had arrived to cheer on their team, watched on dumbfounded, and maybe a little jealous, as Lisbon lost its heart to the boisterous clans of East Glasgow. It was clear that the battle off the pitch had been won. Now all that remained was to triumph on it. For despite such joyous celebrations many felt deep down that the cold, calculated veterans of Herrera's Milanese might just be that little bit too much for Stein's vibrant, if somewhat inexperienced, team at this heady level. For catenaccio was designed to destroy the dreams and aspirations of even the most fervent supporter. The massed congregation of Brother Wilfrid prayed for a miracle.

With Lisbon in safe hands, Stein made camp in the seaside resort of Estoril. Here, tactics were fine-tuned out on the training field. The Scottish champions had but one plan. They would attempt to overwhelm the Italians by hitting them from all angles. Both full-backs, Tommy Gemmell and Jim Craig, had instructions to bomb forward at every opportunity. Inter would be well aware of Celtic's two wingers, Bobby Lennox and the incomparable Jimmy 'Jinky' Johnstone, but the ferocity, sureness of pass and sheer pace which Gemmell and Craig were capable of attaining would surely surprise them. As for Lennox and the simply brilliant Johnstone, Stein instructed them to move infield and attack the Inter rearguard head on. Added to the selfless running of Steve Chalmers and Willie Wallace up front, and the astute promptings of the centre midfield duo of Bertie Auld and Bobby Murdoch, hopes were high that Celtic could get in and amongst Inter. With Stein's total confidence in his two centre-halves John Clark and captain Billy McNeill being able to handle the class and speed of the frighteningly talented Mazzola and the stalking Cappellini?, here lay the masterplan. Behind these two defensive stalwarts stood the remarkable Ronnie Simpson. At the ripe old age of 37, Simpson found himself plucked from reserve obscurity by Stein to become a first-team regular. The son of a former Rangers and Scotland defender, this was a man enjoying an Indian summer of extravagant proportions.

On the eve of the final, Jock Stein gave forth a war cry which stirred the very soul and lifted the hearts of those still in love with the true spirit of the game. 'Win or lose, we want to make the game worth remembering. We don't just want to win, we want to win playing good football, to make the neutrals glad we've done it, glad to remember how we did it.' Such stirring comments set the scene for an ultimate showdown. Helenio Herrera's abhorrent hijacking of the European Cup with a team and system specifically designed to nullify and destroy had taken the game to an all-time low. It had become essential, a crusade even, that he be not allowed to claim this most prestigious of competitions once more and that Celtic, by some miracle, should overcome the wretched policy of catenaccio. Stein received priceless advice from the Liverpool manager and his close friend Bill Shankly. Shankly had tangled with Herrera's Milan before, losing a semi-final in scandalous circumstances, with a referee allegedly performing as if he were wearing an Inter shirt underneath his top. He told his pal that he must resist any Milan attempt at one-upmanship beforehand and, most importantly, not to let himself or his lads appear in any way intimidated by their opponents' big-name reputation. For the man born into the mining village of Blantyre in Lanarkshire 44 years before, footballing immortality stood but one game away. Stein's 11 years down the coal mines saw him work side by side with men he would always rank as amongst the finest he ever met. Against such comparison, players would have to show Stein their worth. That being so, is it really so astonishing that the side Stein selected to take on Inter Milan were all born within the Celtic heartland? Oh yes, there was genius within the ranks: Jimmy Johnstone was a player who many say rivalled Georgie Best for his dribbling skills. Johnstone was a native of Glasgow who, like Best, enjoyed as many good nights off the field as on it. He was a law unto himself, a genius with the ball at his feet. But what truly epitomised the big man's side was heart; a never-say-die streak that refused adamantly to accept the notion of defeat. They say that truly great sides epitomise the finer sides of their manager's character. Jock Stein's men were of such a mould.

The day before the final, Celtic travelled into Lisbon from Estoril to train at the National Stadium, and to check out the playing surface. As they arrived, the Inter team were just preparing to leave. As the Scots took to the field Herrera decided to sneak back and see if he could pick up any hints as to what Stein's tactics might be. As ever on the alert for such ruses, the Celtic manager told his side to swap positions. Defenders played as forwards, midfielders masqueraded as centre-backs. Herrera cut a perplexed figure on seeing Jimmy Johnstone being employed at centre-half! Finally realising that he was being had, he cut short his spying mission. With Herrera gone Stein afforded himself a slight smile and told everyone to resume their normal positions. One up to the big man.

It was in the tunnel that the lads from Glasgow decided to have some fun with their esteemed opponents. Jimmy Johnstone shouted over to the Italian international left-back Facchetti: 'Hey, big man,' smiled Johnstone. 'How about me and you swapping shirts after the game?'

Facchetti, all immaculate with perfectly combed hair and film-star profile, glared across at this diminutive red-haired Scotsman with huge disdain. It was a look that Johnstone was all set to wipe right off his face in the coming 90 minutes. To the furious flutter of beating Italian and Scottish hearts, Celtic and Inter Milan appeared from the bowels of the National Stadium. Led by captains Billy McNeill and Armando Picchi, both sides strode across the running track and into full view of the watching world. With the Portuguese throwing in their lot alongside the Celtic supporters, their Italian counterparts found themselves vastly outnumbered. This tree-lined amphitheatre cut a fine sight with its impressive, wide, sweeping terraces tinged with huge swathes of green and white. Remembering Shankly's wise words, Stein acted fast when the Italians attempted to claim the bench earmarked for Celtic. They were very swiftly removed in no uncertain fashion, helped on their way with a few choice Glaswegian swear words. An infuriated Herrera spat venom in the Scot's direction, but Stein's point had been well made. They would not be intimidated by the Milanese superstars.

It was to be Inter to kick off. The German referee, Karl Tschenscher, signalled to his linesmen and began what was to be an unforgettable occasion. The Italians began with a flurry. Renato Cappellini's cross was headed goalwards by a stooping Mazzola, only to be well blocked by Simpson on his line. The early moments saw Inter showing their undoubted midfield class as they passed the ball amongst themselves with ease. Celtic finally woke up when Johnstone cut inside and shot low at goal, only for the hugely experienced goalkeeper Giuliano Sarti to take it with ease. A further chance swiftly followed when a cross by Bobby Murdoch was headed narrowly wide by Johnstone. Known as 'the flea', the little winger was all set to give his much-lauded man-marker Tarcisio Burgnich a harrowing afternoon in the Lisbon sun.

On seven minutes there was disaster for Celtic when Mazzola's searching pass sent his sidekick Cappellini hurtling into Simpson's penalty area. Looking a certainty to score, the Celtic defender Jim Craig was forced into bringing him down. A penalty for Inter. Billy McNeill led the complaints but Herr Tschenscher had no doubts. Sandro Mazzola strode forward to

nonchalantly roll the ball into Ronnie Simpson's left-hand corner: 1–0. This
was an especially emotional moment for Mazzola, for it was from Lisbon
that his father and the entire Torino side had been killed in an air crash back
in 1949. Immediately, Herrera was off the bench laying down instructions.
The bolt was about to be locked tight. Milan fell back en masse for the
restart. Immediately, Celtic tried to hit back but the sweeper Picchi robbed
Johnstone of possession. Again the Scots advanced. Bertie Auld from
midfield let fly, only to see his effort crash against the Inter crossbar. With
their fans roaring them on, the green-and-white hoops pressed forward,
Murdoch and Johnstone wonderfully setting up the left-winger Lennox to
hit a shot straight at Sarti. Celtic's off-the-ball movement and ability to find
space was already evident. Lennox and Johnstone this time combined to win
a corner for their club. From this Billy McNeill miskicked from just six
yards out. The chances were appearing thick and fast. Celtic appeared to
have the armoury to open up the so-called formidable catenaccio system
with ease. Such were the shockwaves caused by their opponents' ferocious
onslaught that Sarti found himself warned by the referee for time wasting.
This, after 15 minutes!

There was a scare for Celtic when Cappellini chased a hooked clearance,
only to be met by Ronnie Simpson, who thwarted the Italian with an
outrageous back flick to his centre-half John Clark. Such was the confidence
flowing through the Scottish champions. Celtic kept pressing; Auld and
Murdoch lining up the full-back Tommy Gemmell, whose weak effort was
picked up by Sarti. The jinking, weaving Johnstone was driving the Inter
defence to despair. Burgnich's inability to swat this annoying 'flea' was
causing them endless problems. Next up to go close for Celtic was
Murdoch, whose shot, set up by centre-forward Steve Chalmers, flew high
over Sarti's woodwork. It was beginning to resemble a siege. Probing,
patient, but always electrifying, Celtic ripped into the Milanese rearguard.
Half-time arrived with Inter still ahead, but reeling. Herrera looked pensive
as he headed off back down the tunnel. His mind raced with thoughts on
how to stem this raging tide of Celtic pressure. Picchi was involved in
heated discussions with Burgnich. His captain was annoyed about
Burgnich's inability to deal with Jimmy Johnstone. As for Stein, he could
ask for no more from his players. Theirs had so far been a performance to
admire and cherish. He could only pray that the next 45 minutes brought
them a just and fitting reward.

The second half began with Guarneri fouling Chalmers on the edge of
the penalty area. From Auld's resulting free kick, Celtic appeared to have
won a penalty, only for the referee to award instead an indirect free kick –

this after Facchetti attempted to kick Willie Wallace's head off! From almost on the penalty spot, the shot flew in only to be deflected away by an Inter boot. But still they came. Tommy Gemmell won back possession and slashed a drive back across the goal, almost giving Sarti a heart attack as, for a second, the ball appeared to be drifting in – only to be hustled away at the last minute. The pressure was unyielding from Celtic. To try and disrupt their momentum Mazzola went down almost in slow motion after an innocuous challenge by Murdoch. From all parts of the stadium the support for Jock Stein's men rang out. Cries of 'Celtic, Celtic' bellowed out loud. A battling run by Chalmers ended with his shot finally blocked by a glut of dark-blue Inter shirts. An increasingly impressive Auld was outshining any of his illustrious counterparts, his fine pass to feed a rampant overlapping Tommy Gemmell cutting the Milan defence to ribbons. Jimmy Johnstone's cruel tormenting of Burgnich continued unabated, as he dragged him endlessly across the park. From one such instance, Jim Craig linked with Bertie Auld, whose pass to Murdoch ended with the midfielder's shot being deflected wide.

The Italians were becoming ever more desperate. Already reduced to feigning injuries, they appeared ripe for the picking. Picchi once more screamed instructions to his besieged team. Celtic, still brimming with craft and determination, turned up the heat. Johnstone, attempting a one-man wonder show, only came to earth after four Inter defenders mauled him to the ground. With both full-backs screaming forward at every opportunity, the Scots had Inter pinned back into their own penalty area. Johnstone, as ever drifting dangerously, set up a chance for Murdoch. Taking careful aim the Celtic man fired narrowly wide. Sarti erupted at the photographers behind his goal as they immediately kicked the ball back into play, thus saving vital seconds and denying him the chance to waste time. The fight-back continued, Clark passed out of defence to Murdoch, who instantly sprayed it out wide to Jim Craig. Advancing dangerously, Craig laid the ball back to a thundering Tommy Gemmell to at last lash high past a despairing Sarti and into the goal: 1–1! Gemmell's right foot had set the city of Lisbon alight! Sarti fell to his knees, disgusted. Game on.

Herrera looked on glumly as his team restarted. Would they have the necessary fitness to withstand the remainder of the contest and maybe sneak a goal on the break? Immediately, Picchi's long pass was seized upon by a Celtic midfield and the cavalry charge resumed. Bobby Murdoch broke clear into the Inter penalty area to force a stupendous save out of Sarti at his near post. From the resulting corner, Tommy Gemmell hit a fierce, low drive straight at the overworked Italian goalkeeper. Twenty-two minutes remained when Gemmell set off once more on a soaring run. With socks rolled down to his ankles, this most unlikely of heroes was close to exhaustion. But what a performance he had given. Picking up speed, Gemmell's final cross missed a lunging Willie Wallace by inches. Inter Milan were dancing on the precipice of a self-made disaster. And how they had deserved it – sitting cowardly in their cage, waiting to be put to the sword. Celtic would not disappoint them. Catenaccio was cracking. The shade of the late afternoon sun cast ever-increasing shadows looping across Inter's penalty area. A dark, foreboding cloak engulfed Sarti's goal. They were living on borrowed time. Herrera sat motionless, as if waiting for the inevitable . . . It was coming.

Stein's men were now going for the jugular. For the Italians there was no way out. Both Corso and Guarneri gave away easy possession as their thirst for battle began to be eaten up by tired legs and broken spirits. A long, searching cross from Gemmell was misjudged by Sarti who watched in horror as it crashed against his crossbar, only to then fall away to safety. A weary and fed-up Burgnich, tired of chasing in Johnstone's wake, simply hacked him to the ground. In retaliation, wee Jimmy skimmed his marker, played a glorious wall pass with Craig, only to see Sarti block the cross. It appeared impossible that Inter were still holding out. A terrific sleight of foot by Bertie Auld saw Gemmell send a raking ball into the Italian area – only for Inter's saviour, Sarti, to grasp hold. Eleven minutes remained when Auld again flighted a chip onto the head of Murdoch, whose instant flick brought out a stunning save from this magnificent Italian goalkeeper. Celtic were still looking for the winner. Seven minutes from time Tommy Gemmell dummied, laid off a side pass to Murdoch, whose shot was deflected by Chalmers past the flailing body of Sarti and into the net. The Italians fell to their knees. Chalmers found himself mobbed by his team-mates, as around the stadium the Celtic supporters went wild. Photographers rushed past the tearful Sarti to capture forever the scenes of delight amongst the Scottish players. How they had deserved such a moment!

As for Inter, they were but a spent force. The final moments saw near hysteria alongside the touchlines. Stein was forced to leave the bench, simply unable to bear the tension as the seconds ticked away. He returned to watch the dying moments of the contest. Finally the referee called time and the triumphant Celtic players threw their arms into the air. The biggest party in the history of their football club could now officially begin! In a blazing cavalry charge, thousands poured across the running track to salute their heroes. Mayhem erupted on the pitch as the green-clad hordes danced and cavorted with their heroes. Tommy Gemmell cut a fine sight in Sandro Mazzola's Inter shirt and a Celtic bobble hat! As pandemonium reigned, Ronnie Simpson was embraced by Stein. Out of the corner of his eye Simpson noticed John Clark charging past him and heading back towards his penalty area. It was only then he remembered that he had left both their sets of false teeth behind the goal! Not wanting them stolen for souvenirs, Clark went hell for leather to retrieve them. Billy McNeill was involved in a losing battle to keep his shirt from a swarming tide of admirers. It would remain the only battle he lost on that beautiful, sunlit late afternoon in Lisbon.

All that remained for Celtic was to collect their coveted prize. McNeill somehow grabbed for himself another jersey and made his way up towards the presidential box and that huge, glistening trophy. Amidst scenes of untold revelry and chaos, the captain of Celtic finally lifted it high. Parkhead was the new home of the European Cup. With the madness showing no sign of abating, it was decided that it would be impossible for the players to do a lap of honour. Instead they headed off to their changing-room to celebrate amongst themselves. There, the joy became etched with tears as the true measure of this historic achievement struck home. Stein watched the scenes unfold with huge pride. For these were his boys. As his mind drifted, Bill Shankly appeared and walked towards him, holding out his hand. 'Congratulations John,' he said. 'You're immortal.' No finer way to end.

POST NOTE

It is estimated that of the 12,000 Celtic supporters who participated in that epic adventure to the Iberian Peninsula, not all returned home. Indeed the number of red-headed Portuguese residing in Lisbon is now said to be well above the national average! In the weeks following the final, stories abounded of Celtic fans falling out of broom cupboards everywhere! For the simple fact was that nobody wanted to let go of what they had experienced on that unforgettable, magical Thursday afternoon in May 1967. That same evening, a blazing trail of euphoria gripped the city of Lisbon. Never in its long and eventful history had it partied so. For high above the Portuguese capital, the stars that shone belonged to Glasgow. Brother Wilfrid and his merry congregation would dance and sing until morning came. But for now they would enjoy this most special of Celtic nights.

11.

THE SON OF DONDINHO

BRAZIL V ITALY

1970 WORLD CUP FINAL

As in everything, Pele came first. Born in Brazil, the eldest of five children, on 23 October 1940, in a small mining village called Tres Coraces, Edson do Nascimento entered this world. It was obvious to all present, as the baby kicked and screamed, that a footballer had come to the household of Joao Ramos do Nascimento. Known as Dondinho, Joao Ramos never made it at the top level. A serious knee injury saw his dreams of becoming a professional footballer cruelly cut short. Happily his son would go on to live his dreams for him. That October night, a new star suddenly appeared above the shanty towns that lay far inland from the white sands of the Copacabana. Pele had arrived. It was to be a wonderful tale.

First emerging in the 1958 World Cup in Sweden, Pele, even as a 17-year-old, astounded the watching crowds. In the team of the incomparable, bewitching Garrincha, Pele, with blessed ball skills and the deadly instincts of a cobra, enthralled all who witnessed this remarkable boy. After a sluggish beginning by his side, the Brazilian manager, Feola, decided to chance his hand. He would risk all on the extraordinary goal-grabbing genius of this raw teenager. The 1958 World Cup will be remembered for Pele's act of wizardry in the final; a sublime piece of skill as he magically whisked the ball over the heads of three Swedish defenders before scoring with frightening ease. Come the final whistle, and Pele's tears of joy only helped endear him to an already adoring audience.

Four years on and injury prevented him from appearing in the later stages as Brazil retained their trophy in Chile. In 1966, Pele came to England clearly established as the finest footballer in the world, but these were changing times. This was the age of the hatchet men and Pele's talents would not be allowed to flourish. In an encounter with Portugal that year, the great Brazilian was left almost crippled after a vicious lunge by defender Morais.

This treatment by the normally sporting Portuguese left Pele nursing not only physical scars but also mental ones. He bade farewell to the cut-throat atmosphere of World Cup football. The tragic sight of Pele limping off at Goodison Park, with a raincoat draped over his shoulders, was apparently the last that his mourning fans would see of him. Happily it was not the end of the tale, for there was one last chapter.

The years leading up to 1970 saw the Brazilians begin to assemble a mind-boggling array of talent. An all-consuming desire to win back the Jules Rimet trophy was proving overwhelming. If Brazil could win a third title then they would keep the trophy. To Brazilian joy Pele had a change of mind and rejoined the crusade. Alongside him a colossal supporting cast stood ready to do battle amidst the heat and ferocity of the Mexican fiesta: Gerson, the possessor of a left foot which bore fair comparison to that of the great Hungarian Puskas – a man who smoked from dusk till dawn – a smoking gun; Tostao, a centre-forward of small but imperial stature; the captain of captains, Carlos Alberto, a raiding full-back who attacked with the pace of an Olympic sprinter; Jairzinho, a darting, devilish winger with classic ball skills; Rivelino, a man with fearsome curving free kicks and, even more scary, a Mexican bandit moustache. Then there was Pele himself, who played as if he were in love with the ball. Mesmeric dribbling, thundering pace, and a blinding shot, all combined to make this charismatic Brazilian a talent beyond compare. With the ball at his feet Pele danced, jinked and soared past bewildered defenders. In 1966, the son of Dondinho had been cut down. From the depths of despair he had risen, eager to reclaim his mantle. At 30, he was considered a spent force. Little did they realise the fierce passion and desire that still burned within him. The man charged with harnessing such power was Mario Zagallo. Zagallo was a veteran of the Brazilian team who swept to victory in Sweden and Chile. A left-winger of exceptional talent himself, Zagallo extolled the traditional values of his nation's football. The Jules Rimet trophy would be brought to Mexico by the world champions England. It had been away too long. It was time for the Brazilians to return it to its spiritual home – forever.

Far away to the east, in Guadalajara, Brazil came out with all their big guns blazing. Czechoslovakia felt the full wrath of four long, hurtful years. The Brazilians let fly with a four-goal blast. An early scare, when Petras swooped to take advantage of some sloppy defending, only succeeded in reminding the South Americans of just what was at stake. However, as well as serving as a wake-up call, it also showed to a watching world an Achilles heel, which would almost cost them dear. As superb as they were when attacking, their keeper Felix, and defenders such as Clodoaldo were prone to moments of madness. The barnstorming Rivelino, with a typically fierce, bending free kick, brought relief to the hordes watching back home in Brazil. The millions who swarmed around rusty old television sets in the favelas erupted in joy as Rivelino's shot hit home. Shortly before the hour, Pele chested down a sweeping pass from the cunning Gerson and unleashed a thunderbolt that flew low past the Czech keeper Viktor. Five minutes later and Jairzinho roared out of the traps like a greyhound to seal the game for the Brazilians. Leaving three Czech defenders in his wake, Jairzinho smashed the ball home with a sure right-foot shot. Fifteen minutes remained when Jairzinho set off again. With the Czech defence unable to hold him, the flying winger finished with a well-hit shot past Viktor − a perfect encore. Jairzinho had satisfied a rapturous audience. On the opening night this starry cast of performers had brought the house down.

It was during this game that Pele had conjured up a moment to treasure. From inside his own half of the centre circle, Pele looked up, and attempted to catch Viktor off his line. History beckoned as the ball soared high in the direction of the Czech goal. With the crowd holding their breath, it dropped inches wide of the net. Viktor shook his head in disbelief; the master took the applause of the Guadalajara crowd. An audacious effort, Pele was back!

Next for the Brazilians was a mouth-watering clash against the holders. Since winning the title on home ground, England's validity as true world champions had been sneered at by the South Americans. They remained convinced that the sending-off of the Argentinian captain, Rattin, had been an injustice. The final against West Germany only confirmed their opinion that all was not as it should have been. The third English goal in extra time had many shaking their heads in disbelief at the Russian linesman's blatant bias against the Germans. They spoke of conspiracies to ensure the home side won the trophy. It was hoped that the Brazilians could put England in their place. Mario Zagallo oozed confidence beforehand. 'We had too many goals for the Czechs,' he said. 'Maybe we will have too many for the English also.' Gerson, who ultimately did not play against the English because of injury, did not bother to hide his feelings on how much he yearned for victory against the world champions. 'My injury is not too severe at the moment. If I am to damage the leg it is better that I do it against the English. There is always a chance I can help to beat them before I come off.' But as much as the Brazilians ached for a win, England's determination to beat them also could not be underestimated. Alf Ramsey's apparent indifference towards the feelings of the Mexican press had them spitting and snarling venom in the champions' direction. Indeed at the opening ceremony, in the Azteca stadium, the English flag was the only one roundly booed by the Mexican crowd. One newspaper headline adamantly declared: 'England are nothing more than a team of drunks and thieves.' The sad, squalid incident involving England captain Bobby Moore being falsely accused of jewel theft en route to Mexico added to the pathetic sight of the West Brom forward, Jeff Astle, staggering off the plane in a 'tired and emotional state', only increased the depth of feeling against them. As for the state of the playing squad, however, many considered it considerably stronger than the one which had triumphed in the summer of 1966. The majority of the players were still around. Alan Ball spoke with sure-fire cockiness when he declared, 'If we score early, we could win by three or four goals.' Jack Charlton felt, quite rightly, that the Brazilian defenders were prone to ball-watching, and with the calibre of Martin Peters and Geoff Hurst on the prowl they could easily be punished.

It would be a contest of the world's best defence against its deadliest attack. The city of Guadalajara held its breath. In a searing, midday furnace, with a rabid pro-Brazilian crowd screaming for English blood, both teams entered the arena. England in all white were met by a hail of boos and whistles. As for Brazil, they were greeted by the Mexicans as if they were their own. The small scatterings of Union Jacks around the Jalisco stadium were lost among the yellow and green that engulfed the terraces. To the passionate resounding rhythm of the samba beat the game began. For the opening ten minutes Brazil hardly touched the ball as the world champions passed the ball around with an air of strutting arrogance, befitting their status. With the ice-cool Bobby Moore locking up at the back, England appeared supremely confident. Alan Ball and Bobby Charlton both tested the unpredictable Felix in the Brazilian goal. The South Americans had started slowly then, as a panther springs on its unsuspecting prey, Jairzinho awoke. Carlos Alberto's sublime pass down the touchline set the winger away. Jairzinho accelerated past Terry Cooper and cut back a perfect cross for the soaring Pele to head the ball down towards the English net. Pele was already celebrating, shouting 'Goal!', only for Gordon Banks to leap miraculously across his line and claw the ball over the crossbar. It was an outrageous save by the England keeper. The bewildered expressions etched on the faces of the Brazilian forwards spoke volumes. Pele could do nothing but stand there, bemoaning his bad luck. Bobby Moore ruffled the hair of his heroic keeper and suggested to him that he should have caught it! Down the other end of the field Felix applauded, along with the rest of the crowd. Millions watching the drama unfold on television could only look on in astonishment as the quality of Banks's stop was replayed. From this incident England grew even further in stature. With the ageing, but still superb, Bobby Charlton rivalling Brazil's Rivelino for subtlety of pass, and Alan Mullery shadowing Pele's every twist and turn, the battle raged. As well as the champions were playing, the Brazilians still produced moments of genius which made the English appear leaden-footed. The manner of their rapier one-twos and lightning movements on the edge of England's penalty area saw Moore and his defenders ever on the alert. As half-time approached it appeared obvious that the two sides on show were without equal elsewhere in the tournament. With their performance, England had shown that despite all the unflattering propaganda which surrounded them they were indeed worthy world champions. The second half saw no respite in the fine quality of the football. As the blazing sun began to take its predictable toll on the weary English, Brazil began to gain the higher ground. Jairzinho, Pele and Tostao prowled and probed for an opening, but each time they threatened, the immeasurable defensive qualities of Bobby Moore would snuff it out. One instance when he took the ball off Jairzinho's toes in the England penalty area caused gasps from the crowd, such was his immaculate timing. Moore was producing a performance that would enter World Cup folklore. Such was the pressure being placed on them, however, something had to give.

Finally, on the hour, England's magnificent rearguard was breached. Tostao, twisting, turning, surrounded by white shirts, found Pele on the edge of the English penalty area. A racing Jairzinho, hurtling into the enemy territory, was found by Pele, who laid it off for his team-mate to lash a flashing drive past Banks and into the top right-hand corner. The Jalisco stadium exploded in a flurry of colour. Brazil had the lead. England rallied, Colin Bell entered the fray for an exhausted Bobby Charlton, Jeff Astle came on for Francis Lee. The battle recommenced. With fresh legs the champions went in search of an equaliser. Alan Ball hit a shot which crashed against the top of the Brazilian crossbar. Then, the substitute Jeff Astle missed an open goal, which would forever haunt him. An abominable mistake by Brazilian defender Everaldo left Astle clear, only to shoot wide with a whole goal to aim at. The man from West Brom held his head in his hands. With Astle's aberration went England's last chance to save themselves. As Brazil threatened to score again at any moment, the game ended. This monumental clash was seen by many to be a dress rehearsal for the final itself. Brazil now viewed England in a new light. Respect was forthcoming for the world champions, they had earned it. Zagallo was convinced that if World Cup glory was to be theirs, somewhere down the road England would again have to be overcome. Pele and Bobby Moore embraced at the finish. A friendship was formed that day which would last until Moore's untimely death from cancer in 1993. The former England captain could not have been left with a finer epitaph than the memory of his performance in Guadalajara on 7 June 1970.

The final group game against Rumania saw a further brace for Pele, as the

Brazilians ran out 3–2 winners. However, by this time all thoughts had turned towards the forthcoming quarter-final match against Peru. To add further spice to this all-South American clash, the Peruvians were managed by former Brazilian legend Didi. Didi had been scathing in his comments regarding the Brazil of 1970. He claimed they lagged far behind the vintage teams of 1958 and 1962. Such comments aside, Didi was viewed as a traitor by his fellow countrymen. They found it quite incomprehensible that he could plot the downfall of his blood people. Didi knew that to try to defend would be hopeless. His team's strength lay in its ability to go forward. He would instruct them to go out and attempt to out-score the Brazilians. This was to prove a brave if foolhardy tactic. For attempting to outgun Pele, Jairzinho and co would be akin to attacking a tank with a bow and arrow. Playing with dash and no shortage of skill, the Peruvians went for broke. To no one's great surprise, the Brazilians hit them with four goals; one from Rivelino, Tostao with two, and a fourth from an increasingly unplayable Jairzinho. Although Peru stormed back with two themselves from Ballardo and the exciting Cubillas, the result was never in serious doubt. Came the final whistle and the Brazilians returned to the dressing-room not their usual joyful selves, for all ears were tuned to a radio broadcasting the extra time of Uruguay–USSR. Refusing to change out of their football kit, the Brazil players listened intently as the Uruguayans sneaked through at the last. The haunting memories of 1950, and the horrors of the last-gasp defeat by their neighbours from the south still cut deep. The pale blue shirts of Uruguay brought out a paranoia amongst Brazilians which no other nation, not even bitter rivals Argentina, could ever aspire to. Like an itch which they could never hope to scratch, this small nation of just two million people had caused their more illustrious neighbours a generation of hurt. It was time to even the score and end forever the nightmare of 16 July 1950. Pesadumbre. The darkest day in Brazilian football history. Unlike Peru, the Uruguayans had no intentions of taking the game to Brazil. Their manager, Juan Eduardo Hohberg, was the player who famously fainted after scoring a last-minute equaliser for his country in the 1954 World Cup semi-final against Hungary. Hohberg sent his team out with orders to intimidate Brazil in any way possible. Guadalajara was again ablaze with Brazilian yellow and green as the samba beat rose from a whisper to a thunder.

The game began as many had expected, with Brazil full of nerves. The psychological power which the Uruguayans appeared to have over them again showed itself after 18 minutes when an awful mix-up between the keeper Felix and his defender Brito let in Cubilla to put the Uruguayans in front. On seeing the ball hit the net, Brazilian heads dropped. Felix fell on his knees in mortal despair, the image of Moacry Barbosa sweeping before him. Gerson looked aghast; even the captain, Carlos Alberto, appeared a broken man. It was happening again, the curse ('catimbaba') was threatening once more to wreck their dreams. A witch's potion brewed in Montevideo was having its desired effect. Luckily for Brazil they had amongst their ranks a sorcerer of their own. Edson do Nascimento, the son of Dondinho, better known as Pele, ran back through his demoralised team-mates to retrieve the ball and restart the match. As he did so, Pele screamed words of encouragement. The game restarted; the Brazilians began to push the Uruguayans back. The veteran stopper Matoas was defending brilliantly as yellow shirts swarmed around him in desperate attempts to pierce this pale-blue wall of steel. His fellow defenders, Ancheta and Mujica, harassed, kicked, slashed, bit and elbowed in defence of their slender lead. Half-time approached with Brazil still struggling to create anything of substance. Gerson, increasingly desperate to find a way through, urged his full-back Clodoaldo to push forward. Finding himself heavily marked, Gerson then sat deep, thus taking his henchmen with him. It proved to be a masterstroke, for on the stroke of half-time Clodoaldo was played in by Tostao, the defender steadied himself, and from a narrow angle the tall, gangly player smashed an equaliser past Mazurkiewicz in the Uruguayan goal. Clodoaldo found himself buried under an ecstatic writhing mass of yellow shirts. The celebrations that ensued signalled nothing less than the lifting of a curse. The whistle blew to end the first period. In the dressing-room the manager, Mario Zagallo, was crying, such was the emotion brought on by Clodoaldo's goal. Zagallo gave a passionate, rousing address to his players. With tears falling down his face, he issued a call to arms. Uruguay would not know what had hit them. Shortly into the second period, Pele set the standard to which Brazil would aspire until the end of the competition. He had noticed in films of Uruguay that their keeper Mazurkiewicz constantly played out short punts to his midfield. Walking, seemingly uninterested, back to the halfway line, Pele whisked round, eyeballed the keeper, intercepted his pass and almost scored from 40 yards with a waist-high screamer back into his midriff. Genius is not a word sufficient to describe such a moment.

Brazil launched waves of attacks on the Uruguayans, each tipped with the added intensity of history and revenge. On 60 minutes, Guadalajara almost self-ignited as they finally put paid to a 20-year curse. Tostao and Pele combined with equal aplomb to put away Jairzinho. With a flurry of pale-blue shirts trailing in his path, Jairzinho let fly a shot that sent every Brazilian on the planet high into orbit. Uruguay tried to take the game back to Brazil but found themselves being caught endlessly on the break. Finally, with a minute remaining, Pele rolled the ball into the path of Rivelino who, with a thrash of his left foot, saw Brazil into the final. The Jalisco stadium against let loose its feelings for this wonderful team: 3–1. Amidst amazing scenes of joy in Guadalajara, Pele came close to delivering the coup de grace. With revenge for 1950 now complete, there existed only the desire to rub the Uruguayans' noses further in the mire. Racing onto an exquisite through ball from Tostao, Pele dummied a bemused Mazurkiewicz, who followed him instead of concentrating on the ball. In an instant Pele had changed direction, rounded the stranded keeper and, in a moment of divine inspiration, aimed a shot just wide of the net. It defied belief. Pele, in his desire to achieve the ultimate goal, had come within inches of immortality. The team partied along with their Mexican allies well into the Guadalajara dawn. There was one more hurdle. Sadly for all supporters of the three lions, it was not England. For in Leon, against a West German team thirsting for revenge for matters past, England squandered a seemingly impregnable two-goal lead to finish with their hearts sliced wide open. In front of a Mexican crowd roaring on the Germans, the final whistle saw Bobby Moore and his brave men relinquish their precious crown. As Gerd Muller swooped to lash a hooked drive past the unfortunate Peter Bonetti, the city of Leon celebrated the demise of England's four-year reign. As the lion lay slain, the pretenders to the crown moved with haste to stake their claim. As Brazil put paid to Uruguay, the Germans' reward for their dismissal of England was to be the 'catenaccio'-obsessed Italians.

'Catenaccio' translates roughly as 'lock out'. Originating in Austria, it was adopted with relish by Italy. No other nation in the world breeds better defenders than the Azzuri. Catenaccio is the ultimate defensive system. Involving all outfield players, it is designed to strangle the life out of opposing forwards. The Italian team which travelled to Mexico had amongst their ranks footballers of style and class to rival anyone in the competition. Allesandro 'Sandro' Mazzola was the son of the great Valentino Mazzola, who had been Italy's and Torino's leading light before his early death in the tragic Superga air crash of 1949. To avoid painful comparisons with his late father, Sandro chose to ply his trade with Inter Milan. There he would cover himself with glory as his goals helped to bring titles, and later three successive European Cup wins. In 1968, Mazzola converted to midfield to help the Azzuri win the European championships. In 1970, Sandro was 28 years old and at his peak. Along with captain and left-back Giacinto Facchetti, and the golden boy of all Azzuri supporters, the magnificent inside-forward Gianni Rivera, Italy's pedigree could not be faulted. However, their reliance on catenaccio would heap enormous pressure on the hefty but heavily outgunned shoulders of lone striker Luigi Riva. The deadly left foot of Riva would reap tremendous dividends if given half a chance. Sadly, opportunities would be hard to come by as the young Caligari hitman from Sardinia found himself fighting against overwhelming odds. Four years previously, the Azzuri had returned home to a midnight welcome committee at Genoa airport, all armed with rotten fruit. Humiliation at the hands of North Korea saw them vilified by their countrymen. The dread of failure seeped into every sinew of Italian preparation for the 1970 World Cup. A distorted notion that catenaccio would bring success in Mexico would prove a grave error.

Italy emerged from their first round group with a grand total of one goal. A 1–0 victory against Sweden, plus two goalless draws via Uruguay and the minnows of Israel, proved thinly sufficient to set up a quarter-final against Mexico. It was against the enthusiastic Mexicans that the infuriating catenaccio would blow a fuse. An early goal for Gonzales rocked the Azzuri and forced them to change tack. The remainder of the contest showed Italy in an altogether different light as they mauled Mexico in a pulverising display, full of class, poise and attacking football. Two goals from the much lauded Riva, one from Rivera, and an own goal sent the hosts crashing out of their own tournament. This Jekyll and Hyde showing by the Azzuri only helped to enrage all those who knew of their true potential. Given the right state of mind, Italy possessed the firepower to take on and beat the best. Sadly, their insistence on using catenaccio whenever danger threatened left them as a team almost schizophrenic in personality.

The semi-final saw them pitted against the Germans in the Azteca. In a roller-coaster encounter, the Italians finally sneaked through 4–3 after extra time. A gruelling contest, littered with twists and turns, meant players on both sides finally fell victim to the blistering heat. As fatigue set in, mistakes made for an extraordinary goal-scoring finale.

The fun began early in the first half when the strong-running Boninsegna charged through the German defence to shoot the Azzuri into the lead. To nobody's great surprise this was the signal for the Italians to fall back en masse and shut up shop. Catenaccio reared its ugly head. Marshalled by Franz Beckenbauer, West Germany took over the midfield and began to bombard their opponents. For almost the entire remainder of the game, the Azzuri found themselves under pressure. Chances aplenty appeared as the temperature touched melting point. The ever-dangerous Seeler and Grabowski both missed good opportunities to equalise as the Italians rode their luck. As the match entered injury time, it appeared once again that a single goal would prove ample for Italy. But just as all seemed lost, a desperate Grabowski tried one last time to break through. His cross found the advancing, tall, blond German defender Schnellinger who, to the abject horror of the Italians, shot past Albertosi. In typical, never-say-die style, West Germany had saved themselves.

With cramp and tiredness setting in, an abundance of goals followed. Within five minutes of the first period of extra time, the lightning reflexes of Gerd Muller shot the Germans in front. Their lead lasted four minutes before the Azzuri defender Burgnich blasted home from close range to make it 2–2. A fine poacher's goal from Riva then put Italy back in front as a watching world gasped in astonishment at the goal feast. By this time Beckenbauer was performing with his arm in a sling. The 'Kaiser' had been chopped down in cynical manner, downed by an Italian rearguard while accelerating with menace towards their goal. Come extra time, and even the Kaiser appeared all but spent. However, there still remained a double sting in the goal-scoring tail. From a corner, Muller again swooped from point-blank range to beat Albertosi. This incredible semi-final reached even further levels of drama when, just four minutes from the end, the dapper features of Gianni Rivera side-footed with great calm past a despairing Sepp Maier. Even the resilient Germans could not raise themselves to come back. The exhausted but exuberant Italians would go forth to take on the Brazilians. They, like Brazil, would be handed the privilege of keeping the trophy if successful. Their two previous triumphs back in the 1930s had set the scene for a winner-takes-all scenario. Against West Germany, the Italians had shown once more that when forced to come out and play they had few equals. The Azzuri remained the ultimate footballing enigma.

THE FINAL ACT

It was the morning of 21 June 1970. Mexico City, though never peaceful, had yet to come properly to life. Three days of rain and low-cloud thunderstorms had left puddles on every pathway. Despite a brave effort the sun was failing in its attempts to break through. The morning of the World Cup final had arrived. For millions of Brazilians and Italians around the world, this was a very special day. Brazil, free from injuries and raring to be let off the leash, appeared to have the entire planet (Italy apart) willing them to victory. At their training camp, beaming faces and cocky smiles hid fierce determination.

From their opening night, this all-star cast of Pele, Jairzinho, Tostao, Gerson and Rivelino had earned rave reviews. But all the plaudits and adulation thrown their way would amount to nothing if they were to fall at the last. Catenaccio would again be brought to the party by the Azzuri. Italy would enter into the Azteca cast as chief villain. Whereas Brazil played the

game in a manner which captured the heart and soul of football supporters
across the globe, the Azzuri, and their wretched policy of catenaccio, saw
them castigated by neutrals. It was felt their one chance of success against the
rampant Brazilians would be to shed their cloak of darkness and attack from
the off. But how does a leopard change its spots – especially when it hardly
needs to do so? Italian philosophy would be to sit, wait and pray for the rare
chance of a breakaway. With such a morbid, negative outlook, the Azzuri lit
the flame for their own funeral pyre.

At the moment of destiny, the Azteca stadium found itself drenched in the
bright yellow and green of Brazil; Mexicans and Brazilians together as one,
many wearing outrageous sombreros, prepared to roar Pele and his team to a
historic victory. The vivid, rapturous colours and melodies of the South
Americans swamped the massed terraces of this magnificent footballing arena
– a truly fit setting for a World Cup final. The small, vociferous bands of
Italian supporters were hopelessly out-shouted amidst such furious backing
for the Brazilians. The teams appeared to a tremendous reception. Well over
a hundred thousand people greeted the finest two exponents of their trade.
Pele juggled a football on his forehead, seemingly oblivious to the bedlam
erupting around him. Hundreds of cameramen lined up opposite the two
sides, capturing their images for posterity. At the opening ceremony, balloons,
all draped with the colours of the competing nations, had been released into
the heavens to signal the start of the tournament. Now, as the last two of
Brazil and Italy drifted high above the Azteca, it was time to write the last
chapter of what had been an astonishing fiesta of football.

Once all formalities had been taken care of, both teams broke away to
begin their final warm-up. In a calculated gesture, the Azzuri ran across to the
touchline and hurled bouquets of flowers into the crowd. This display was
greeted with jeers and no small degree of scepticism. To a crescendo of noise,
the players took up their positions and prepared to play winner takes all.
Seconds before the East German referee, Herr Glockner, opened proceedings,
the impatient Gerson ushered the last dozen photographers off the field. The
Azzuri began the final. It was they who threatened first; Mazzola's pass found
the left foot of Riva who, from 25 yards, let fly a flashing shot, only to see
Felix tip it over the crossbar. The Brazilians appeared to have misjudged the
damp surface, for in the early stages many of their players struggled to keep
their feet. Rivelino, in particular, suffered as an early attempt with a free kick
went horribly awry. The Italians began in promising fashion. Showing scant
regard for Brazil's reputation, the early signs were that the Azzuri had come
out to play and not, as many feared, disappear into their defensive shell.
Mazzola was matching Brazilian cunning and sleight of foot in midfield,

Facchetti was raiding dangerously down the left, whilst Riva looked up for a fight. Slowly, after a shaky opening, the yellow shirts of Brazil built up a rhythm. As the beat of the samba drums echoed down from the terraces, Jairzinho started to pin back Facchetti's runs, thus leaving space for Carlos Alberto to swoop in. Panicking, the Italians retreated, abandoning any illusion of taking on their opponents. They would lock out and rely on scraps – catenaccio. The normally plundering Gerson was sitting deep, apparently unwilling to risk straying across the halfway line. A previous meander in the opening moments had failed to be picked up by his Azzuri bodyguards. The quick-thinking Gerson noted this and swiftly retreated into his own half. He would return.

Brazil settled – Carlos Alberto's fine cross found Pele, only for Albertosi to dive bravely at his feet. Pele, ever the sportsman, patted the Italian goalkeeper on the head. The Azzuri hit back. Riva broke out to lash a low drive straight at Felix, who fumbled badly before grabbing at the second attempt. It was end-to-end football. Again the Italians lashed back and Mazzola had a shot blocked as the Brazilians struggled to clear their lines. The action, despite Italian reluctance to commit themselves, was non-stop – and Tostao roared clear to place pressure back on the Italians and only a fine clearance by Facchetti at the expense of a throw-in saved the day.

Tostao threw the ball to a lurking Rivelino. His precise cross found the head of a rising Pele, who soared above his marker Bertini and lashed a bullet header past Albertosi and into the goal. Mobbed by his ecstatic team-mates, Pele disappeared underneath a crowd of yellow shirts. Gerson gazed towards the heavens and gave thanks to his Maker. Any script worth its salt would surely suggest that Brazil go on and hand out to the Italians the lesson their sullen, sterile obsession with catenaccio richly deserved. Such was the enormity of the prize at stake, however, that there still existed a nervousness amongst the South Americans which could cost them dear. Lifted by such obvious frailty in the Brazilian defence, the Azzuri went in search of an equaliser. Led by the imaginative, strong-running Mazzola, they hit back. Riva stole past a stumbling Brito to drive a shot two feet wide of the post. Zagallo, watching with his clipboard in hand, appeared pensive. Seven minutes before half-time Brazil committed footballing suicide. Lazily stroking the ball around in his own half, Clodoaldo attempted a back flick which was swiftly intercepted by Boninsegna. Chased in frightful desperation by Carlos Alberto and Brito, the Azzuri midfielder streaked away into the Brazilian penalty area before laying off a pass to the stalking Riva. The Sardinian failed to control as Felix came roaring out of his net to crash into him. To the goalkeeper's horror, the ball fell loose back at the feet of Boninsegna, who

gleefully steered his shot into an empty net. Clodoaldo held his head in shame
– his terrible error had resulted in disaster. If the Italians could find the
courage to purge their defensive mentality and attack the shell-shocked
Brazilians, then a most unlikely victory could well be theirs. History beckoned
for the Azzuri. On the stroke of half-time, Pele again had the ball in the net,
only to see the referee disallow his effort. The electronic clock in the Azteca
showed seven seconds remaining when Pele's low drive flew past Albertosi.
The furious Brazilians surrounded Herr Glockner, but he simply waved them
away. Still reeling from the Italian equaliser, the South Americans headed
gloomily off the pitch: 1–1.

A tearful Clodoaldo sat heartbroken in the dressing-room. Mario Zagallo
walked across and gave him a playful cuff on the ear. Hugging his defender,
Zagallo whispered words of encouragement. Speaking before the game, the
Brazilian manager had ordered his team to reserve precious energy in the first
period, for he was certain the heart-stopping altitude of Mexico City would
have an adverse effect on the Italians. Having had only four days to recover
from their epic contest against the Germans, Zagallo gambled that the Azzuri
would begin to fade in the second half. When this occurred he wanted his
players ready and primed to take full advantage. The time had arrived for
Brazil to stamp their authority on an Italian side who, despite some attacking
moves, still steadfastly refused to abandon their defensive ideals of catenaccio.
Only Pele's early strike had forced them to appear from behind their
barricades. Gerson, however, was preparing to lure them out into the open,
and to end stubborn Azzuri resistance. He had discovered a chink in Italy's
defensive set-up, but being astute bided his time to strike, so as to give no
chance of repair when he did make his move.

The second half began with the sun winning its drawn-out struggle to
break through. With renewed determination, Brazil swept forward. Jairzinho
fed his captain, who swept menacingly down the right-hand touchline.
Alberto's fine cross into the Italian penalty area was met thunderously by Pele,
who succeeded only in putting his shot wide. Their desire to win back the
Jules Rimet trophy meant Brazil was going straight for the Azzuri jugular. The
reply from Italy was swift and succinct. With relish they launched themselves
at the unsuspecting Brazilians. From one such foul on Pele, Robert Rivelino
let fly from way out, only for Albertosi to dive to his left and save well. Pele
was beginning to scare the Italian defence to death. Picking up the ball in his
own half, the son of Dondinho would create havoc as he marauded forward
with the ball glued to his dancing feet. Gerson moved up with deadly intent.
Now playing solely in his opponent's half, he caused alarm bells to sound on
the Italian bench. The manager, Ferlucchi, cut a fraught and worried figure as

Gerson probed deep into enemy territory. The pressure on Italy was increased further when Jairzinho was brought down giving Rivelino yet another opportunity to have a thrash at Albertosi. From a full 30 yards the Brazilian unleashed a pile-drive which careered into the Azzuri crossbar. The Azteca rose to applaud Rivelino's stupendous effort. Italy fought desperately to keep Brazil at bay, but such was the pressure upon them it was surely only a matter of time before they cracked. On 66 minutes, the tactical nous shown by Gerson was about to reap rewards. Cutting inside from the Italian left-hand touchline, Jairzinho played in Gerson who, from 20 yards out, dragged the ball onto his esteemed left peg and flashed a snarling drive past Albertosi. The Azteca went wild. Gerson's wonderful show of self-contained opportunism had proved invaluable for his country's cause. Italy's reaction to their misfortune saw Pele horribly hacked to the ground by Domenghini in the centre circle. It was an outrageous tackle by the Italian which seemed to show that the Azzuri were running out of steam. Zagallo's masterplan was coming to fruition. Five minutes on and Gerson himself found Pele's head, whose knock-back into the six-yard box was scrambled home by a non-rushing Jairzinho. There appeared little doubt now that the World Cup was on its way back to where many considered was its spiritual home. Jairzinho dropped to his knees and made the sign of the cross. Far away in Rome, at the Vatican, a Brazilian pope fought with all his heart to remain neutral. A slight smile on the pontiff's face probably showed where his true allegiance lay.

Twenty minutes remained for the Italians to endure. By now it was showtime for Brazil. The flicks, dummies and tricks on display from the show-boating South Americans mocked the alleged fortress of catenaccio. Gerson, who by now was having the time of his life, set up a chance for the darting Tostao, only to see him miss by a whisker. Not yet content with his apparent one-man demolition job, Gerson this time played in defender Everaldo, only to see him shoot straight at Albertosi. With four minutes left to play, one of the defining images of this or any World Cup occurred. Dribbling clear of four chasing Italian players, Clodoaldo atoned for his first-half moment of madness. Playing his way into the annals of World Cup history, the Brazilian defender danced and jinked before caressing a pass out wide to the prowling Jairzinho. With an arrogance befitting his wonderful performances throughout the tournament, Jairzinho stroked a pass inside to Pele, midway inside the Azzuri half. Pele quite nonchalantly played a ball without even looking into the path of a roaring, barnstorming Carlos Alberto. Screaming into the Italian penalty area, the Brazilian captain of captains smashed a ferocious low drive past a helpless Albertosi, to seal a quite magnificent victory: 4–1 to Brazil and a legend was born. During the final moments the referee had to quell a flurry of pitch invasions, as supporters, photographers and well-wishers continually rushed onto the field of play. Beaten and battered, the Azzuri continued to push forward to salvage some pride. When Riva shot high over Felix's crossbar deep into injury time, the ecstatic crowd decided to keep the ball. When a replacement finally arrived, Herr Glockner ended Italian agony and blew for time. His whistle signalled a cavalry charge onto the field. The Brazilian players found themselves mobbed as supporters charged in their hundreds towards them. Pele was hoisted high. A Mexican sombrero was placed upon his head as a very public coronation took place. However, for some the situation would turn nasty as Tostao was violently stripped by over-eager fans hunting for mementos. The goalkeeper Felix sobbed uncontrollably as the realisation of their achievement struck home. Rivelino collapsed in a heap, a mixture of exhaustion and emotion. An exuberant supporter staked a Brazilian flag in the penalty area where Carlos Alberto had smashed home their fourth and utterly decisive goal.

Back on home soil, the carnival had begun in earnest. In the shanty towns and poverty-hit favelas which covered the country, celebrations would last forever and a day. A long-held ambition had been fulfilled. The Jules Rimet trophy would now take up permanent residence in Brazil. Countless hearts burst as Carlos Alberto lifted the World Cup high, his joyful smile a defining image of Mexico 1970. The festivities commenced. The Brazilian lap of honour was accompanied by a mass of supporters and photographers who were intent on partying with the champions until they reached the blessed sanctity of the dressing-room. Pele, sipping quietly on a glass of water, caught the eye of his coach Zagallo. With the party in full swing around them, both men came together and shared a tearful embrace. With the World Cup back in the proper hands, and his place in history assured, Pele at that moment decided that the time was right to retire from international football. There would be no comebacks. The son of Dondinho had done his father proud; there was nothing left to prove. The night the dream ended, the star which shone above Tres Coraces when Edson de Nascimentes was born dimmed a little. Then it vanished altogether from the jet-black Brazilian sky. The final chapter had been written. The fairy tale was over.

12.

FOOL'S GOLD

SCOTLAND V HOLLAND

1978 WORLD CUP

My name is Ally Macleod, and I am a winner.

Long after the final whistle had blown on Scotland's ill-fated World Cup campaign, a lone, tearful piper remained behind on the empty terraces to lament his country's demise. The haunting, whirling melody in sad mournful echoes swept across Mendoza, weeping for a lost dream. Swept along on a tidal wave of hype and delusions of self-grandeur, the tartan army had travelled to Argentina chasing fool's gold. What they were to experience was a journey into footballing hell.

Sewn into the rich tapestry of Scotland's long and bloody history are enduring images of dramatic last stands and fallen heroes – William Wallace betrayed at Falkirk, hanged, drawn and quartered at the frightening whim of a dying, mad English king; the redcoats gleefully slaughtering the wounded at Culloden. In the summer of 1978, the call went out once more for the tartan army to unite; for Argentina beckoned. Roused by wild promises of glory, the Scots began to dream the dreams of madmen. Such illusions became imbued with a heavy dose of reality when, on being grouped with Holland, Peru and Iran, the manager and self-proclaimed guru, Ally Macleod, publicly declared that 'Scotland will win the World Cup'. From south of the border there came gales of laughter from a nation of 50 million, compared to Scotland's five, which had not even made it to Argentina. In a manner laced with jealousy, the English press attacked their Scottish counterparts as merely fans with typewriters. Maybe their inglorious defeat at Bannockburn still cut deep? This notwithstanding, the media frenzy which exploded in the wake of the Scots' final qualifying match against Wales only confirmed for many that something strange seemed to have occurred beyond Hadrian's Wall. Lingering north of the border, there lay optimism for success. As Rod Stewart sang, 'Ole ola, ole ola, we're gonna bring that gold cup back from over there', the tartan army even attempted to rent a submarine to take them to Argentina. The lunatics had not only taken over the asylum, they had succeeded in convincing the world they were sane. Immortality beckoned for Ally's army, but sadly not in the manner they would have desired. All together now, 'Ole ola, ole ola'.

The tale began on an unforgettable night at Anfield on 17 October 1977. In a shameful episode, the Welsh FA abandoned their country for money. Stadiums such as Wrexham's racecourse ground were deemed of insufficient size to accommodate the hordes of supporters desperate to witness the showdown. Both Scotland and Wales stood level on points. The Welsh decision to move the game to Merseyside saw any advantage they might have gained on home territory vanish completely as the tartan army travelled down in droves to snap up the tickets. On the night of the match the city of Liverpool lay under Scottish occupation. Of the 51,000 present at Anfield, over three-quarters swore allegiance to the flag of St Andrew. The bright red shirts of the Welsh were swamped amidst the masses of their Celtic blood brothers from the far north. Both countries had done remarkably well to see off the not inconsiderable challenge of the third team in the group, the reigning European champions, Czechoslovakia. It would now be a fight to the death between the remaining two. As kick-off approached, and the boisterous Scots drank Liverpool pubs dry, expectations had reached such monstrous levels that any notion of failure was simply scoffed at. An air of over-confidence bordering on arrogance had begun to sweep dangerously through the massed ranks of the kilted hordes. The Liver bird itself risked being dismantled if victory was not forthcoming. The city of Liverpool braced itself. They need not have worried, for despite a brave Welsh challenge, Lady Luck shone down on Scotland when they were awarded a late controversial second-half penalty. This dubious decision had the livid Welsh supporters alleging the referee's Scottish ancestry, amongst other things. A handball given against defender Joey Jones, when it appeared clearly to have been Scotland's Joe Jordan who committed the offence, dealt Wales a cruel blow. With just 11 minutes remaining, Derby County midfielder Don Masson was given the opportunity to put his country into the World Cup finals. Masson stepped up to lash his shot past the Welsh keeper, Dai Davies, and send Anfield wild with delight. In a last effort to save themselves, Wales threw caution to the wind and stormed forward. Three minutes from time, with the stadium gloriously awash with blue and white, Manchester United defender Martin Buchan crossed wonderfully for Kenny Dalglish to smash a flying header past the flailing arms of Davies. Scotland were there! Dalglish, on his own Liverpool stage, had sent the tartan army soaring into dreamland.

Argentina beckoned, but even that fine Scottish bard Robert Burns, after whom the DC10 which would carry Scotland to the 11th World Cup finals was named, would have struggled to pen the tragic events about to envelop his fellow countrymen. On 25 May 1978, on a warm summer's evening at Hampden Park, 20,000 members of the tartan army gathered to wish their heroes good luck in their quest for World Cup glory. The Scottish players travelled around the running track in an open-top, double-deck bus. Many appeared visibly embarrassed by the whole charade, fully aware that the time for shouting the odds was after the prize had been won, not before. Players who plied their trade down south, in the English first division, feared what lay in store. Free from the mass euphoria which had engulfed their clansmen, they still had the ability to see through the hysteria and view the truth. An exuberant Ally Macleod indulged himself as he took the acclaim of his adoring public. When asked what he would do when Scotland actually won the World Cup, Ally replied in all seriousness: 'Retain it!' In the centre circle, the stirring tones of a pipe band drifted over the cheering crowds on the terraces. Amidst such emotional surroundings, Glasgow bade a proud, tearful farewell to Ally's army. Macleod had promised to make their wildest dreams come true. Heaven help him if he failed to deliver!

PERU

Scotland were based in the small hill town of Alta Gracia. On arrival they received a heroes' welcome from the inhabitants. The ordinary Argentinians threw open their hearts to the visitors from foreign shores. Sadly, the iron fist of General Jorge Videla's military junta was never far away, lurking menacingly in the shadows. Trigger-happy soldiers ringed the grounds of the Sierras Hotel, with orders to shoot first and ask questions later. Many a journalist risked life and limb if they attempted to enter without permission. Even the players themselves dared not move out for fear of being used for target practice. Such circumstances quite rightly infuriated the besieged Scottish party. This, allied to the poor facilities of the hotel, meant Ally's army, even at this early stage, were showing signs of open rebellion. The pathetic sight of a swimming-pool filled only with cockroaches, and bedrooms resembling little more than dormitories, soon saw morale dip alarmingly. To add further fuel to an increasingly smoking fire, an earth tremor which rocked Alta Gracia was said to be the worst to hit the region for over half a century.

The more superstitious began to whisper of omens. They were right to do so, for arriving in the city of Cordoba, eager to knock the Scots off their self-made perch, were Peru – Cubillas, Munante, Oblitas and all. Cordoba lay an hour's drive from Alta Gracia. It was here that Scotland began their ill-fated campaign.

In a gesture bordering on absurdity, Ally Macleod refused publicly the opportunity to go and view Peru live, preferring to rely on a handful of videos and second-hand snippets of information, most of which turned out to be incorrect. The dream was all set to turn into a nightmare. Saturday, 3 July 1978. Scotland and Peru walked out to do battle in the Chateau Carreras stadium in Cordoba, greeted by 37,792 people. Across the steep concrete terraces the strength of the tartan army could be measured in hundreds rather than thousands. Such was the drunken bravura which had gripped the Scots following Anfield, close to 30,000 were said to be planning a summer jaunt across the Atlantic. It soon became apparent that the sheer length of such a journey, not to mention cost, had meant many stayed at home to watch on television. Macleod was without three of his regular back four. Both full-backs, Manchester City's Willie Donachie and the supreme Danny McGrain, from Celtic, plus centre-half Gordon McQueen of Manchester United, were all denied him through injury. In their place was Aberdeen's Stuart Kennedy, Manchester United's Martin Buchan and Nottingham Forest's Kenny Burns. In midfield Macleod again placed his trust in the reliable but ageing Derby duo of Don Masson and captain Bruce Rioch. Most controversially, the Scottish manager preferred the predictable menacing presence of Joe Jordan rather than the on-form, on-fire Derek Johnstone of Rangers. Johnstone was coming off the back of a sensational season, in which he had scored 41 goals for his club, plus two for his country in the recent home internationals. Macleod's utter refusal to listen to anyone's opinion but his own meant Johnstone was left on the sidelines.

It could not have started any better for the Scots. On 19 minutes, Joe Jordan stabbed home from close range, after a left-foot snap-shot from Rioch was badly fumbled by the goalkeeper Ramon Quiroga. A deserved booking for the defender Velasquez, after a lunge on Jordan, might have shown that Peru were rattled by Scotland's bustling centre-forward, but just when it appeared to be going to script, an ill wind whistled low over Cordoba. Macleod's inept attempts to do his homework on the Peruvians soon became obvious as their speedy wingers Oblitas and Munante began to run at his two replacement full-backs. Both Kennedy and Buchan, who was being played out of position, found themselves forced onto the back foot against the trickery and pace of each. Buchan would hardly have been surprised to learn that

Munante was in fact an Olympic-class 400-metre runner. The Manchester United centre-half, hardly renowned for his speed, suffered tremendously against the lightning Peruvian who sped past him in a blur. Operating through the midfield to deadly effect came Teofillio Cubillas. Cubillas was a survivor of the 1970 World Cup. Still only 29, he laughed at the label of veteran which had been placed upon him by badly informed European journalists. This was a player performing at the peak of his powers. Peru's flashing one-twos and quick-fire footwork had the Scots retreating in panic. Shortly before half-time, Peru grabbed a deserved equaliser. Again, wonderful approach work by the Peruvians finally allowed the whiplash Cueto to smash low past the much maligned Alan Rough. The small tartan-clad groups around the stadium watched with growing trepidation. The half-time whistle left them reeling with the realisation that after all the hype the simple truth was that they were not really that good.

Hardly inspiring with his half-time talk, Macleod's only words of wisdom were for Alan Rough to kick the ball longer and harder. Shell-shocked players sat in stunned disbelief as their manager appeared unable to explain to them how to deal with the ever-growing threat of Peru. The second half, however, saw Scotland rally. Jordan had a header crash onto the post, while a strangely subdued Kenny Dalglish finally awoke to trouble Quiroga with a lashing drive that flew off a Peruvian defender. On seeing their team roar back into life, the tartan army sang their hearts out for the lads in blue and white. On 63 minutes, Bruce Rioch found his legs taken from beneath him by Diaz, and the Swedish referee Eriksson awarded Scotland a penalty. Don Masson would be handed the chance to put the Scots back in front. Peru's keeper, Quiroga, basked in the nickname of 'El Loco'. His madcap forays upfield caused heart attacks amongst his defenders, none more so than captain and legendary centre-half Hector Chumpitaz. He was also a shot-stopper of top quality, for Masson's half-hearted penalty attempt was easily parried away by Quiroga as he dived low to his right to break Scottish hearts. From that moment Peruvian confidence soared. Launching all-out attacks on Alan Rough's goal, they went for the kill. With Oblitas and Munante ripping Macleod's team to shreds on both flanks, Scotland found themselves under siege. This was not how Ally Macleod had planned world domination. Inevitably it was the magnificent Cubillas who masterminded the Peruvian breakthrough. His wickedly, curling shot, hit with great venom with the outside of his right boot, saw Rough totally flat-footed as the ball swerved demonically past him. Almost immediately Scotland substituted Masson and Rioch, and brought on Lou Macari and Archie Gemmill. Both had been pushed by journalists beforehand to be included in the line-up. It made little difference as the Peruvians continued to cut Scotland's defence to ribbons. Macleod watched on glum-faced, seemingly unable to believe what was happening to his team. Fourteen minutes from time, Kennedy was forced into bringing down Duarte on the edge of the penalty area. A slight smile crossed Cubillas' lips. The Scottish wall was formed with the diminutive Lou Macari placed quite inexplicably on the end. After a team-mate's dummy run, Cubillas strode forward to stroke a masterful effort with his right foot past a dumbstruck Rough: 3–1 and the game over. Scotland had been outclassed. The Peruvian manager, Marcos Calderon, wore the smug grin of a man who knew his team had proved the critics wrong. The final whistle saw the Scots slouch embarrassedly off the field. At the press conference Macleod went on the defensive, publicly slating his players. Claiming that eight of them did not perform, he refused to accept any responsibility for Scotland's pathetic showing. The tartan army showed their disgust for the team by hammering on the side of the coach as they attempted to leave the stadium. Spitting and snarling at the ashen-faced players, they felt cheated and let down. It was all a long way from the triumphant scenes at Hampden Park only a few weeks before.

The next morning it was open season on Ally Macleod and his beleaguered team. Newspapers both sides of the border cut loose with a vicious torrent of abuse. The English press took great delight in twisting the knife deep, for Macleod had never been slow to remind them that England had failed to qualify for Argentina. Hammered from all directions, the Scotland party closed ranks and retreated to Alta Gracia. Their lacklustre showing had supporters shaking their heads in disgust.

Things were not to improve. Immediately following the final whistle, the Scottish winger Willie Johnstone was taken by FIFA officials for a random drugs test. The nippy West Brom winger had been one of Scotland's few successes against the Peruvians. Johnstone, when questioned if he had taken any stimulants, was honest enough to admit that he had taken some pep pills called Reactivan. This was not illegal in Britain, but to the Scotsman's horror he was informed that it was on FIFA's banned list. The secretary of the Scottish FA, Ernie Walker, acted swiftly in sending Johnstone home in disgrace. Walker's attitude was akin to a public execution for Johnstone, for his name would forever be tarnished by an incident in which he was merely careless. In claiming his actions were to protect the good name of his country, Ernie Walker fed Willie Johnstone to the Fleet Street wolves. On returning home, Johnstone lost much sympathy when he sold his tortured soul to a Sunday tabloid. A shabby affair. Almost daily different stories emerged in the media claiming disarray amongst the Scots. Wild tales of late-night drinking sessions and womanising were emblazoned across the front pages. Based close by, the Mexican World Cup squad spoke of how certain Scottish players had indulged themselves in all-night parties. Most of what was written has been dismissed as mere fabrication, but at the time all was taken as gospel by a Scottish public seething with indignation. Events in the next game would hardly help to improve matters.

IRAN

Elsewhere in the group Holland began comfortably, casually dismissing Iran 3–0. The Iranians appeared to have little to offer. The Scots were expected to see them off with some ease. Macleod made five changes from the team which had flopped against Peru. In a ghostly atmosphere, with only 8,000 present in the Chateau Carreras stadium, the teams emerged. The Scottish players appeared pensive. The tartan army had once more gathered to back them. A victory against Iran would put their World Cup back on the rails.

The game started well for Macleod's men. The opening minutes saw chances appear for Dalglish and Macari. Both would go begging as Iran looked unable to cope with Scotland's early momentum. However, Scotland's play quickly became riddled with sloppy passing and individual errors. Suddenly recognising that their opponents were there for the taking, the Iranians gained in confidence and began to attack. Faraki almost put them in front when his low shot was blocked by Rough. Scotland appeared disorganised and dispirited. A typical example of disjointed play occurred when Willie Donachie collided with Martin Buchan, cutting his head open in the process. Buchan would later comment: 'Willie is my best mate. I suppose it sums up how things are going when he nearly kicks my head off!' Two minutes before half-time a hilarious own goal by Iranian defender Eskandarian gave the Scots an undeserved lead. Sitting on his backside on the penalty spot, the hapless Eskandarian somehow contrived to kick the ball into his own net. Even he appeared not to know whether to laugh or cry.

The second half saw no improvement in Scotland's performance. Indeed, on the hour Iran rocked Macleod's men on their heels when they grabbed an equaliser. On seeing the ball strike the back of the net, Ally Macleod put his head in his hands. Scotland, under his leadership, had finally hit rock bottom. They were now in real danger of actually losing the game. The closing minutes saw the Iranians finishing the stronger side: 1–1. The final whistle was greeted with a hail of jeers and boos by the tartan army. Once more as Scotland's coach left the stadium it was serenaded by angry supporters singing, 'We want our money back'. Many were in tears, unable to believe the shambolic state of their team. Others vented their frustration on the team coach, rocking it to and fro, trying to turn it on its side. Only the swift intervention of Argentinian riot police prevented them from doing so. The Scottish supporters could forgive a bad performance, but they could not stomach a lack of fight amongst their team. This was what fuelled their anger, and this was ultimately what broke their hearts. The following day at Alta Gracia, while waiting for a press conference to begin, Ally Macleod resembled a rabbit caught in the headlights of a speeding car. Trying in vain to lighten the atmosphere he ushered a stray dog towards him and began to stroke it. 'At least the dog still likes me,' quipped Macleod, only to regret his words as the stray turned nasty and bit him!

HOLLAND

While Scotland plunged to the depths against Iran, Holland and Peru fought out a goalless draw; a result that suited both, and one which meant the Scots would have to beat the Dutch by a margin of three goals to stay alive in Argentina. Due to his fear of being kidnapped, Johan Cruyff had refused to travel to South America, but even without their 'Prince of Orange' Holland still had amongst their ranks the calibre of Krol, Rep, Haan, Resinbrink, the van der Kerkhoff twins and, of course, the mercurial heartbeat of their team, Johan Neeskens. Indeed eight of the team who took the field against Scotland had played in the previous World Cup final. All Holland now had to do to qualify was to avoid defeat by more than three goals.

To the utter delight of all concerned, the Scots bade farewell to Alta Gracia and headed off to meet their destiny in Mendoza. The city of Mendoza lay in the foothills of the Andes. The San Martin stadium was itself built into the side of a mountain. High above, the peaks of the Andes, shrouded in mist, gave the arena a real sense of drama – a perfect setting for Scotland's last stand.

Following the débâcle against Iran, Ally Macleod fell into a pit of despair. For three days he hardly ventured out of his room. The fresh-faced Ally, always quick with a quip, appeared to have gone forever. In his place came a gaunt, depressed figure, whose ravaged features were those of a man bereft of both heart and spirit. Never had he felt more alone. The joke flying around Glasgow was that Mickey Mouse had taken to wearing an Ally Macleod watch! He had further cast himself adrift from public sentiment by signing an exclusive deal with the *Scottish Daily Express*, for £25,000. Previously he had refused such offers, giving each journalist an equal share of the pie; but as the walls of his castle were breached, Ally took the bait. Once this leaked out the personal scorn and abuse heaped upon his head by rival newspapers was both unfair and cruel, for despite Bill Shankly's inane talk of life and death, football was, after all, just a game. While Macleod had stalled on cashing in, his players had wasted little time in hawking their stories around various tabloids. Bickering over bonuses further sapped morale amongst the squad. It was a mess. Now, players who had disgraced the country they purported to represent had one last chance to win back some dignity. A sense of anti-climax drifted over Scotland as the game against the Dutch drew near. One wag when asked about Scotland's chances replied, 'How are we going to convince the Dutch to score three own goals?'

Throughout the tournament, Scottish journalists and supporters had repeatedly complained about Ally Macleod's refusal to play Liverpool's classy midfielder Graeme Souness. Only a month previously, Souness had created a goal for Kenny Dalglish with a sublime pass which secured his club a second successive European Cup. It appeared to all outsiders that Macleod simply did not rate Souness. Possibly blinded by loyalty, he had continued to rely on the stalwart Don Masson. Sadly, Masson had been shown to be past his best. Against the Dutch Souness would be given his chance. The team which the critics and fans had craved would finally take the field in Mendoza. But surely it was all too late? On 11 June 1978, Scotland and Holland began the finest match of Argentina 1978. Showing a patience and subtlety of passing sadly lacking in their first two matches, the Scots attempted to scale Mount Everest wearing carpet slippers. The clans had gathered one last time as they prayed for a miracle; and yet, as Scotland pinged the ball around with new-found confidence, many found their spirits roused. Holland had come out determined not to be messed around. Some of their early challenges verged on assault as they appeared unsettled as to how to approach the game. The Scots surged forward, and Rioch looked dismayed as his fine header thudded against the Dutch crossbar. Dalglish, finally showing the skills which made him such a superstar for his club, was unlucky to see his own effort ruled out. The noise reverberating around the San Martin made it clear that Scotland had the neutrals on their side. Inspired by such raucous support, they threw caution to the wind and charged! Behind it all was Souness. How his countrymen

wished that Macleod had picked him against Iran, for surely they would not
now be in this dire state, chasing fool's gold. On 34 minutes, Scotland's
world came crashing down, when Kennedy and Rough between them
brought Robbie Resinbrink to earth inside the penalty area. Resinbrink
made the Scots pay by blasting home the thousandth goal in the World Cup
finals. Could they really have expected anything else? Scotland kicked off,
and still they probed, looking for a way through. By this time Holland had
lost Neeskens through injury. On the stroke of half-time, Souness lashed in
a high cross which Jordan headed down in the direction of Kenny Dalglish.
Showing great technique, Dalglish volleyed a terrific shot past Jan
Jongbloed in the Dutch goal to level for Scotland. Maybe the dream had
died but pride was still intact.

So began the second half. A minute after the restart Souness, again the
thorn in the Dutch defence, found himself bundled over in the penalty box
by Willy van der Kerkhoff. A penalty for Scotland. Up came Archie Gemmill
to smash low and hard past Jongbloed; 2–1 and Macleod, who had been
reduced to a figure of ridicule, appeared momentarily a man reborn. Surely it
was asking too much? Holland were rattled. The loss of Neeskens, plus an
unsure game plan saw them uncertain how to deal with the rampaging Scots.
The tartan army, after being forced to endure so much heartache, roared out
in defiance. This night might not be a Bannockburn, but by God they would
go down fighting.

Again Scotland went forward, and Kenny Dalglish found himself
outnumbered by three Dutch defenders as he was robbed of possession. The
loose ball fell to a lurking Archie Gemmill who, on the edge of the penalty
area, side-stepped Wim Jansen, jinked past Krol, nutmegged Poortvliet, and
as Jongbloed advanced, slipped a shot ever so sweetly into the Dutch goal: 3–1
to Scotland! High in the television gantry, commentators from every nation,
Holland apart, sprang to their feet when wee Archie's stupendous effort hit
the net. Maybe there did exist a crock of gold at the end of the rainbow? Then
again, maybe not. One more goal was required to see the Scots through.
Holland argued amongst themselves – this was not a team in harmony. Back
on native soil, a feeling of excitement, tinged with more than a little
bewilderment, swept across the land. Twenty-two minutes remained for
Scotland to score again and send the Dutch hurtling out of the competition.
As euphoria draped itself across the celebrating Scottish supporters, Johnny
Rep won possession for Holland, and from fully 30 yards let fly a screamer
past the despairing fingertips of Alan Rough. Game, set and match. If there
had been any doubts before, they had now been dispelled. Scotland were
going home. Adios. On seeing the ball hurtle past Rough, Macleod gave a

heavy sigh and prepared, one suspects, for a lifetime of self-doubt and mockery; but without his grand notion that he would prevail, Scotland would never have lived the dream. Ally Macleod had given hope where there was previously none. He chanced his arm, and for this should be applauded; good for him. We can all dream.

13.

A FISTFUL OF DOLLARS

ARGENTINA V PERU

1978 WORLD CUP

It is Peru's duty to safeguard the decency of the competition.
– Hector Chumpitaz (Peru's captain)

As night-time's veil drew across the dark Rosario sky, and a half moon made its first dramatic appearance of the evening, Argentina held its breath. The date was 21 June 1978. Inside the Codviolo Rosario stadium 38,000 Argentines prayed for a miracle. The host nation needed to score four times to reach the World Cup final. This was due to Brazil's decisive 3–1 victory over Poland that same afternoon. The Brazilians led by two points and, more importantly, possessed a vastly superior goal difference. The odds favoured heavily the three times world champions. Argentina's destiny now lay solely in their ability to destroy Peru. Cesar Menotti's team entered the stadium to be greeted by a tumultuous snowstorm of blue and white confetti. Led by their captain, Daniel Passarella, the Argentine players looked around in amazement and disbelief. Masses of torn paper glittered under the blinding-white glaze of floodlights. The 11 men chosen to wear the blue and white hoops dared not fail amidst such passionate support. A huge burden rested on the shoulders of their two star forwards. The skilful, long-legged Mario Kempes and the lethal predatory instincts of the huge, mustachioed Leapoldo Luque. These two had fired the bullets which had shot their nation to within sight of the final. It had been a rocky ride. Dogged by controversy throughout, they had been helped by some questionable refereeing, and at times been forced to rely on sheer good fortune. All this was in the past, for now they stood on the brink of making their country's wildest dreams come true.

Throughout the playing of the national anthems it was clear that the frenzied atmosphere that had enveloped the stadium had affected the players.

The Argentinian faces looked etched with passion and desire. It was well known amongst them that they had never played for higher stakes. Each understood the prize for victory; but they also understood clearly the cost of failure. As thousands of flags waved in the cool night breeze the players broke to take up their positions, eager to get on with the match. Throughout the tournament the Peruvians in flashes had played some crisp, delightful, attacking football. Their humiliation of a much-hyped Scotland in the early rounds had sent shock waves rippling through the Mundial. Cubillas, Munante and the flying Oblitas had ripped to shreds a bedraggled Scottish side and now huge respect was being paid to this exciting team with the dashing red stripe. In defence the Peruvian captain, Hector Chumpitaz, made sure that his fellow defenders' excursions upfield were carefully watched and covered. Even the immensely experienced Chumpitaz would shake his head, however, when he saw his keeper Ramon Quiroga ('El Loco') performing his dubious party tricks. His hurtling out of goal at times had severe consequences for his side, but in Quiroga's defence he was also a superb shot stopper. Up until now.

As the spare balls were kicked off the field, the Peruvians looked apprehensive. The explosive, intimidating atmosphere of the Rosario had clearly got to them. The lean, languid figure of Cesar Menotti lurked anxiously near the Argentinian dug-out. From this moment on he was helpless. Taking his place on the bench, this chain-smoking, long-haired Argentinian guru could only keep his fingers crossed. Four goals were required. Four goals. It was a hell of a mountain to climb. The referee from France, M. Robert Burz, checked his watch, put his whistle to his mouth and began one of the most infamous games in World Cup history. Peru opened brightly. After only two minutes, Munante sped through a panicking Argentinian rearguard and chipped a shot against the post. The ball rebounded to safety and was hastily hacked clear. As Munante's shot headed towards the goal an eerie silence had descended upon the Codviolo Rosario. Many a rosary bead was gripped tight to keep that ball out of the net. It had been a close shave. These Peruvians looked like they had failed to read the script. On the crowded terraces Argentinian hearts skipped a beat. The country's leader, General Jorge Videla, looked on anxiously. Shuffling uneasily in his seat, Videla cut an uncomfortable figure. Peru threatened to ruin the party and send Argentina's suicide rate through the roof.

Minutes after, there was yet another scare for Argentina when Oblitas ran through and shot dangerously across Ubaldo Fillol's goal. The home side were edgy and showing signs of stage fright. The captain Passarella roared at his defenders to concentrate. The tension from the terraces was in danger of overwhelming them. Menotti too looked edgy. Puffing as ever on a cigarette, he knew his side needed the boost of an early goal, otherwise the cause would be hopeless. He need not have fretted. Argentina pressed forward. The Peruvians began to have terrible difficulties in pinning down Kempes. Quiroga's goal was becoming the target of increasing pressure. A breakthrough began to look likely and on 21 minutes, to the relief of every Argentinian, it finally arrived. Twisting and turning on the edge of the box, Kempes danced his way through and shot low past Quiroga into the bottom right-hand corner. With his trusted left foot Kempes had began the rout. There would be much more to follow. As Peru visibly wilted the Argentinians swarmed forward. A second goal looked a certainty. On 43 minutes, Taranti stooped low to send a diving header past a badly fumbling Quiroga. They were halfway there. Further chances followed as Kempes and Luque threatened to run riot. However, as the referee blew for half-time there had been no further goals. As a full moon hovered high over the stadium, the Argentinian fans danced all through the interval. The omens looked good. Something was badly wrong with the Peruvians. Their baffling performance after such a blistering start had neutrals shaking their heads.

On 49 minutes Kempes played a one-two with Bertoni and unleashed a flashing drive to beat a hapless Quiroga: 3–0. With Peru apparently lying down, the Argentinians trampled all over them. Another goal had to follow. With the crowd on the point of madness Kempes headed down for his partner in crime Luque to scramble home the fourth and most important goal. An ecstatic Rosario crowd roared out in joy. The Argentines kept up the pressure. Almost inevitably another opportunity arrived when Oritz broke clear and laid it on a silver platter for the substitute Houseman to make it five. Four Peruvians seemed content to stand and watch. They did everything but applaud. This was not the team who had thrilled the watching world earlier in the tournament. On 72 minutes Luque crashed home number six with a sparkling hit. It was carnival time for Argentina. At the final whistle the stadium was awash with blue and white banners waving in delight at their team's sensational victory. The home side were in the World Cup final. Only Holland now stood between them and heaven on earth, but at what price was this gained?

The Brazilians were understandably aggrieved by the disturbing non-performance of the Peruvians. Their manager Claudio Coutinho was calm but pointed in his fury at Peru. His damning remarks that the Peruvians would feel no pride when they next heard their national anthem at the World Cup would hurt much more than any slanging match. The Brazilian newspapers let fly with both barrels. Not for them Coutinho's soft but stinging approach.

Accusations of bribery and rumours of under-the-table dealings were hurled in the Peruvians' direction. The pre-match words of Hector Chumpitaz, the captain of Peru, that he and his team-mates 'would safeguard the decency of the competition' had in the end proved worthless and cheap. Something was not right. Peru pleaded their innocence. Ramon Quiroga in particular was crucified by the sceptics. The Argentinian-born keeper released a statement on behalf of himself and his team-mates swearing that they had given their all during the game. However, such was their total ineptitude and obvious lack of willingness to compete, this was greeted with disdain. The Peruvians were stoned by their own supporters when they returned home to Lima. It had been a shabby and disgraceful end to their World Cup campaign. All fall down?

Were Peru, as was widely rumoured, bribed to take a fall, or was the truth that the Argentinians simply outclassed and overran them? All through the tournament the host nation had benefited from some bizarre decisions. In the first round appalling refereeing by the men in black had gifted them victories over Hungary and France. Sadly for Argentina, in their third outing, against the Italians, the Israeli referee, Mr Abraham Klein, was a man cut from superior cloth. The impressive Klein was beyond reproach and indeed, more importantly, beyond approach. The result of such an appointment was that the host nation was deservedly beaten. The Azzuri grabbed a highly credited 1–0 victory courtesy of a Roberto Bettega strike. In all honesty, this was scant reward for their fine display. The Argentinians, denied a helping hand by the man in the middle, were shown up to be a side that were clearly no world beaters. In view of all this, just what on earth did go on during that curious evening in the Codviolo Rosario stadium?

It was the early morning of Sunday, 18 June 1986. The day of the England–Argentina World Cup quarter-final. An article appeared on the front page of *The Times* newspaper. Written by Argentinian journalist Maria Avignol, it alleged that during the 1978 World Cup finals her country's military junta had bribed Peru to lie down against the host nation, thus allowing Argentina to reach the final. Avignol claimed that the Peruvian players were under strict instructions to gift the home side the four goals required to leapfrog fierce rivals Brazil. In the end it was a total of six goals which was smashed past Peru's goalkeeper Ramon Quiroga. In return Peru allegedly received 35,000 tons of free grain, plus the Argentinian central bank released $50 million for the Peruvian generals to use at their whim. In addition, a cargo of military arms was to find itself heading over the border and in the direction of Lima. Some deal, but was it true? Strange dealings did in fact occur during that fateful evening. Cesar Menotti barred his keeper and his substitutes from the team talk. Peru played in plain red shirts instead of their dashing white with red stripe. To ease the shame? Was this significant; an act of surrender maybe?

Ramon Quiroga, the Peruvian keeper, was born in the same town as Menotti. Although he had lived most of his life in Peru, doubts had to be raised about his state of mind before such an emotional occasion for his blood country. Quiroga's performance was, to say the least, erratic. Unpredictable at best, Quiroga's nickname of 'El Loco' was well earned. The Argentine military junta had close links with their fellow generals in Peru. With the Peruvians already eliminated it is not out of the question that a deal was indeed struck; and that Peru to their lasting shame raised the white flag and allowed Kempes and Luque to walk all over them and their country's honour. Avignol's sources, although never named for obvious reasons, were thought extremely credible. Two senior civil servants to the junta risked all to reveal their country's shameful secret. There existed another source. The Peruvians' reserve goalkeeper Manzo revealed whilst on a drinking spree in his home city of Lima that his team-mates did accept dollars to throw the game. However, next day when sober and clear headed, Manzo retracted his whole story. He obviously valued his life more than a clear conscience.

In 1978 Argentina was a dangerous place to express an opinion. The country was under the heel of a ruthless military dictatorship. A gang of senior army officers led by General Jorge Videla had seized power back in 1976. Isabelita Peron's civilian government found itself the victim of a military coup. Videla's henchmen, with their neatly pressed uniforms and row upon row of medals, were in all but appearance nothing more than a bunch of gangsters; a gang of thugs who were simply out to line their own pockets. However, such was their frightening hold over the Argentinian people, criticism was rarely heard. No one dared speak out. The merest slur against Jorge Videla and his hoodlums dealt mercilessly. A visit in the dead of night, torture and a bullet in the back of the head was Videla's idea of justice. Also much favoured by the junta was making bodies disappear by dropping them from helicopters into the vast expanses of the River Plate. During General Videla's corrupt reign an estimated 11,000 people vanished. Amongst these were hundreds of teachers, priests and doctors, almost certainly murdered by death squads.

Any man, woman or child considered the slightest danger to his junta would receive a visit by Videla's hated secret police. What happened to them afterwards was reminiscent of Hitler's Nazi regime. Concentration camps were secretly set up where people were systematically tortured and then disposed of. In such a country, bribing a team to lose a football match is a small matter. There were also accusations of drug abuse. Throughout the

Mundial rumours raged that Argentinian players, when called by FIFA to take part in routine testing, were handing over ready-made samples. Indeed one story got out that an Argentinian player, according to his urine sample, was actually pregnant! Amphetamines were known to be in widespread use by players involved in their national championship. More rumours flew after the Peru game that Kempes and Tarantini were still hyped up and running around their dressing-room a full hour after the game had finished!

Videla needed the World Cup. Victory had to be achieved at any price. Every method at his disposal, both lawful and unlawful, would have been used to make this possible. The Peruvian players were, it seems, mere pawns in what was the ultimate disgrace. Whilst the tournament ran its course, the concentration camps were moved lock, stock and barrel, the blood was wiped off whitewashed walls, and the mothers of the disappeared cried themselves to sleep at night. Ladies and gentlemen, I give you the 1978 World Cup.

Avignol's brave accusations have never been proven, and most probably never will be. South American politics have a tendency to stray down murky pathways. In the continent of the sun and the shadow the truth is never easy to find.

14.

THE PRODIGAL SON

Italy v Brazil

1982 WORLD CUP

Say it isn't so, Paolo.

When confronted with the dreadful accusations, Paolo steadfastly refuted them. He claimed it was all some horrendous mistake. It mattered little, for the evidence appeared overwhelming. Paolo Rossi was as guilty as sin. Whilst playing for Perugia he was found guilty of taking money, along with many of his team-mates, to fix a 2–2 draw with Avellino. Rossi was said to have gone along with the scam only after insisting that he be allowed to score his side's two goals. For his crime Rossi was handed a three-year ban. A career that had promised so much had ground to a tragic halt. The ban was later reduced to two years. It ended as the 1982 World Cup finals loomed large. With the great silver-haired warrior Roberto Bettega injured, the Azzuri manager, Enzo Bearzot, decided to risk all on the rusty but still extraordinary goal-poaching prowess of Paolo. With only three games under his belt for new club Juventus, Rossi was given the chance to wipe the slate clean. Redemption was at hand.

The beat of the samba drum had fallen silent. In its place had sounded the sombre tones of Wagner, to be followed four years on by the exuberant melodies of the Argentinian salsa. Twelve long, lean years passed with the Brazilians forced to watch as other countries laid their hands on a trophy they considered their own. That glorious sun-drenched, Technicolor summer of 1970 was now but a fading memory for the people of this football-mad country. West Germany they could just about stomach, but Argentina? It was time to reclaim what was rightfully theirs. The boys from Brazil arrived in Europe meaning business. España 82 prepared to welcome them into the fold with open arms. Paolo Rossi, however, stood ready to break their hearts.

In 1974 the Brazilians appeared unrecognisable in their tawdry blue shirts as they bowed out in an unsporting and despicable manner to Johan Cruyff and his mercurial Dutchmen. In 1978 there was little improvement. Where had the magic gone? The dreary path Brazilian football had taken under Claudio Coutinho could not be allowed to continue. Coutinho's dismissal and tragic early demise by drowning cleared the way for the appointment of Tele Santana. Now this was more like it! Santana was a footballing romantic. His mind raced with vivid images of Loenidas, Ademir, Pele, Garrincha, Jairzinho. This was how he would bring back the glory days. Brazil should not be afraid of anyone. Unfortunately for Santana and his countrymen they lacked a forward capable of living in such esteemed company. They had instead the cumbersome but extremely willing Serginho. Santana had suffered bad luck when the rapier-like Reinaldo was injured in the run-up to the tournament. There was only one alternative. Serginho was a mere battering ram when compared with the traditional style of Brazilian centre-forwards. All was not lost; for in midfield lay an attacking quartet unequalled since the son of Dondinho and his blood brothers had run riot in the Azteca. Falcao, Socrates, Cerezo and the man nicknamed the 'White Pele', Artur Antunes Coimbra, better known as Zico. Adding to such frightening ability was the explosive attacking left-winger Eder and the overlapping, eccentric but electrifying full-back Junior. With such a supporting cast ready to supply the ammunition it seemed nonsensical that any forward could fail to deliver the goods; any, that is, except the much maligned Serginho. The idea that the Brazilians had nothing better to offer caused onlookers to shake their heads in disbelief; an opinion that was widely shared by the players themselves, and none more so than an exasperated Zico. Santana received unmerciful stick from Brazilian journalists for his decision to pick Serginho, but in all honesty he had little choice. Oh for a Pele! Serginho was all set to prove a donkey, if not indeed a scapegoat or, more cruelly, a mere ass!

The Azzuri arrived in Spain engaged in a bitter war of words with their press. Accusations flew from all angles regarding the attitude, behaviour and quality of Enzo Bearzot's men. A fierce stand-off had occurred. Outraged at their treatment by certain journalists, the Italian players refused to have any dealings with the media. A poor run of form leading up to the tournament, plus rumours of huge financial bonuses being demanded by the squad, had seen Bearzot's side slaughtered. The coach's decision to recall Paolo Rossi from the wilderness had headline writers screaming vitriol in his direction; but Bearzot had incredible faith in Rossi. This was a player who was blessed with the ability to be in the right place at the right time. The Azzuri closed ranks. They elected a spokesman to speak for all of them. The man chosen was captain and Italian football legend Dino Zoff. The 40-year-old goalkeeper became the front man for the entire squad. The 1982 World Cup finals were to be Dino's swan song. No one deserved more than he to finish as a champion. But as the arguments raged and the headlines blazed indignation, such thoughts appeared mere folly. Most Italians felt that their team would struggle to make it beyond even the first phase. The Azzuri would prove difficult to overcome. With defenders of such calibre as the fearsome Gentile, Cabrini and Collovati and the magnificent sweeper Gaetano Scirea, Italy had few equals at the back. Indeed, even by Italian standards this was a rearguard of exceptional quality. In midfield there was the imaginative schemer Giancarlo Antognioni, aided by the ruthless but immensely skilled Marco Tardelli. On the left-wing the Roma forward Bruno Conti would maraud with deadliness. But who would score the goals. Rossi? The *tifosi* had their doubts.

The Italians found themselves grouped with Peru, Poland and first-timers Cameroon. They began in Vigo against the Poles. It was a dreadfully dull affair. Poland, with Zbogniew Boniek amongst their ranks, appeared as reluctant as the Azzuri to open up. Boniek had recently signed a hugely lucrative contract to ply his trade with Serie A giants Juventus. Juve must have wondered if they had wasted their money as their new man appeared totally uninterested. Cynics might have suggested that he had no wish to upset his new paymasters. Rossi made an enthusiastic showing, and there was a typically solid performance from Zoff in this, his hundredth international appearance; but there was little else. It appeared that the twelfth World Cup had little to fear from this shot-shy team of Bearzot's. Matters hardly improved in the second match against the Peruvians. Indeed they got worse. A crashing drive from Conti, after a sublime piece of skill on the edge of the penalty area, had given the Italians a spectacular lead. The Azzuri closed shop and appeared to be coasting when, with five minutes remaining, Diaz struck home a deserved equaliser for the South Americans. Another draw meant the disgruntled hacks once more unscrewed their poison pens. This time out Paolo Rossi had proved a huge disappointment. Indeed he was so bad that Bearzot withdrew him early in the second half. The momentum of his return had sustained Rossi facing the Poles; but against the Peruvians Paolo's lack of match practice was cruelly exposed. For Bearzot it was time to build the sand-bags even higher; and yet for as much as the critics raged the Azzuri were still unbeaten. A point in the final game against the Africans of Cameroon would prove sufficient to see them through. Cameroon themselves were unbeaten, but this was not the team who would thrill the world eight years on in Italia 90. If such a thing was possible, the Africans were equally as negative as the Italians themselves. Sadly, the foul smell of corruption again began to contaminate the atmosphere.

On 23 June 1982, the Azzuri and Cameroon fought out a stale, shabby 1–1 draw. It was enough to see Italy into the second round and send the Africans home, albeit unbeaten. Bearzot's side qualified above the Cameroon, courtesy of scoring one more goal. Seventeen thousand watched as the veteran Graziani headed past a fumbling Thomas Nkomo to put his country in front. Before the Azzuri had time to bang down the shutters the Africans hit back, Mbida smashing home from six yards past a helpless Zoff. The next day the Italian media let fly with both barrels. Despite their team's progress into the next round, the flak flew thick and fierce. Again Rossi, who had done himself no favours whatsoever with his performance against the Africans, was heavily criticised. Dark rumours began to be whispered regarding the Cameroon performance. Their refusal to open up and go for a second goal, thus staying in the tournament, appeared strange and confusing. Why did the manager's wife return home with a large plastic bag crammed with various foreign currencies? Behind Bearzot's back journalists spoke of a ruthless, criminal betting ring deep in the south of Italy offering the Africans money to throw the match. Amongst those allegedly approached was the Cameroon centre-forward Roger Milla. Milla later denied these accusations vehemently. The allegations reached the ears of FIFA officials, who failed to act, since there appeared to be no hard evidence. The frightening tentacles of the Camorra (the Neapolitan Mafia) spread far and wide. It would not have been beyond them to have tried such a trick. The Italians took flight and headed off for Barcelona, their venue for the second phase. Awaiting them would be the formidable South American giants, Brazil and Argentina. The *tifosi* shook their heads in horror. They feared the worst. They feared humiliation.

As the Italians bored the watching world to tears, Brazil were setting the tournament ablaze. Based deep in the south, in Seville, Tele Santana's men opened against the USSR. The Russians, managed by the wily Konstantin Beskov, arrived with a battle plan to tame the Brazilians. Their side brimmed with world-class ability. Players such as their captain and wonderful defender Alexander Chivadze, Bessonov, Shengelia and the legendary attacker Oleg Blokhin meant they could never be taken lightly. Against Brazil, despite the South Americans enjoying most of the possession and creating many openings, it was the Russians who struck first. After several missed opportunities, all by the lambasted Serginho, the Soviet midfielder Bal shot home from the edge of the box. His effort was fumbled terribly by Waldir Peres in the Brazilian goal, who could only watch as the ball rolled over the line. The second half wore on and still the Russians held firm. As well as Brazil were playing, Beskov's team looked worthy of their slender lead. Coming into the competition on the back of a 22-game unbeaten run, the USSR looked set for a shock opening win. Fifteen minutes remained when the Brazilian captain Socrates picked up the ball 25 yards out and took aim. The lanky, bearded player side-stepped two Russian defenders before letting fly a magnificent drive high into the corner of the USSR goal. It was a tremendous strike and nothing less than Brazil deserved. The captain had saved the day. This man who received extra payments from his club Corinthians for joining in on goal celebrations did not need much persuasion to celebrate that particular effort. As the Russians tired, Brazil went for the winner. It arrived three minutes from time and was well worth the wait. Falcao dummied and Eder's dipping volley from the edge of the area sent the Brazilian supporters into ecstasy. Tele Santana had remained true to his word. They were back.

Four days later they took the field once more against Scotland. The Scots had begun well with a 5–2 drubbing of New Zealand. Their manager, Jock Stein, made wholesale changes for the match against the Brazilians. Amongst these was the Dundee United defender David Narey. The versatile Narey would play at right-back and try to counter the threat of the sublime trickery of Eder. As kick-off approached in the Benito Villamarin stadium, both sets of supporters mingled happily together on the terraces. The teams appeared to huge cheers. The Scots were determined to put on a good show. To the delight of the tartan masses they took a shock lead in the 18th minute. To the disbelief of his countrymen, David Narey ran through onto a John Wark header and smashed a terrific shot past Waldir Peres. The Brazilians refused to panic. In the stifling early evening heat they passed the ball around with a touch and technique that bewildered the chasing Scots. As hard as they tried Stein's men failed to win back possession. On 33 minutes they conceded a free kick on the edge of their box. Zico sized up his options. With frightening ease he curled a marvellous shot past Alan Rough in the Scottish goal: 1–1. Half-time arrived and to the eternal fury of all Scotsmen, the BBC's Jimmy Hill dismissed David Narey's wonder strike as nothing more than a mere 'toe poke'. In the Brazilian dressing-room Santana could not fault his team. He knew well that it was just a matter of time. Three minutes into the second half Brazil took the lead.

Junior's in-swinging, near-post corner kick was met by the big defender Oscar who headed home powerfully past Rough and into the net. Now it would be simply a case of how many. On 65 minutes Eder chipped home a classic third over a stranded and prostrate Scottish goalkeeper; a touch of class that summed up this Brazilian team. Scotland were chasing shadows. This command performance by Santana's men was crowned superbly by Falcao who smashed home a low drive from 30 yards: 4–1, and game over. A memorable, balmy evening in Seville finished with Brazilian and Scottish supporters partying together long into the night, each sporting the shirts and flags of the other. Brazil completed their group matches with a 4–0 canter over a badly outclassed New Zealand. The highlight was a stupendous acrobatic, overhead kick by Zico. Even Serginho managed to force one over the line, to his and his countrymen's huge relief. The reward for their 100 per cent record was a second-round place alongside deadly rivals Argentina and a badly misfiring Italy. Santana had good reason to be confident. The samba drum beat loud and proud. Brazil were closing in on a fourth World Cup trophy. On to Barcelona.

It was a three-way shoot-out. The Italians and world champions Argentina would be first in the ring. Cesar Menotti's men had yet to reach the form of four years earlier. They had recovered sufficiently to qualify after losing their opening game to the unfancied Belgians. Menotti was scathing in his pre-match criticism of the Azzuri. 'They are one of the greatest teams in the world,' he said stone faced, adding sarcastically, 'that is until they cross the halfway line!' The Argentinians were hugely confident of beating the sterile Italians. They had seen nothing so far to fear. It appeared beyond argument that the crucial game would be against the Brazilians. The backbone of the 1978 team was still around: Fillol, Tarantini, Passarella, Ardiles, and the hero of the Pampas, Mario Kempes, had been joined by a new kid on the block – a stocky, curly-haired 22-year-old by the name of Diego Armando Maradona. This was Maradona's first major appearance on the world scene. During the previous Mundial he had missed out on his country's finest hour. Menotti had come under tremendous pressure to include the precocious 17-year-old. It was he who handed Maradona his international début at the tender age of just 16. It was during that game Menotti realised that despite all Maradona's mind-blowing skills, his physique and mental state were not yet ready to stand up to the intensity of World Cup competition. In short, he would have been kicked from pillar to post. Maradona's career could well have been finished before it ever got started. In typical hysterical style, Diego reacted quite spectacularly to the news of his exclusion. He declared that Menotti had betrayed him, and that he would now retire from the game. All this at 17! Happily, and not too surprisingly, he was to change his mind. One week later he smashed home a hat trick for his club Bocca Juniors. Diego would have his day in the sun. España 82, it was thought by many, would grant him the chance to show his true worth. The game against the Azzuri would prove for him a magnificent opportunity to lay down his marker as the world's greatest player. Maradona, however, had yet to come face to face with one of the most inaptly named defenders of all time – the Neapolitan hatchet man, Claudio Gentile.

Born in the slums of downtown Naples, Gentile learned his trade kicking a ball around the cobbled alleyways that swamp that fair city. His talent as a defender of fine technique and fierce, no-prisoners attitude was put to good use in the famous black and white striped shirt of Juventus. There he performed with great tenacity alongside similar characters such as Cabrini, Cuccureddu and the classy, but ruthless, sweeper, Gaetano Scirea. It was during the 1978 World Cup finals that Bearzot first used the formidable prowess of Gentile. Italy had been drawn against the host nation in the early stages. He had earmarked the young Neapolitan to man-mark Argentina's great hope and superstar, the swift and deadly Mario Kempes. The story goes that Bearzot simply walked into the Azzuri dressing-room before the match and asked, 'Who feels like stopping Kempes?' Claudio Gentile stood up and looking his manager in the eye declared menacingly, 'Me!' The Argentinian number nine found himself shackled by the biting, snarling Gentile. With their most potent threat under lock and key, the South Americans lost 0–1 to a highly impressive Azzuri. It was time to renew old acquaintances.

The games would be played not, as expected, at Barcelona's magnificent Nou Camp, but instead at the much smaller home of Español, the Sarria stadium. Hosting only a capacity of 44,000, it was jammed to the rafters for all three encounters. The crazy decision not to use the Nou Camp astounded all three camps. However, the Sarria would more than play its part in the dramatic events that unfolded. The Italian players' rift with their media showed no sign of healing. They had voted 18–4 to continue their cold-shoulder attitude towards fuming, frustrated journalists. The situation was hardly helped by widespread criticism of bonuses paid to the squad for reaching the second round. Paolo Rossi, for one, was finding himself pilloried for his performance so far; but Enzo Bearzot refused to join in with the lynch mobs that screamed for his centre-forward's head. He remained faithful to Rossi. Many called it blind faith. The more outspoken called it blatant stupidity.

The match against Argentina began as expected with the Azzuri shuffling back to form a defensive wall of blue. A special camera had been arranged to focus in on the battle of wills between Maradona and Gentile. It proved X-rated viewing as the Italian specialist marker pulled every underhand trick in the book to frustrate the young Argentinian maestro. It was a frightening display of controlled violence by Gentile that did not so much stretch the rules, but more bend them backwards. Events around the duelling pair also threatened to explode as nerves on both sides frayed. The first half brimmed with reckless tackles and dangerous over-the-top lunges. The stakes were high. An English journalist, John Roberts writing for the *Daily Mail*, said, 'This match contained all the exaggerated violence of a spaghetti western, although the acting was much better!' The Rumanian referee, Nicolae Rainea, appeared oblivious to the muggings and assaults that passed for challenges across the field. Astonishingly, Gentile avoided a yellow card as he went about his merry way hacking and slashing an under-siege Maradona. Come half-time there had been only one effort of note; a snap-shot by Ramon Diaz which was smartly turned over the bar by the evergreen safe hands of Dino Zoff. Something was dreadfully wrong with the world champions. They seemed deflated. It was not so much events on the field, but matters which had taken place many miles away in the Falkland Islands which had affected them. Their nation's humiliating surrender to the British task force had cast a dark shadow over their attempts to hold onto their crown. Even though they were standing up to Italian strong-arm tactics, the will to express themselves as was their natural wont had sadly gone astray. They had the appearance of a team playing with a broken heart.

The Azzuri began the second half a side transformed. Throwing off their defensive shackles they went for Argentina's throat. Suddenly Bruno Conti came to life and began to threaten dangerously down the left wing. The Italian supporters sensed a change of attitude amongst their team. Rossi began to make dangerous runs into the world champions' penalty box, finally receiving half decent service. On 57 minutes they roared into the lead. Conti fed the fleet-footed Antognoni. The Azzuri midfielder played a long, silky pass to put the full-speed Marco Tardelli clear in the penalty box. Tardelli took aim and smashed a fierce low drive past Fillol and into the net. At long last the deadlock had been broken.

Argentina hit back. Maradona, for once escaping from the clutches of Gentile, shot hard against the Italian crossbar, to be followed shortly by his captain, Daniel Passarella, also striking the woodwork. The familiar languid features of Cesar Menotti watched anxiously. Menotti had further reason to look worried when on 67 minutes Graziani played Paolo Rossi in for a clear run on goal. Staying true to form, Rossi fluffed the opportunity, only to see Conti control the rebound off a stranded Fillol and place a neat pass inside for Cabrini to slash into the empty goal: 2–0 for the Azzuri. The semi-finals beckoned. The Italians shut up shop. A pent-up Maradona found himself booked as he lashed out in sheer frustration at his inability to shake off the shadow of Claudio Gentile. Seven minutes from time Passarella drove home a 25-yard free kick past Dino Zoff, who was clearly still organising his defensive wall. Nonetheless the goal stood. The final moments saw the South Americans trying desperately to forage an unlikely equaliser. It was not to be. The referee Rainea called time and the Azzuri began their celebrations.

Written off as no-hopers beforehand, they had rammed the words of their critics back down their throats. Argentina were as good as out. For them it hurt like hell. They were left with an all-or-nothing, do-or-die clash with their most hated foe in order to stay alive in the competition. Three days later Brazil and her supporters would gleefully embark on finishing off the world champions. As for the Azzuri, it was time to rest. Bearzot knew well their greatest task still lay ahead.

As many expected, the reign of Argentina as world champions was extinguished by an on-fire Brazilian side. In a performance that delighted their fans and, indeed, the whole world, Brazil cut loose in terrifying fashion. The goal spree began as early as the 12th minute. Eder's 35-yard free kick bent quite alarmingly as it thumped loudly against Fillol's crossbar. The rebound was pounced upon by Zico as he pushed in front of a bumbling Serginho to make certain of the opportunity. Artur Antunes Coimbra had little time for his lumbering sidekick. His looks of contempt as Serginho messed up repeatedly spoke volumes. 'The ball is square when Serginho plays,' wrote a mocking Brazilian journalist, an opinion obviously shared by Zico. With Falcao and Socrates in devastating form, the Brazilians turned on the style. The Argentinians battled hard but found themselves being overrun by their opponents' outstanding midfield quartet. Maradona was anonymous against such skilled opponents, his frustration clearly rising as the men from the Copacabana gave him short shrift. To them he was a mere upstart.

As the first half wore on it was clear that Argentina were in big trouble. Half-time came and went and the footballing lesson for the world champions continued. On 68 minutes Brazil deservedly doubled their lead. A deft touch from Zico put Falcao clear on the Argentinian right. The tall, imperious figure of Falcao crossed wonderfully for Serginho to power a thunderous header past Fillol. This was a moment to cherish for the Brazilian centre-forward as he found himself mobbed by his team-mates, this time for the right reasons. Argentina collapsed. Six minutes later the Brazilians twisted the sword deeper when they scored again. Once more it was Zico, threading a sublime pass through for the dashing full-back Junior to charge clear and shoot past Fillol: 3–0 and humiliation complete for Argentina. Not quite. Three minutes from time Diego Maradona was shown the red card for an outrageous challenge on the substitute Batista. The sight of him trudging off the field with his head down remains one of the enduring memories of the 1982 World Cup. But he would be back. With only seconds remaining, Ramon Diaz flashed a shot past Peres to grab one back for Argentina, but the match was already won. At the final whistle the massed ranks of partying yellow-shirted supporters on the terraces, dancing and swaying to the rhythmic beat of the samba, bore dramatic comparison with the sight of tear-stained Argentinians mourning the loss of their world crown. A trophy won four years before, albeit in dubious and, some might say, scandalous circumstances, had been torn from their grasp. It was time to go home. As for Brazil, they were ready to hand out the same type of footballing master class to the Azzuri. Due to their superior goal difference the Brazilians required only a draw against Italy to qualify for the semi-finals. This their fans claimed could be achieved sleepwalking. Little did they realise that Paolo Rossi was about to awake from his slumber and hand them the shock of their lives.

Enzo Bearzot watched the Brazilian annihilation of Argentina with great interest and more than a little trepidation. He had already gone on record as saying that Brazil would win the World Cup. Now he was faced with the absurd notion of having to prove his prediction incorrect; and yet he remained confident that his lads could pull off a surprise. The Brazilians, for all their attacking brilliance from midfield, were fragile at the back, and clumsy up front with the leaden-footed Serginho. If Tardelli, Antognoni and Conti performed to their peak, Socrates and his illustrious trio of performing artists would find themselves in the game of their lives. But Bearzot required more. For to overcome a side such as Brazil he would need goals. It was time for Rossi to repay the debt to his manager. This young man had performed throughout as if the worries of the world were weighing on his slim shoulders. Redemption was proving somewhat difficult to attain. As for the Brazilians, this time around it would be the turn of Zico to suffer at the hands of the infamous but highly effective Claudio Gentile. Surprisingly, when not reprising his role of on-field psychopath, Gentile was a cultured footballer; but it will be his performances as villain for which he will be remembered.

The Azzuri were primed and ready to go. Enzo Bearzot was ready to shock the footballing world with his tactics. This brave man, who always had handled himself with great dignity, was ready to cast away the defensive shackles which had haunted his nation's team for decades. In a move of staggering courage Bearzot had decided that his team would go against the grain. They would attack.

THE GAME

Hours before the game began, the Sarria stadium teemed with supporters of both sides. The beat of the samba drummers rang loud. A mass blanket of yellow shirts swamped the steep terraces where the supporters of Brazil danced themselves into a frenzy. The Italians were also there in force. The green, red

and white tricolour of the Azzuri was clearly evident in large numbers around
the ground. Half an hour before kick-off the Italian players appeared to
inspect the pitch and soak up the atmosphere. On seeing their heroes the *tifosi*
exploded in delight. Flags waved, whilst firecrackers banged in the stifling
heat of the Spanish sun. The footballers of the Azzuri watched in
astonishment as their fans staged a heart-stopping show of defiance and
loyalty. In that instant their already immense determination to win the day
increased ten-fold.

Shortly after, amidst a cloud of smoke-bombs and deafening cheers, both
teams entered the arena. Forty-four thousand people held their breath as the
Israeli referee, Abraham Klein, signalled to each of his linesmen and began
what was to be one of the finest matches ever seen in World Cup competition.
The Azzuri started where they had left off against Argentina. Bruno Conti
probed intelligently looking for a way through. With less than five minutes
on the clock, the little Roma winger swept a cross-field ball to the raiding full-
back Cabrini. Cabrini put in a dipping cross from the left wing deep to the
back of the Brazilian penalty area. Arriving unnoticed was Paolo Rossi.
Stooping low, he aimed a precise header past Waldir Peres and into the back
of the net: 1–0 to Italy! Finally the centre-forward had begun to repay his
manager's loyalty. The Brazilians looked aghast. Where on earth had Rossi
come from? His ability to ghost into goal-scoring positions had returned at
the perfect time.

Brazil restarted, eager for swift retribution. The gangling but supremely
talented Socrates glided smoothly over the halfway line and played a pass
forward to Serginho. Showing an unusually sweet touch, Serginho beat off
Gentile's challenge but quickly returned to form by losing possession. Luckily
for the Brazilians the ball spun clear to Zico. As the Azzuri retreated to cover
their area, Zico split them wide open with a precise flick to put Serginho
through with just Dino Zoff to beat. As his country held its collective breath
the hapless centre-forward risked eternal infamy by blasting horribly wide.
Zico failed to hide his disgust at seeing his team-mate fluff such an
outstanding opportunity. He screamed abuse at the forlorn-looking Serginho.
Once more the ball was square.

On 12 minutes, to the utter delight of their massive support, Brazil pieced
together an equaliser of the highest order. Again it was Socrates who forced
the Italians to back-pedal. Playing a pass inside to Zico, the 'white Pele'
produced a moment of skill that had everyone off their seat in the Sarria. As
if on ice, Zico sped past his tormentor Gentile and played in a return pass to
Socrates. The captain of Brazil tore into the Azzuri penalty area and unleashed
a low drive that thundered past Zoff at his near post; a breathtaking goal that

set the stadium alight: 1–1. A sea of yellow and green flags waved in frantic salute; and no little relief. Incidents came thick and fast. The Italians refused to bow before their illustrious opponents. The referee, Mr Klein, booked Gentile for a gruesome foul on Zico. The battle raged. On 24 minutes the match took yet another twist. A careless Cerezo lost possession to Paolo Rossi who, unable to believe his luck, raced into the Brazilian penalty area and shot powerfully past a despairing Peres. This extraordinary game once more swung back in Italy's favour. Rossi was mobbed by his fellow Azzuri. Bearzot leapt off the bench in disbelief. His boy was back in business!

Again Brazil restarted. Cerezo immediately tried to make amends when he crossed for a leaping Socrates to power a header straight at Zoff. On 34 minutes the Italians were forced into making a substitution. The stalwart Collovati went off injured and on to take his place came 18-year-old Giuseppe Bergomi of Inter Milan. Bergomi took up his position alongside the accomplished Scirea. Bearzot had little fear about throwing this prodigiously talented young defender in at the deep end for he possessed the heart of a true Azzuri. His orders were to pick up Serginho. Shortly after coming on he complained to his goalkeeper and captain, Dino Zoff, that he was having difficulty breathing. Zoff calmed him down and Giuseppe Bergomi went on to play the game of his life. Entering into the fray with a hunger to win tackles verging on fanatical, he wasted little time laying down his marker on Serginho's shins. As half-time drew near, a let-off for Italy occurred when Gentile ripped the shirt off Zico's back inside his own area; a clear penalty. Fortunately for the Azzuri the referee had already blown for offside. The interval allowed time for both players and supporters to catch their breath.

The second half began. Zoff was immediately forced into three saves in rapid succession as the Brazilians threatened to turn the screw, the best when he hurtled off his line to thwart an oncoming Cerezo. Cerezo was performing like a man possessed in order to make up for his costly first-half error. Zico, trying desperately to break free of Gentile, escaped for a fleeting moment to play in once more his worst nightmare Serginho. Serginho again fumbled his effort as he shot half-heartedly at a relieved Zoff. The Brazilian fans howled in derision at seeing yet another good chance go begging. They poured scorn down upon the distressed but totally out-of-his-depth Serginho. Brazil continued to hammer away at a magnificent Azzuri rearguard, Cerezo again going close in his one-man mission to rescue his country's cause. The Italians, however, were now full of confidence. They were no longer scared of launching swift counter-attacks of their own. On one such breakaway, Graziani ran clear on the left and put in a fine cross to an unmarked Paolo Rossi. The Azzuri hitman shot inexplicably wide when it would have been easier to score. Rossi buried his head in his hands. Brazil were still alive. As their supporters bayed, prayed and pleaded for their team to equalise, the atmosphere inside the Sarria stadium threatened to overwhelm all present; the flair and sorcery of the Brazilians, against the magnificent technique and sheer, stubborn determination of the Italians. On 68 minutes a Brazilian who plied his trade in the eternal city of Rome escaped from the Azzuri shackles and sent his countrymen once more soaring into carnival mood. Dribbling in from the left-hand touchline, Junior swept a pass across field to the advancing Falcao. The Azzuri defence dropped off. Falcao beat one, side-stepped another and thrashed an outstanding left-foot drive past Zoff from the edge of the area. Falcao disappeared under a sea of yellow. The entire Brazilian bench ran onto the field to join in the celebrations. Once again it was advantage to Brazil. There were just over 20 minutes left to play.

To make matters even better for the South Americans, Santana substituted Serginho and brought on a right-winger, Paulo Isidoro. Isidoro moved into midfield whilst Socrates took up an attacking position. They had no intention of shutting up shop, for it was simply not in their nature. The Italians, however, were now left with no option but to open up. Bearzot regrouped his troops. Antognoni began to make skirmishes into the Brazilian half. Also Zico had begun to tire badly. The constant close attention of the octopus-like Gentile was finally taking its toll. But still the chances appeared. The substitute Isidoro was foiled at the last by a remarkable, brave stop from Dino Zoff. His had been a captain's role. The Azzuri surged forward. A corner was earned. Fourteen minutes remained when Conti's cross flew high into the Brazilian box, and landed at the feet of Marco Tardelli. Tardelli's weak effort back into the danger area was pounced on by Rossi, who swooped to smash it low into the net. The Brazilians fell to the ground in utter disbelief. Paolo Rossi had snatched a sensational hat trick. The fans and journalists who had handed out incessant abuse to this one-time outcast of Italian football were being forced to eat their words. The *tifosi* in the crowd could hardly bear to watch the events unfurling before them, for this was not the Azzuri they had grown accustomed to. Bearzot's newly found attacking philosophy might be good for the soul, but it tended to cause terrible problems for Italian hearts. Tele Santana stood on the touchline, urging his men to keep going. The yellow masses had fallen silent, but soon the drums of the samba once more began to beat out their rhythm. There was still time. Anything could yet happen.

Gaetano Scirea had marshalled his defence with all the strategic brilliance of a five-star general. Now, as the Brazilians launched their final bout of assaults, he prepared once more to repel all boarders. Brazil came forward with a fury bordering on panic as the clock ticked. Socrates had an effort disallowed for offside. Throwing caution to the wind, the South Americans were being effortlessly picked off by the Azzuri, as they broke out with deadly intent. From one such move the magnificent Antognoni shot home from nine yards, only to see it cancelled out, also for offside. Antognoni had been superb throughout, easily the equal of anything in a yellow shirt. Two minutes remained as the Brazilians laid siege to the Azzuri goal. Their supporters screamed and roared themselves hoarse in a vain attempt to force an equaliser, and ultimate salvation; but the Italians remained unyielding. The noise level increased as an Eder free kick jetted into the Azzuri penalty area. Cerezo rose high to smash his header goalwards, only to see Zoff break his heart. Could this man do anything more? It was a barnstorming finish by the Brazilians. A corner was earned. An under-par Eder sprinted over to take it. Many supporters could hardly bear to watch as he took aim and put in a wickedly curling cross. Zoff launched himself heroically into a mass of writhing bodies to punch clear. The Azzuri pleaded with Klein to end the torment, but still it continued. This was not catenaccio; this was sheer desperation. Finally the referee called time on what had been a truly epic occasion. The Italians rushed as one to embrace the hero of the hour. Paolo Rossi found himself swamped by jubilant team-mates and officials alike. Tears flowed on both sides. Even amongst the neutrals the passion and drama of this epic battle had seeped under the skin. Bobby Charlton, commentating for BBC television, finished the game with tears rolling down his cheeks. His fellow broadcaster, John Motson, was forced to continue alone as Charlton struggled to control his emotions.

The Brazilian players were inconsolable. Eder slumped in a heap, whilst a shaken Socrates watched the joyful Italians in a state of shock. Zico lay with his head in his hands. His almighty tussle with Gentile had finally ended in desolation. As fine a side as Brazil most certainly were, they were out. There was to be no carnival in Rio that night. A side brimming with world-class individuals had been struck down by its inability to stop careless defensive errors. Over-confidence bordering on arrogance had in the end proved their downfall. As for the contribution of the wretched Serginho, the least said the better. It was 14 years before the Brazilians finally laid their hands on the World Cup trophy again. The Brazil of Socrates, Zico, Falcao and Eder was destined to stand alongside the greats of Hungary and Holland as amongst the finest never to win the biggest prize of all.

What about Enzo Bearzot and his courageous Azzuri? Came the final whistle and the whole of Italy erupted in joy at their team's heroic performance. Rossi was praised to the heavens. The sins of the past were forgiven, if not totally forgotten. Bearzot was now a footballing tactical genius, his former accusers now lining up to praise his achievement in guiding the Azzuri past Brazil and into the semi-finals. His brave decision to stick with Rossi as he struggled to find his form was now being viewed as a classic piece of man-management. But Bearzot was no fool. He knew defeat in the next round against Poland would see them turn on him again. Happily this was not to be, for the Italians swept the Poles aside with some ease. Two goals from the rejuvenated Rossi were enough to see them into the final against a shattered West Germany, their semi-final epic with the French having left them drained of all energy. On a glorious night in Madrid, at the Bernabeu stadium, goals from Rossi, Tardelli and Altobelli saw the World Cup trophy return to Italian soil. As for the prodigal son, his spell in the wilderness was at an end. Paolo Rossi was going home. Redemption had been gained.

15.

SCOPA

ARGENTINA V ENGLAND

1986 WORLD CUP QUARTER-FINAL

n Naples they have a card game called Scopa. It is played endlessly by old men who sit quietly smoking their roll-ups and sipping steaming-hot coffee outside the harbour bars and restaurants. As the inhabitants of this enchanting but dangerous city hurtle past on screeching mopeds, and local fishermen glare at American tourists who have dared to take their picture, the old men study the hand that fate has dealt them. Scopa is a game of many strange rules but no scruples. At its dark heart lies rule number one: 'Always try and glimpse your opponent's hand.' In short, anything goes. The atmosphere, therefore, can at times become a little strained, if not downright murderous. Indeed if the competitors were 20 years younger blood would almost inevitably be spilled. Played by men of questionable values and quick temper, the simple game of Scopa possesses the capacity to wreak mayhem. To win you have to cheat, lie, curse, and join forces with Old Nick himself; but there are times when the price is just too high to pay.

The story of Scopa begins not as expected on a football pitch, but far away on a barren, God-forsaken, desolate group of islands in the middle of the southern Atlantic. A cold, inhospitable area that for a short but tragic period in 1982 became stained with the blood of hundreds of British and Argentinian servicemen. This was Scopa played for the highest stakes imaginable. The Argentinian military junta, led by General Leopoldo Galtieri, found itself in big trouble on the domestic front. Coming to power in the aftermath of the evil and sadistic regime of Jorge Videla, Galtieri had inherited a nation on the verge of collapse, and a population seething with discontent. The general needed a crusade; something to appease the masses. An empty stomach can be forgotten temporarily if the heart can be made to soar. Galtieri fished around his options. Each time he and his army advisers

would come back to the thorny issue of the Malvinas; officially the property
of Her Majesty's government, but locked away in every Argentinian psyche
as belonging to them. Every school child was and still is taught in Argentina
that the Malvinas were stolen from them by English pirates back in the
1860s. For Galtieri this was the perfect scenario; but it would be
tremendously risky. It involved pulling the tail of the still-feared and
respected British bulldog. Faced with little choice, the general made ready
his plans; but as Galtieri prepared to play God with the lives of thousands
of untrained, ill-equipped young conscripts, rumours were already sweeping
London regarding the Argentinian plan. It would never be allowed to
succeed. The British could ill afford such a loss of face. The 'Iron Lady',
Prime Minister Margaret Thatcher, had been handed an ace card to save her
own neck. For like her Argentinian opponent, she too had problems
threatening to overwhelm her on the home scene. There was nothing like a
good war to galvanise the voters. For the sake of two egomaniacs'
desperation to hold tight onto the reins of power, the Falklands conflict was
initiated, ignited and embraced with relish.

With brass bands playing Rod Stewart's 'Sailing', the task force set off in
a southerly direction. Wives, girlfriends and mothers waved farewell to their
loved ones. The nagging fear that they were sailing out of sight forever
would sadly for many prove true. It was thus in Argentina. Despite what the
Tory press reported at the time, not all Argentinians were fanatics who lay
in bed every night dreaming about the Malvinas. For the ordinary soldier
and sailor on both sides the next 60 days would defy all logic. As politicians
preached and newspapers screamed absurd headlines, the people who knew
better shook their heads in sadness and despair. As the body count mounted
and HMS *Sheffield* made it 1–1 with the retreating *Belgrano*, it appeared for
a short period that the lunatics had taken over the asylum. Whilst the
Falklands' huge population of penguins and sheep stared impartially at the
new arrivals, the kid gloves came off; the white dove of peace was shot out
of the air; and the killing began. The superior British forces, although
heavily outnumbered, battered the Argentinians into an inglorious
surrender. It was a total mismatch. The highly trained professional soldiers
of the crown fought ferociously to end brief but at times fierce resistance
from the Argentinians. In the end the South Americans were sent scuttling
for safety under a white flag raised over the island capital of Port Stanley.
General Mario Benjamin Menendez was the man placed by Galtieri in
charge of the ill-fated invasion. He listened in horror to reports of his
shattered army being chased from the mountains surrounding Stanley.
Despite orders to the contrary, he had no intention whatsoever of fighting

to the last man. Menendez would not sacrifice his raw recruits for the sake of this freezing, miserable, wind-swept excuse of an island. It was simply not worth the price.

On 2 May 1982, the Union Jack was once more raised over the Falklands. Back in London Thatcher took the applause of her yuppie puppets from the safety of No. 10 Downing Street. She ordered everybody to 'rejoice', but nobody rejoiced, except maybe the relieved island's penguins and sheep which had been so rudely disturbed. For years after, however, they were being blown to bits by the thousands of mines left by the retreating Argentinians.

As the war drew to its bitter end, the Argentinians were losing yet more face far away on the football fields of the 1982 World Cup finals. Their grip as holders of the World Cup had been loosened by a magnificent Brazilian side who took great pleasure in plunging the knife deep. To rub further salt into the wound their emerging young superstar, Diego Armando Maradona, was sent off. The prodigious Maradona had lashed out in belated fury, not so much at Brazilian foul play, but more likely at British superiority on the battlefields of Goose Green and the steep slopes of Mount Tumbledown. Argentina was plunged into a state of deep national mourning. The crowds reappeared to demonstrate against Galtieri. Buenos Aires seethed with indignation at what they viewed as monumental humiliation in the Malvinas. This tyrannical despot had seen his temporary popularity disappear overnight. Galtieri's at best dubious hand of Scopa had failed miserably. Argentinian redemption would eventually arrive on a football field, at the dancing feet of one of its greatest sons.

In the years following the Argentinian invasion of the Falklands, the islands were slowly transformed into a fortress by the British army, making futile any further attempts by Buenos Aires to restore face with acts of force. The Malvinas existed only on Argentinian maps and in the hearts of historians who steadfastly refused to alter their textbooks. Four long years passed. The atmosphere between the two nations remained unhealthy. An unofficial state of war still existed. Argentinians gazed misty-eyed towards the Malvinas. How they ached for revenge.

It was during a World Cup qualifying match in hostile Colombia that Diego Maradona first made known his determination to take no prisoners in his quest to lead Argentina back to the promised land. Whilst engulfed in the midst of battle on the pitch, a Colombian supporter, incensed with his team's lack of ability to cope with this Argentinian menace, threw an orange in his direction. Diego saw it coming. Catching it on his thigh, he picked out the appropriate guilty party and with an almighty whack sent the orange hurtling back in his direction, missing by an inch. The home crowd applauded. They may have hated his guts but by God they had to respect his genius. Pele, di Stefano, Puskas, Eusebio, Cruyff. Maradona's God-given talent had yet to yield any worthwhile trophies. There remained nagging doubts as to whether 'el Diegrito' would ever enter such annals of greatness; but in the blazing heat of the Mexican sun Maradona banished such doubts forever. The crowning of a king is always an occasion for huge pomp and ceremony. When such an event occurs over a full month the temptation to judge whether he's worthy can prove overwhelming. Maradona was no angel. A brief foray at Barcelona had been dogged with controversy. Indeed it was during his stay there that he was first introduced to the cause of his ultimate downfall – cocaine. A falling-out with the Barca hierarchy saw a parting of the ways inevitable. The chic, sophisticated Catalan way of life was not for this kid born and raised in the slums of Buenos Aires. Napoli came calling. This ailing southern Italian giant splashed out a world record fee to land the troublesome superstar. It would be amongst the Neapolitans that Maradona would truly fulfil his potential. His ability to explode like lightning past bewildered opponents, with the ball glued as if by magic to his left foot, had Serie A defences retreating en masse. The terraces of the San Paolo roared out in acclaim at their saviour. In no time at all the little Argentinian had the local inhabitants worshipping at his feet. The citizens of Naples took him to their hearts. Diego Armando Maradona expressed his thanks as only he seemed able; by ripping to shreds the hated northern giants of Milan and Juventus every time they came to town. Despite being diminutive in height, Maradona possessed the bulk and firepower of a battleship.

In the summer of 1986 Argentina travelled to Mexico with a team of ten decent players and one talent extraordinaire. The manager, Carlos Bilardo, would base his entire team strategy around the brilliance of his number ten. As a player Bilardo had a notorious reputation as a hatchet man. He had used his dubious talent for the infamous Estudiantes side of the late 1960s, memorably assaulting a beleaguered Nobby Stiles in the World Cup championships in Buenos Aires. As a manager his no-nonsense, take-no-prisoners, anything-goes attitude had stayed with him. This was a man who would stoop to any level to ensure victory; yet even a hard nut like Bilardo found himself strangely moved by the beauty of Maradona's genius. Argentina found themselves in a first-round group with South Korea, Bulgaria and world champions Italy. They, along with the Italians, were favourites to progress. Opening against the underdogs of Korea, their captain set up all three goals in a comfortable 3–1 win. In their next game, however, Italy was sure to test Maradona and his team to the full. The Italian manager, Enzo Bearzot, had earmarked the unenviable task of shackling Maradona to his Napoli teammate and close friend Salvatore Bagni, who set about his job with some relish. All thoughts of friendship were forgotten as the game got under way. Maradona led his fellow Neapolitan a merry dance for most of the contest. An honourable 1–1 draw was obtained, with Diego himself grabbing a fine equaliser; a typically astute finish from the Argentinian captain as he drilled it low past the Azzuri goalkeeper Galli. At the end of the game the two friends embraced. It had been a fair but hard-fought tussle. Italy finished satisfied with a point. Bagni was to find himself heavily criticised back in Italy for his 'kind treatment' of Maradona. The northern-based newspapers claimed that this Neapolitan had betrayed his country in not giving the Argentinian a harder time, though Maradona's battered state at the end of the game appeared to contradict this.

Argentina wrapped up the group with a straightforward 2–0 win over Bulgaria. Goals from Valdano and Burruchaga saw them safely through to the second phase. Maradona was again dominant as he mercilessly tortured the Bulgarian defenders with his pace and trickery. It had been a trouble-free passage for the Argentinians; but it was from this point that the competition would begin in earnest. Now they were entering the minefields of the second phase – sudden death. Argentina had been drawn against the tournament's bad boys – Uruguay. Throughout the first-round matches the Uruguayans had disgraced themselves with some despicable behaviour. In their final match against Scotland they finally overstepped the mark. The Scots went into the game needing a win to qualify; the South Americans requiring a draw. Uruguay made clear their intentions when after only 55 seconds Batista was sent off for a dreadful foul on Gordon Strachan. For the next 89 minutes the Uruguayans scratched, kicked, mauled, punched, spat and slashed their way to a turgid 0–0 draw. It was quite simply a scandalous display. The fun continued after the final whistle when several of the Uruguayan players tried to assault the referee. This after qualification had been assured! It defied belief. They could not be allowed to get away with it. The Scottish manager, Alex Ferguson, refused to shake hands with his South American counterpart, Omar Borras, at the final whistle. Borras did his best to calm the whole situation down when he turned round and called the French referee, Quiniou, a 'murderer'! Ferguson raged in the post-match conference: 'If Borras defends his team he is sitting there lying, cheating and uttering a load of rubbish. I can't even wish him the best of luck.' Ferguson, never a man to mince his words, had the Uruguayan journalists quaking.

FIFA acted swiftly in throwing the book at Borras and his guilty players. They threatened them with expulsion. Any further trouble and they would be on the next flight out of Mexico and on their way back home to Uruguay, to what would have surely been an interesting reception committee. A match against their great rivals from across the vast expanse of the Montevideo river would test their new image to the full.

On a treacherous, rain-lashed surface, unveiling previously unseen tricks, Diego Maradona set the 1986 World Cup finals alight. In the midst of a terrifying electric storm, in which streaks of lightning flashed across the dark Puebla skies, Maradona danced, teased and tormented the Uruguayans into humiliating submission. Showing great bravery as well as wonderful ability, he ran repeatedly at the heart of Uruguay's defence, almost as if he were tempting them to hack him to the ground. Mindful that they were out only on bail, Borras's bunch of hooligans stuck ruefully to the rules of the game. However, the irresistible temptation to put this little Argentinian upstart into orbit proved at times almost overwhelming. There were moments when the contest threatened to explode, history dictated nothing less, but overall Uruguay behaved. The FIFA officials watched intently from the stands. The Uruguayans had been forced to water down their act. Like a blue comedian having to rely on clean material they never quite looked like pulling it off. Denied the crippling of Maradona, Uruguay resorted to sly off-the-ball digs and pulling at his shirt. On this form, however, Maradona was unplayable. The winning goal arrived for Argentina from their left-winger Pasculi in the 40th minute. A snap-shot effort that was nothing more than their superior football deserved. In reality they should have won by a bagful.

It had been a fine all-round performance by Bilardo's well-drilled and highly determined side. With Maradona on song they had begun to resemble potential World Cup winners. The Uruguayans vanished from the scene to be missed by no one. The Argentinian players hugged and embraced. Bilardo ran onto the field to engulf his captain in a bear-hug. A trophy lost four years before amidst much back-stabbing was back within their sights. In Buenos Aires the Argentinian blue and white flag flew high and proud; car horns blew noisily in triumph as thousands danced and sang in salute of their team. Argentina's reward for ridding the World Cup of Omar Borras and his boorish Uruguayans was a clash against an old foe. On 22 June 1986, in the vast cauldron of Mexico City's Azteca stadium, the Argentinians found themselves up against Bobby Robson's England. For many it signalled a return to the Falklands/Malvinas conflict.

Behind the scenes FIFA officials were in a panic. The governments of both countries met at the highest level to discuss what was a powder-keg situation. They had hoped that this doomsday scenario could have been avoided by one or both of the adversaries being eliminated; but it was not to be. The showdown would take place.

To say the English made hard work of a mediocre first-round group of opponents is an understatement. Thrown in with Poland, Morocco and Portugal, England contrived all manner of disasters to make sure they went home early. Robson's men began against a Portuguese side who were so upset about bonuses offered them by their FA that they had threatened up until the last minute to withdraw from the competition. It mattered little. England lost 0–1. In doing so they were spectacularly awful. Expectations had, as ever, been huge. Coming into Mexico 86 with a fine, long, unbeaten run, they fell to defeat courtesy of a Carlos Manuel breakaway goal 15 minutes from time. Just when the English imagined events could not get any worse, along came the fiasco against Morocco. Here it appeared to all football supporters watching around the world that these Englishmen had finally lost the plot. After suffering the loss in the first half of their captain, Bryan Robson, to yet another nagging, accursed shoulder injury, the normally placid Ray Wilkins showed an amazing uncharacteristic flash of schoolboy petulance. Wilkins quite inexplicably threw the ball at the referee after a decision had gone against him. His disappearance piled even more pressure on his bedraggled team-mates. We then had the amazing scene of English players punching the air after achieving a heart-busting, gut-wrenching 0–0 draw with the mighty Moroccans. Sadly, the tabloid newspapers failed to share these opinions. Bobby Robson and his badly under-achieving side were mercilessly pilloried by their national press. The headlines screamed out a nation's disgust: 'Bring them home! You're a disgrace!' England had one last chance to save themselves. They daren't fail.

The final match was against the Poles. A victory would be sufficient to see England off the hook. But such had been their insipid form throughout, their supporters feared the worst. Indeed the squad's flight back to England was provisionally booked before the game with Poland had even begun. Robson, after heated discussions with his senior players, made several changes to his line-up. Most importantly in came the astute and probing Peter Beardsley. Beardsley would come in for the more traditional centre-forward Mark Hateley; traditional being another word for awkward, cumbersome and, particularly in Hateley's case, hopelessly out of his depth. Beardsley would be expected to feed the rapacious goal-scoring appetite of a badly misfiring Gary Lineker. The pairing worked an absolute treat. In true Lazarus style England roared back from the dead to hammer Poland

3–0. A born-again Lineker smashed home a deadly hat trick of goals, all scored within the limits of the six-yard box. It had been the first time that an English player had scored a hat trick in the World Cup since 1966. It was a performance that revived England's hopes. At last they had given the impression of a well-organised, sophisticated international team; not a rag-tag bunch of 11 individuals.

In the second round they were drawn against Paraguay. Played in the daunting surroundings of the Azteca stadium, it turned out to be a thrilling match, with a rejuvenated England finally winning through 3–0. But the scoreline in no way told the true story of the game. The Paraguayans were a typical South American concoction of sublime football and wretched defensive thuggery. Their skilful attacking players, Cabanas and Mendoza, repeatedly caused the English defence problems with their movement and pace; whereas at the back their defenders verged at times on the psychotic. Their centre-half Delgado at one stage caught Gary Lineker with a karate chop across the throat. They were an unpredictable bunch. When the Paraguayans concentrated on playing their football they looked capable of causing an upset.

As this gripping contest unfolded, however, the remodelled midfield of Hodge, Reid, Hoddle and Trevor Steven began to dominate. The poaching talents of Lineker finally came to the fore as the tide turned in England's favour. The deadly centre-forward twice proved too quick for the rugged Paraguayan defenders as he struck a further brace from close range. A third from Beardsley put the game far out of reach of the South Americans. Although theirs was undoubtedly a brave challenge, the Paraguayans finished a well-beaten team. They had, however, made their mark on their opponents, in more ways than one. It was 20 years since England had last won the World Cup. Twenty long, unconvincing years. In that time managers had come and gone and tournaments had passed them sadly by. For all the hard-luck stories which inevitably seem to attend every English set-back, the truth was that they were simply not good enough. The black and white footage of the late great Bobby Moore lifting aloft the Jules Rimet trophy appeared at times to resemble an epitaph for English football, rather than the beginning of some fantasy golden age. It was time once more for the lion to roar.

'Look, mate, I play football. About politics I know nothing,. Nothing, mate, nothing.' The unconvincing words of Diego Maradona nobly pretended that the forthcoming quarter-final with the English had no hidden meaning. His comments came at a press conference when asked by a journalist from *The Times* for his thoughts regarding the upcoming encounter. Maradona played it cool. He was no fool. 'When we go on the field,' he claimed, 'it is the game of football that matters, and not who wins the war.' Maybe el Diegrito missed his vocation in life, for he sure as hell gave a startlingly good impression of a politician. Diego was toeing the party line; but others were not so keen. Their defender Jose Luis Brown was slightly more forthcoming. Not surprisingly, with his Irish roots, Brown did not hide his true feelings. 'We all had cousins and friends that fought in the Malvinas,' he said. 'Not all of them came back. They will be in our thoughts when we take on the English.' Brown's comments lit the touch paper. He had said what privately all the Argentinian players were thinking. As the game drew closer others opened up on what was really in their hearts. The goalkeeper Nery Pumpido declared: 'To beat England would be a double satisfaction for everything that happened in the Malvinas.' Back in Buenos Aires plane-loads of the notorious Argentinian hooligans known as the 'Barras Bravas' were draping themselves in the flag of their country and heading for Mexico seeking English blood. With the supporters of St George not exactly shy when it comes to a rumpus, tensions were running high amongst the authorities. The old saying that 'football is war' was in imminent danger of being proved true on this particular occasion. As an Argentinian newspaper *Cronica* declared on their front-page headline that Maradona was their very own Exocet, the peace-makers on both sides shook their heads. What was the point? In England matters were hardly any better. The tabloid newspapers transformed Bobby Robson's men into an updated version of the Falklands task force. Papers such as the *Sun* and the *Daily Star* appeared determined to restart the conflict on a football pitch.

The night before the game Maradona could not sleep. His every bone ached for victory. He was prepared to do anything necessary to bring this about. By fair means or foul, it mattered little to him. There are times when all that matters is to win. This would be a contest where for Diego Maradona a different set of rules would apply; the rules of Scopa. His time amongst the Neapolitans would serve him well.

Bobby Robson devised a system in which he hoped the threat of the Argentinian number ten could be dealt with. Instead of placing the responsibility of such a difficult task with one individual, Robson came up with a plan to spread the load. Whoever happened to be closest to Maradona would take him. The English midfield and defence were instructed to 'crowd him, don't let him breathe, cut off his air'. In other words suffocate the little Argentinian so-and-so! The thinking behind this was simple. Stop Maradona and you stop Argentina. Curtailing the threat of one such as him was so much easier to plan than actually pull off. Robson could not stress enough the importance to his players of the need to keep their feet and, most importantly, their nerve when dealing with Diego.

Apart from the odd minor scuffle there was little incident off the pitch before the match. The Mexican police and security forces had a reputation for being heavy-handed. They would stand for no nonsense. The slightest sniff of trouble and the riot shields and batons would appear. They watched keenly from behind their visors as the supporters of both sides sang their war songs, songs in which the Falklands or Malvinas tended to figure heavily. On 22 June 1986, England and Argentina entered the legendary Azteca stadium. England were playing in the unusual strip of white tops and blue shorts. Argentina were in dark blue. Peter Shilton and Diego Maradona shook hands in the centre circle. It was polite but nothing more. The referee, Mr Ben Nasser from Tunisia, cut a nervous figure before the kick-off. Indeed he looked more tense than the players. Bobby Robson had bad vibes almost from the off as England's centre-half Terry Fenwick found himself yellow carded early on for a foul on – guess who? Robson sensed an Argentinian bias in the official. His fears as the contest unfolded would sadly be proved correct.

As the game began, both teams looked intent on giving nothing away. It was cat and mouse. England's much lauded rebuilt midfield found itself redundant as their defenders hit a shower of long balls in the general direction of Gary Lineker. It was a hopelessly outdated tactic which inevitably was dealt with effortlessly by the Argentine rearguard. Carlos Bilardo had assigned the fearsome Batista to man-mark Lineker. Batista took to it with relish as the England number nine was harassed to within an inch of the law. His every run was blocked by Argentinian defenders who queued up to help out their team-mate. It was a tension-stricken first 45 minutes, full of cautious play and minor petty fouls. The intense pressure of the occasion had clearly taken hold. From open play there had appeared only one chance of note, a snap-shot by England's Peter Beardsley which flew into the side netting. This apart neither side had an opportunity worth mention. Diego Maradona had probed patiently and gently. He was biding his time, looking for a weakness. When in possession he was crowded by the English midfield as they sought to kill any threat at birth. As the half-time whistle blew Maradona had been all but anonymous. In a game as tight as this it would require something extraordinary to break the deadlock – a slice of fortune or a piece of magic to swing the odds. Six minutes into the second period, Diego Armando Maradona chanced his luck and produced a hand of Scopa that rocked this quarter-final.

Maradona had the whiff of English blood in his nostrils. With increasing menace he attacked the heart of their defence, striking panic amongst the centre-halves Butcher and Fenwick. Steve Hodge dropped back from midfield to help out his colleagues; but in trying to hook the ball to safety he succeeded only in mishitting it back towards the advancing Peter Shilton. As Shilton came thundering out, Maradona challenged and with a deft flick of the wrist punched it into the unguarded English net. Hand-ball, surely? But wait! As Diego ran off with his arms raised in triumph, time appeared to stand still. Shilton ran towards the referee to point out Maradona's act. To his and every Englishman's absolute dismay Ben Nasser decided to allow the goal. It was a scandalous decision and was shown with television evidence to be totally incorrect. England's pleas for justice were met with deaf ears. It was to no avail. The goal would stand. After this fiasco Nasser would never referee in international football again. Bobby Robson watched these surreal goings-on from the touchline. His pre-match intuition about Nasser had proved to be horribly spot on; but nothing was going to change history. Robson urged his team on. With well over 30 minutes left to play England still had plenty of time to save themselves. Four minutes later they were dead.

In Argentinian folklore there exists a charming tale of a colourful character by the name of Enrique Garcia. Many years ago Garcia scored a goal that was sprinkled with gold dust. A magical weaving run mesmerised his opponents and left them paralysed with rage and admiration. Impressed with himself, Garcia, whose nickname was 'el Cheuco', picked the ball out of the net and headed off back to the halfway line taking in the applause, stopping only to dust down his original tracks, so that no one could ever copy his wonder goal. Enter Maradona.

The English had been shaken badly by the terrible injustice inflicted upon them. Before they had a chance to pull themselves together, Maradona hit them with the greatest goal in the history of the World Cup. Receiving possession inside his own half on the right-hand side of the field, Diego flew like the wind, leaving a flurry of white shirts wondering where the hell he had gone. Evading challenge after challenge he swooped down upon a terrified English rearguard. Butcher, Fenwick and Steven were all left for dead as a blazing Maradona hurtled into the history books, and shot past a despairing Peter Shilton. It was a truly magnificent goal by the Argentinian captain. Single-handedly he had taken on and destroyed the entire English side, leaving in his wake a trailing path of stardust that would forever linger in the memory.

Robson brought on the Liverpool winger John Barnes to try and galvanise the comeback. It worked. As Argentina set out their tactics to hold on to their lead, Barnes, with orders to run at the Argentinian defenders, began to have an effect. He was terrorising his marker Giusti. The left-wing became England's main source of attack as the young winger ran the hapless Argentinian ragged. English hearts soared as a ray of hope suddenly shone through. Ten minutes from time, Barnes again roared past a glut of defenders to cross perfectly for Lineker to pull one back with his head: 2–1. There was still time to save it. The English supporters screamed themselves hoarse. The dream of an equaliser was alive and well as it became obvious that the Argentinians simply could not cope with the pace and trickery of John Barnes. Maradona clenched his fists and implored his men not to throw it away. They had come too far to lose everything at this late stage. In the final moments Barnes one last time slaughtered the South Americans on the left and played in a marvellous cross which again found the head of Gary Lineker. Lineker, looking a certainty to score, was foiled at the last by the death-defying challenge of Jose Luis Brown. Risking life and limb to stop the Englishman, Brown somehow did enough to keep the ball out of the goal. His Irish grandfather would have been truly proud of him. It was the final act in a memorable if tremendously controversial quarter-final.

As England fought desperately, Ben Nasser signalled the end of the match. All of the Argentinian players went in search of their captain, for he more than any had brought about this moment of glory. Victory was theirs. A semi-final place had been earned; but more importantly the hidden agenda had been served. Pride was seen to have been restored for the disaster in the South Atlantic. Although nobody would ever quite come out and admit this, the scenes in the Argentinian dressing-room left little doubt as to their true feelings. It was Maradona waving his shirt wildly above his head who led the singing of his country's national anthem, his place amongst the immortals forever assured after his epic second goal. The captain had played his hand of Scopa to perfection. To win at all costs, that is the name of the game. Cheat, lie, steal, do what you have to do to gain an advantage. Maradona's later claim that it was not he but the 'hand of God' which put the ball in the net was to inflame the English. But what did he care? Revenge had been gained. Immediately following the match, Maradona and Terry Butcher were chosen by FIFA officials for the routine drug testing. To help them along they were each offered fluids. Butcher chose a beer, whilst Maradona, with a beaming smile, said that he preferred Coke. Happily the irony was lost on the English centre-half!

In late 1999 Diego Armando Maradona tottered on the brink of death. The ravages of his cocaine addiction had finally taken its toll. Years of abuse had left him seriously ill. Argentinian specialists warned Diego in no uncertain terms that unless he cleaned up his act he was a dead man. Maradona now faces his toughest opponent – himself.

16.

TEARS OF A CLOWN

ENGLAND V WEST GERMANY

1990 WORLD CUP SEMI-FINAL

As if given a new lease of life, Bobby Robson's punch-drunk, but still-standing England staggered triumphantly into the semi-finals of Italia 90. Their near-death experience at the hands of the magnificent, if suicidal, Cameroon had left them with genuine optimism for success. With the host nation committing hara-kiri in Naples, against Maradona's average Argentina, England's odds had been dramatically cut to actually win the World Cup. Robson's side prepared to face an old foe in Turin – Franz Beckenbauer and his powerful West Germany. History beckoned for the three lions.

SARDINIA

It was a strange World Cup for the English. The fear of hooligans had forced them to play their opening group matches on the island dust bowl of Sardinia. The Italian *carabinieri* had made Sardinia into an island fortress. The majority of the English supporters had travelled solely to cheer on their team, but there remained an unhealthy number whose malicious intent meant innocent fans were dragged into the trouble. Such was the fear these morons caused that any supporter who associated himself with the three lions risked a good hiding from a police force which hit first and asked questions afterwards. In such an atmosphere of bitterness and intimidation, the English prepared their assault on the 14th World Cup.

A stand-off had occurred between the England camp and the press. They had arrived in Italia 90 at war with a cynical and hostile army of newspaper hacks. The manager, Bobby Robson, was the target of a vicious campaign to undermine his role. Two papers in particular, the *Daily Mirror* and the *Daily*

Mail, went after the affable Robson's head with frightening venom. The news that he had signed a contract to go to PSV Eindhoven after the World Cup campaign had made them reach for their poison pens. Astonishingly, such was the determination of certain journalists to oust Robson, a feeling emerged that some even wanted England to lose. As the searchlights of the *carabinieri* helicopters lit up the Sardinian night-time sky and the wailing of police sirens pierced the air, a feeling of despondency gripped the English; and this before a game had been played!

In the midst of a fierce electric storm, England opened up against the Republic of Ireland. As lightning bolts streaked into the surrounding Sardinian mountains, both teams bored a watching world to tears. A 1–1 draw was greeted with disdain by the press and media. Jack Charlton's hardly inspiring but hard-working Irish side had England pinned back for almost the entire second half. An early poacher's goal from Gary Lineker was deservedly cancelled out by an arrowing Sheedy strike. The Republic would finish satisfied with a point. It had been a typical British encounter, played with a scarcity of skill or finesse. The ball players of the English, such as Waddle, Barnes and Gascoigne, had all performed their duty in the trenches; but this was the World Cup. It was time to step out of the Dark Ages. The senior players in the England squad met with Robson and insisted that a sweeper system be brought in. The manager, although at first reluctant, realised this was the best way ahead; for next on the agenda were Guillit, Rijkaard, Koeman and Van Basten. Holland were making their way to Sardinia.

With the sweeper system installed, England rejoined Italia 90, and a young, manic Geordie exploded like a supernova on the world scene; for it was in the game against the Dutch that Paul Gascoigne would lead Holland's much vaunted midfield a merry dance. Displaying the skills and technique English footballers were supposed to lack, Gascoigne produced a dazzling cv of his talent. His dancing feet weaving intricate paths past befuddled orange shirts was a fair sight for all Englishmen. Gazza's alert football brain was always aware of the swift give and go, the little swerve, a cunning through pass – a footballer born in Newcastle, but made in Heaven. It was once written of the great Brazilian Garrincha that he could never pass an exam but, my God, he could pass a ball! The same quote could easily have been applied to Paul Gascoigne. A generous soul who would hand over his last pound, Gazza was also the possessor of an anarchic sense of humour. No one was safe from his mad pranks. Originally, Bobby Robson had suffered deep misgivings on whether he could trust Gascoigne in the no-prisoners atmosphere of the World Cup. Gazza had a notoriously short fuse. In the minefields that would have to be crossed in Italia 90, Robson required players on whom he could completely rely. It was only a late friendly against Czechoslovakia at Wembley which secured Gazza his ticket. It was a sparkling, seductive display, which in the end convinced Robson to take him along.

Against Holland, the entire England team appeared reborn. As Gascoigne ran amok, the three lions marauded forward. With five at the back, there existed an air of confidence about England's normally stoical defence. Mark Wright, Terry Butcher and the electric-heeled Des Walker, flanked by Stuart Pearce and Paul Parker, dealt comfortably with anything the Dutch threw at them. Up front, better finishing by the usually lethal Gary Lineker and England could well have been celebrating a famous victory, instead of an honourable 0–0 draw. Gascoigne was simply outstanding. With an exquisite piece of deft skill, he left a Dutch defender limp and bedraggled as the famous Johan Cruyff twist and turn was reinvented, Geordie style. He even found time to ask the great Ronald Koeman what he was earning at Barcelona. Koeman's reply has never been printed! A memorable win was almost clinched with a dramatic last-minute free kick from Stuart Pearce, which was disallowed for being indirect. Sadly, as pride was restored on the football pitch, events off it continued to tarnish the image of the three lions.

As the white shirts played with new-found style and class, the hooligans who purported to support them stayed rooted in the Dark Ages. As trouble exploded, the *carabinieri* let fly with tear gas and baton charges. Many an innocent Englishman, draped in the flag, or wearing an England top, found himself a victim of over-zealous policing, which at times itself verged on thuggery. The English gutter press feasted on the appalling scenes that were occurring in Sardinia. Rumours abounded amongst supporters of a certain journalist even inciting the trouble. It was said that he offered fans a brick with a large sum of money tied to it. This would be theirs if they smashed a shop window. A photographer stood close by, ready to capture the moment. Luckily, the reporter in question was told in no uncertain terms what he could do with his brick. Such stories spread like wildfire amongst English followers. It is a certainty that on the nights when the fighting raged, some idiot would have taken up the crass offer. Somewhere, far away on the mainland, the rest of Italia 90 was revelling in a party atmosphere. As the *carabinieri* helicopters hovered menacingly over the English camp sites, Sardinia appeared more of a war zone.

Results elsewhere had left the qualifying situation tense for all concerned. With the Republic of Ireland also earning a point against a resilient and surprisingly decent Egypt, all four countries were level going into the final round of games. If England beat the Egyptians in their last outing, they would be through. If not, depending on the result of Holland and the Republic, they could be forced into the situation of drawing lots.

During the match against the Dutch, England captain Bryan Robson had been forced to leave in the midst of battle. The perennially unlucky Robson appeared cursed. Throughout his storming career with Manchester United and England, he had been troubled by a never-ending succession of serious injuries. Four years before in Mexico, he had been laid low with a damaged shoulder; now it was his Achilles heel which meant he had to withdraw from the squad and return home. It was the young midfielder from Aston Villa, David Platt, who stepped in for Robson against Holland. Immediately he impressed as he foraged endlessly alongside the flamboyant skills of Gascoigne. Although no Bryan Robson, the young Aston Villa midfielder possessed a good eye; a talent which would serve his country well as England progressed. For the match with Egypt, Bobby Robson reverted to 4–4–2. The Egyptians had to be beaten. Robson felt the best way to achieve this was to return to a normal back four (so much for revolution). The veteran Steve McMahon would replace the inexperienced David Platt, while Gary Lineker would be joined up front by the battering ram from Wolves, Steve Bull. Back to basics. It was a turgid first half. An Egyptian team had come to Sardinia with the sole intention of sneaking a draw. England, appearing bereft of inspiration, looked like granting them their wish. As the English struggled badly against a fast and highly disciplined rearguard, with the Irish and the Dutch also level, the dreaded possibility of drawing lots was fast becoming a reality. Finally, with tension increasing by the minute, Paul Gascoigne engineered a breakthrough. His free kick found centre-half Mark Wright. Wright's header flew hard and strong past the Egyptian keeper, Shoubeir. Gazza ran over to celebrate with the English bench. He found himself mobbed by the substitutes. Peter Beardsley planted a kiss on his forehead, while Bobby Robson ruffled the head of his young maestro. The relief was clear to see. As news of England's goal reached Palermo, the scene of the Holland–Irish match, both captains, Ruud Guillit and Mick McCarthy, agreed to a cease-fire. A draw saw each through. Due to the bizarre qualification rules, only the Egyptians would go out. The rest would go on. England, after an awful beginning, had finally made it off this accursed island. It was time to bid *arrivederci* to Sardinia.

BELGIUM

In a scintillating, end-to-end battle, England sneaked past the Belgians by the skin of their teeth. Reverting to a sweeper system, Robson watched as his team played with a level of technique and sophistication lacking in their previous display. Gascoigne was all over the field, creating, scheming; Waddle and Barnes stalked the flanks, effortlessly interchanging, while Lineker prowled ominously. In short, England resembled a team again. But as well as they were playing, the superlative Belgians, led by the magnificent Scifo, always appeared to have a slight edge. Scifo caused heart failure amongst the England supporters whenever he took control of the play. One almighty strike from the little Belgian almost snapped the English post in two. The evergreen Jan Ceulemans also smashed a tremendous effort against Peter Shilton's woodwork. England also had chances. John Barnes had a snarling volley deemed inexplicably offside, and Lineker also had an effort cancelled out by over-zealous refereeing. The English were producing form reminiscent of the Holland match, but the Belgians appeared at times to have just that little more. With 15 minutes remaining, David Platt was brought into the fray to replace a tiring Steve McMahon. The tough-tackling Scouser had battled against the tide all evening in desperate attempts to pin down the genius of Scifo. Gascoigne also was beginning to feel the strain. In what would prove fateful for events later in the tournament, he found himself being booked for trying to curtail the threat of Belgium's red tempest. Compared to the class act of Enzo Scifo, Gazza at times resembled a puppy snapping at his master's ankles. A marvellous, exciting contest finished scoreless. The tiring excesses of extra time and the fearful prospect of penalties lay in wait.

Encircled by huge swathes of black-uniformed *carabinieri*, all armed to the hilt, the English supporters sang out in praise of their team. The flags of St George, emblazoned with the names of various towns and cities, lay spread across the terraces of the Renata dall Ara stadium. Both sets of players appeared drained. Only the day before, Bobby Robson had admonished the hyper-active Gazza for playing tennis in the blazing sun, when he should have been resting. Looking absolutely shattered, Gascoigne must have wished he had taken his manager's advice. Extra time would be nothing more than a battle for survival. As the clock ticked, the prospect of a penalty shoot-out began to rear its ugly head. There was less than a minute to play when Gazza set off on a final gallop. The 36-year-old defender Eric Gerets brought him crashing to earth just inside the Belgian half. As the referee checked his watch, Gazza placed a precision cross into Belgium's penalty area. Waiting to swoop was David Platt, who hit it gloriously on the turn and into the back of the net. The English supporters danced jigs of joy as the Belgians and their fans stood dumbfounded. Seventeen seconds remained when Platt's effort hit the back of the goal! It had been that close. In a sporting gesture, the legendary manager Guy Thys sought out his opposite number, Bobby Robson, and embraced him. On the field Gascoigne led the players in saluting their much-put-upon supporters. Waddle and Butcher did a dance in the centre circle, both with beaming smiles. Typically, Gazza played a mock violin to the grief-stricken hordes of Belgians. Cruel! Robson would dedicate Platt's winner to his captain Bryan Robson. 'That was for you, Bryan,' said an ecstatic Robson. 'That one was for you.' Now it was on to Naples and a quarter-final against the indomitable lions of Cameroon.

CAMEROON

How England ever managed to overcome an exuberant Cameroon is one of the World Cup's most enduring mysteries. In all but the scoreline, the wonderfully talented Africans slaughtered Bobby Robson's side. In scenes resembling nothing less than a siege, England from the first whistle found themselves in a battle royal. Another precious strike from David Platt and two penalties from the ice-cool Lineker would prove just enough. But it was a gruelling match. Cameroon, in the way they attacked, did themselves much credit. The appearance off the substitute bench of the 38-year-old Roger Milla helped galvanise what was already a pulsating performance. The days when people scoffed at African football finished forever on 1 July 1990. Roared on by a Neapolitan crowd, they overran a bedraggled England. In the end it was only the predatory instincts of Gary Lineker which saw the English through. Where people could fault England's technique in comparison to Cameroon, no one could possibly ask questions about their heart. Mark Wright finished the contest with blood pouring from a head wound, and Lineker had been kicked, mauled and kicked again by the ferocious Massing. After one challenge, Massing left England's centre-forward lying in a messy heap on the ground. As he glared up he saw only the furious features of Massing staring madly down at him. 'Do not touch me,' growled the African giant to a wide-eyed Lineker. Sensible as ever, England's finest simply dusted himself down and proceeded to see his country into the semi-final, because no matter how many plaudits were piled on Cameroon, they were out. England were the team to go on. The three lions now faced their ultimate test for, in Turin, at the Stella delle Alpi, destiny had decreed another showdown with the old enemy – the Germans.

In the previous two tournaments, the Germans had fallen at the last hurdle. In 1982, an exhausted team crashed to a Paolo Rossi-inspired Azzuri team in Madrid. An epic semi-final with the French in Seville had left them victorious, but spent. Four years on they again fell short, Diego Maradona's Argentina breaking German hearts in the magnificent setting of the Azteca stadium. The pain of having to watch as others celebrated cut deep. Such agonies could not be allowed to happen a third time.

Under the masterful control of Franz Beckenbauer, West Germany efficiently arrived at the semi-final stage. The outstanding performance of the captain, Lothar Matthaus, had only confirmed his position amongst the world's best. Matthaus was the heartbeat of this German side; a midfielder of class, pace and perception. Up front Beckenbauer's side had in its armoury the awesome fire power of Rudi Voller and Jurgen Klinnsman. Without doubt this was the finest German team since 1974. Italia 90 had watched in awe, and a little fear, as they opened in deadly fashion against Yugoslavia. This highly fancied team from the Balkans were terrified into an inglorious surrender by the ferocity of West Germany's display. Two goals from Matthaus, one a blistering strike from long range, brought the Yugoslavs to their knees. A final scoreline of 4–1 saw the Germans lay down their marker in fine style. A comprehensive destruction of the United Arab Emirates followed next. The hapless Arabs were toyed with by West Germany, a 5–1 massacre which didn't do justice to the gap in class between them. Victory confirmed their place in the next phase. It was all looking rather daunting. Without breaking sweat, 'der Kaiser's' stormtroopers had sauntered through. The final game saw Colombia snatch a 1–1 draw off the sleepwalking Germans. Italia 90 breathed a collective sigh of relief. They were human after all!

Now came the Dutch. After their party piece with the Irish, Holland received their just reward. Matches between these two old adversaries never failed to ignite, and this proved no exception. The Dutch always played against the Germans as if their very lives depended on the result. Memories of a time when their nation fell under the Nazi jackboot galvanised the orange shirts of Holland to perform for something far more than simple World Cup glory. The San Siro in Milan provided an electrifying atmosphere as these warring neighbours began their spat. In what turned out to be a classic encounter, West Germany finally won the day 2–1, but only after a tumultuous struggle. It was to be the dashing Jurgen Klinnsman, in the performance of his career, who would prove the difference between the two.

Klinnsman scored once and led the line magnificently for his country. However, the game would be forever tarnished by a double sending-off. An outraged Frank Rijkaard spat at Rudi Voller in revenge for an alleged racist remark by the German. Both players left the pitch still arguing. It was a shameful episode which soured what had been a sublime game of football. Andres Brehme's late curling drive meant West Germany was home and dry; but it would be Klinnsman's heroic showing, and the pathetic brawl between Rijkaard and Voller, which would be remembered.

On a blazing hot Milan afternoon, a lone Jurgen Klinnsman penalty was sufficient to see off a disappointing Czechoslovakia in a tepid quarter-final clash. The effort put in by Beckenbauer's men in putting out Holland showed itself as they struggled in the Milan heat. But at the final whistle thoughts had already started to turn towards Turin. Franz Beckenbauer would not underestimate England, history had taught him that much. The Germans were not playing as well as they had done, and this gave Beckenbauer slight reason to worry. This was the English, though. His players would be ready.

England had come a long way from the dust bowl of Sardinia. Despite being ravaged by injuries, and the incessant problem of hooliganism following them around Italy, they were still battling away. The time when the tabloids had ridiculed the players and manager had gone; for as is the way of things in the English media, the improved tides of fortune saw headlines change overnight. Yesterday's villains suddenly became today's heroes. The same journalists who had castigated the players for their opening performances against the Irish, now praised them to the hilt. Bobby Robson was worried. His most precious talent was a booking away from suspension. Robson had preached to Gascoigne endlessly of the importance of walking away from trouble. Gazza's fiery temper would have been clearly noted by the Germans; they also would be aware of his disciplinary tightrope. His manager could only pray that Gascoigne, who had done him proud throughout the competition, would ignore German gamesmanship; for as sure as night follows day, they would endeavour to get him booked. For Gazza to miss the final through suspension would have been a crime. A wave of euphoria was sweeping across England. The 'World in Motion' single by New Order had caught perfectly the mood of the nation. The bars, pubs and clubs in every city and town filled up with supporters desperate to cheer the lads to a second World Cup final. 'Respect yourself, it's one on one,' sang New Order. It was time to go back to war with the Germans.

WEST GERMANY

As kick-off on 4 July drew near in the Stella delle Alpi, the bedraggled, weary, ragged hordes of St George continued to roar their support for England. The smattering of Union Jacks were surrounded by black-helmeted *carabinieri*, who watched them like hawks, all just waiting for the slightest opportunity to wade in and crack a few English heads together. Above, in the red-lit Turin sky, a surveillance helicopter buzzed the stadium. Treated as criminals since their arrival on Italian soil, these loyal fans had earned the right to be present as England prepared to mount their last stand – Cockneys, Scousers, Mancs, Geordies and Brummies. A long, perilous journey, in which they had been herded around like cattle, had seen small regional differences melt away. For one night and, God willing, maybe two, they were all Englishmen together. Deep in the bowels of the Stella delle Alpi, Bobby Robson was still busy instilling into Gascoigne the importance of discipline. He warned him of the danger Lothar Matthaus would pose, of how, if he strayed from position, Matthaus would come storming through the gap like a demon. 'Leave him to me, boss,' was the confident Geordie's reply. 'No problem!' Robson could only trust this young man who, if on form, could tear the Germans to pieces.

The teams appeared from the tunnel to a marvellous reception. Due to the unfair distribution of tickets, the German supporters were by far the majority. Far away to the north of the stadium stood the impressive mountain peaks of the Alps, and beyond them Switzerland, where Hungary had been ambushed by the Germans many years before. (Some things never change.) England were in traditional white, West Germany in green. The game began and the noise and tension inside the delle Alpi chilled the blood. In the first minute, Paul Gascoigne let fly a crashing volley, which the German keeper Illgner tipped over the bar. Gazza bossed the midfield with a mixture of exquisite skill and gritty determination. Bobby Robson's pre-match concerns of whether Gascoigne was capable of looking after Lothar Matthaus appeared to have been unfounded, for in the early stages it was Matthaus who spent his time chasing after Gazza. England were looking superb. Peter Beardsley, probing intelligently alongside Gary Lineker, was picking holes in the German defence. The first half-hour was theirs – Lineker went close, Waddle put Paul Parker through to shoot over, and the inimitable Gazza nutmegged the great Matthaus! The German appeared rattled as the English came at them. Franz Beckenbauer, elegant as ever, with arms folded in a smart short-sleeved shirt, was watching his team being outplayed. Still, though, England had not made the breakthrough. Stuart Pearce fired a rocket inches wide of Illgner's under-siege goal, and Chrissy Waddle attempted to score from the centre circle!

Confidence flowed through the English ranks. Ever so slowly, West Germany, as the first half drew on, began to grab a foothold back in the game. Peter Shilton had to make a fine save from the darting Olaf Thon, followed by a tremendous stop from Augenthaler's free kick. In typical, smooth freewheeling style, the Germans began to motor through midfield. As the whistle blew for half-time, the klaxons were blowing with a new confidence. The 40-year-old Shilton, who for the first half-hour hardly touched the ball, suddenly had become England's busiest player. Both sets of supporters took time to catch their breath. The stakes had been pushed even higher by Italy's demise in Naples against Maradona's Argentina. If victory could be achieved here in Turin, each nation knew they were more than capable of dealing with a half-fit Diego and his average side. Germans and English both had unfinished business with 'el Diegrito'.

West Germany began the second half as they had ended the first. In ominous fashion, Lothar Matthaus began to dominate proceedings, but still England held their own. On the hour Stuart Pearce was forced into bringing down the troublesome Thomas Hassler on the edge of the English box. As the delle Alpi held its breath, Hassler squared the ball for the defender Brehme to hit it. Brehme's shot deflected wickedly off Paul Parker and ballooned over a stranded Shilton: 1–0, the deadlock was broken. The Germans ran joyfully towards Brehme as flares and rockets exploded among their supporters. England rallied, and Waddle almost made it through, only to be stopped at the last. Robson took off the old warrior Terry Butcher, to replace him with the attacking midfielder Trevor Steven. Still the English fans refused to give up hope. 'God Save the Queen' and 'Come on England' came roaring down from the terraces. Depending on who you supported, time was either frozen or moving twice as fast. Bobby Robson looked on in animated fashion. He checked his watch; ten minutes remained for England to save themselves. Paul Parker played a long, searching pass high into the German penalty box. The normally unflappable centre-half Jurgen Kohler for once failed to control the ball, and was forced to watch in horror as Gary Lineker took it off him. With lightning control, Lineker took the ball high on his thigh and unleashed a low drive past Illgner: 1–1. England's golden boy had saved them at the last. Bedlam erupted amongst the English supporters. How they had ached for that moment. Many had already given up, convinced they had left Lady Luck in Naples, in defeating Cameroon. Extra time would be called for. Robson urged his players to keep going. Beckenbauer walked amongst his troops, ushering out advice learned over a glorious career. All those years of experience were now paying dividends for both managers. Just 30 minutes more.

Extra time saw no let-up in the furious pace and drama. Klinnsman was held off by Des Walker when he appeared certain to score. Suddenly it was all the Germans. Gascoigne was battling manfully to stem the tide of green shirts as they marauded through from midfield. In a rash challenge Gascoigne caught the flailing Thomas Berthold directly in front of the German bench. Berthold went down as if he had been hit by a sniper. Players hurtled towards the touchline urging the referee to book the Englishman. Gascoigne has been well and truly booked. Out came the yellow card and a legend was born. Gazza was inconsolable, his face a mixture of rage and grief. For a second it appeared he had gone completely. Lineker came across to console him. He urged Bobby Robson, 'Have a word with him.' Tears fell down the young Geordie's face as the cruel reality of his situation hit home. Should England come through this mighty night in Turin, then their brightest light would not be able to play in the final. Clearing his mind, Gazza threw himself wholeheartedly back into the fray. As the English fans roared his name, Paul Gascoigne sent Waddle dashing clear in the German penalty area. Waddle took aim, and unleashed a ferocious drive that smacked against the inside of the post, came back out and missed the in-rushing Platt by an inch. Maybe England had left their luck in Naples after all? The second period of extra time ticked ominously away. With both sides close to exhaustion, chances began to appear thick and fast. A screamer from Brehme just cleared the English crossbar; Buchwald lashed a shot against Shilton's post. Platt had the ball in the net only to see it disallowed. It was pulsating drama, and no team deserved to lose. There would be no breakthrough, for the final whistle blew and after two hours of unrelenting drama a penalty shoot-out would decide the winners. All eyes and cameras focused in on the broken-hearted Gascoigne. As huge applause rang out around the delle Alpi, Bobby Robson gave Gazza a consoling hug before steadying himself for what lay ahead. Working for British television, back in London, Bryan Robson commented that 'they should take the cameras off him'. Sadly there were to be more English tears shed before this remarkable night in Turin was over.

Gascoigne insisted to his manager that he was okay to take the sixth penalty, if required. England's initial five would be in the order of Lineker, Beardsley, Platt, Pearce and Waddle. All the players of both sides gathered in the semi-circle. By now the Turin sky had lost its red glow and had turned black, littered with stars. The two goalkeepers made the walk to the chosen goal. Shilton and Illgner chattered happily away – the pressure lay more with the men chosen to try and beat them. It was Gary Lineker who went first. In typical manner, Lineker clinically put his spot kick away – England led. Brehme came forward to lash his shot past Shilton. This classy defender levelled proceedings. Now Peter Beardsley, a fine effort: 2–1 to the English.

Lothar Matthaus strode forward in confident manner to take his turn. Not surprisingly, the West German captain never gave Peter Shilton a hope. David Platt, the scorer of a brace of important goals in the run-up to the semi-finals, now risked his hand. Platt's penalty smashed past the diving Illgner. In the centre circle many could hardly bear to watch. Karl Heinz Riedle, his face etched in concentration, stepped forward. Riedle's effort left Shilton without a prayer, as the ball was hammered past him with great precision. Stuart Pearce was a sure-fire certainty to blast in his effort. Illgner stood as if frozen. Up came Pearce to crash a drive straight at the keeper's body. Advantage West Germany. The distraught defender made his way back to the centre circle to be consoled by his team-mates. Peter Beardsley rushed forward to place a comforting arm around his shoulders. Olaf Thon, without, it appeared, a nerve in his body, strolled forward with great conviction, and sent his penalty soaring into the top corner of the net. It would all be down to Chris Waddle to keep England alive. With his long, loping style, Waddle strode up to the ball and sent his shot woefully high over the crossbar, and in the direction of the Alps. It was all over. Waddle slumped tragically to his knees. The Germans rushed as one to mob their goalkeeper. Only Matthaus took the time to stop and console the crying Waddle. Franz Beckenbauer shook hands with an ashen-faced Bobby Robson. Beckenbauer, with typical style and grace, congratulated the England manager on his team's fine performance. 'What a pity it had to come to this,' he said. The England manager choked back his disappointment to wish his dignified opponent all the best in the final. The English supporters started up an emotional rendition of 'You'll Never Walk Alone' and a choked, weary Gazza went across to salute them. His face filled with tears, Gascoigne bade a final farewell before disappearing out of sight. The dream was over. Italia 90 had ended in glorious despair for England.

As expected, West Germany went on to beat a rancid Argentina in a final forever stained by the thuggish antics of the South Americans. The Germans claimed the trophy seven minutes from time with a penalty from Brehme. As Maradona and his countrymen lost their heads and what remained of their reputation, West Germany kept their nerve to take the mantle of world champions. In Rome, with Maradona sobbing crocodile tears, Lothar Matthaus raised high the World Cup trophy. England went on to lose to Italy in a highly entertaining third-place contest; a much more joyful occasion, as Gascoigne orchestrated a Mexican wave for both sides at the end of the game. At one stage Gazza even had the English bench joining in with the crowd as the wave swept around the San Nicola stadium in Bari. Gazzamania had arrived! Paul Gascoigne had the entire nation at his feet. At 22 years old, Gazza returned home a hero. Arriving back at Luton airport to a rapturous reception, the England squad were met by a press frenzy. Thousands lined the surrounding roads as the players took their applause from an open-top bus; but there was really only one who the crowds had gathered to see – a grinning young Geordie who had decided to celebrate the moment by wearing a gigantic pair of plastic boobs! Everybody loved Paul Gascoigne.

In the summer of 1998, Gazza, now 31, was left out of England's World Cup squad. A career that had promised untold glory had turned horribly sour. As the vultures gathered for the death knell of Gazza's England career, thoughts went back to a hot, balmy night in Turin, many years before. What was going to be the first step on a wonderful journey would be remembered as Paul Gascoigne's epitaph. The tears of a hero turned into those of a clown. But what a player!

17.

THE TREASURE OF SAN GENARO

ITALY V ARGENTINA

1990 WORLD CUP SEMI-FINAL

Rascals, vagabonds, cut-throats and thieves. Shadowy figures in darkly lit doorways. Streets full of crime and intrigue. This is a place were the devil would need a bodyguard. Gangs of hoodlums on mopeds tear up and down endless back alleys. Mean-faced characters in shades sit lazing around outside cafés and bars. Old men, with piercing eyes that have seen too much, play cards. Welcome to Naples.

Naples, a city as beautiful as it is dangerous; where from almost every shop devils and harlequins stare back at you; a city whose patron saint refuses to die. Twice a year San Genaro answers the prayers of all Neapolitans as his blood miraculously liquefies live on television. In a broadcast shown unedited throughout the southern peninsula, a miracle occurs. San Genaro is held in huge esteem by all Neapolitans. It is claimed that when the miracle fails disaster will strike the region. In times of dire trouble, and there have been many, on the terraces the supporters of Napoli FC have even taken to praying en masse to their holy saint. '*San Genaro, quitaci tu*' ('San Genaro, please help us') has echoed many times within the San Paolo stadium during the lean and troubled years. In the summer of 1984 these prayers were answered.

To a swirling haze of blue and white flags and scarves waving in his honour, Diego Armando Maradona descended from the heavens. Fifty thousand poured into the San Paolo stadium, all desperate to pay homage to their new messiah. At first just a tiny speck in the Neapolitan sky, Maradona's helicopter swooped low over the bay of Naples, giving the young Argentinian a dramatic view of what was to become his kingdom. He gazed below at the white spray of speeding motor-boats cutting a dash through the waters of the Tyrrhenian Sea. Just a short distance away, on the Isle of Capri, a Maradona look-alike was busy trying to keep the paparazzi off the real 'el Diegrito's' trail. Naples was a city set to burst with anticipation. For hours the fanatical supporters of Napoli FC had sung and danced on the terraces of the San Paolo, awaiting the arrival of their saviour.

The brooding hulk of Mount Vesuvius loomed over this Babylon by the sea. This is a region whose beauty is in stark contrast to the dark and bloody history of its most prominent city. The southern peninsula which Naples proudly dominates was this day preparing to welcome the world's finest into their close-knit clan, for Maradona, raised among the slums of Buenos Aires, was viewed as a kindred spirit by the Neapolitan *tifosi*. With his help their ailing club Napoli FC would rise up and roar their defiance against the hated northern powers.

For generations Napoli had been forced to endure the jeers of teams north of Rome. Viewed as barbarians and a sore on the face of Italy, the Neapolitans raised two fingers at the mocking northerners; but at times someone spitting in your face was hard to take. Whenever Napoli travelled north insults would inevitably be hurled in their direction. On one famous occasion the supporters of Perugia, whilst playing host to the southerners, unfurled an enormous banner displaying, 'Stop Nuclear Tests in the Pacific. Hold them in Naples.' The Napoli supporters replied by waving flags of the American Confederacy, demonstrating that they had no wish to be part of Italy.

The reception that greeted Maradona as he stepped out onto the hallowed turf of the San Paolo had a profound effect on him. He felt like he had arrived at his spiritual home. The snobbery of Barcelona was not for Diego. He was a child of the back alleys, a creature of the streets. Here amongst this city of two million anarchists, where cheating and trickery are an integral part of everyday life, Maradona would flourish. To tumultuous acclaim he wrapped a Napoli scarf around his neck and took the applause from the centre circle. This was a marriage made in heaven. Surrounded by a frightening array of photographers and cameramen, Maradona blew kisses to the adoring Neapolitan masses. In that moment he promised himself that he would make these people's dreams come true. Such a show of unrestrained love deserved nothing less.

Thrown a football, he proceeded to juggle it and perform a few party tricks, sending the 50,000 Napoli *tifosi* to even further levels of adoration. Fireworks exploded, whilst blue and white flares engulfed the Neapolitans in a blurred haze. Enjoying every moment, Maradona set off on a lap of honour. This was nothing less than a coronation. The newly crowned king of Naples let loose a string of light-blue balloons that drifted high above the San Paolo stadium and off in the direction of Vesuvius. Among the crowd the president of Napoli FC, Corrado Ferlaine, watched these amazing scenes unfurl with bursting pride; for it was he who had orchestrated Maradona's transfer. Ferlaine, a man himself born in the shadow of the volcano, had declared enough was enough. In 1984 there was only one man who could help revive his slowly dying club. Diego Armando Maradona, who at that time was plying his magical trade amidst the politics and intrigue of Barcelona, had to be brought in. A series of bad injuries and a fall-out with the Barca president made Ferlaine confident that Maradona could be prised away from Catalonia. A swoop for the great Argentinian would galvanise not only his football team, but indeed the whole city; for Naples was still recovering from a devastating earthquake only four years previously.

Vesuvius awoke in anger on 23 November 1980. Over 5,000 people were claimed by the disaster. For all Neapolitans it was a ghastly premonition of what could lie ahead for them as they lived out their lives in the shadow of such a menace. The misty hidden peaks of Vesuvius play a large part in how the people of Naples see life. Live for today as there may well be no tomorrow. Incidentally, the year of 1980 was one of the very rare occasions when the miracle of San Genaro, to the horror of all Neapolitans, failed to occur. Shortly after, the earthquake hit, causing untold grief and misery throughout the region. In a city as superstitious as Naples it was not totally unexpected. Deciding that he would not take no for an answer, Corrado Ferlaine approached the Maradona camp determined to get his man.

At first he found their demands wholly unreasonable and far beyond what Napoli FC could ever afford. It was only when Maradona himself insisted that a deal be done that progress was achieved. An initial fee of $13 million would be paid to Barcelona whilst the player himself received $6 million. It was a pirate's treasure for the Argentinian and easily smashed any previous transfer fee record. The means by which Ferlaine obtained the cash to pay for Maradona lay hidden in the murk of Neapolitan life. The poverty-stricken neighbourhoods that sprawled at the foot of Vesuvius lay under the frightening control of the Camorra. This was the Naples equivalent of the Cosa Nostra, the Mafia. The Camorra, it was said, were known to be even more ruthless than their Sicilian brothers. Frightening rumours linking Ferlaine with the Camorra were whispered around the city.

After the 1980 earthquake the Napoli chairman's building companies were controversially involved in the rehousing of thousands of Neapolitans. As billions of lira poured into the region to help with the rebuilding, much of the cash never reached its intended target. The people of Naples had little doubt about what had happened to it. The Camorra spread their tentacles to include all parts of Neapolitan life, including their football team. They desired the purchase of Maradona for their own needs. The Camorra had big plans for the little Argentinian.

After extensive discussions, banging of tables, threats and name-calling, a deal for 'el Diegrito' was finally struck. The Neapolitans had their man, or so they thought. The Barcelona officials decided at the last to complicate matters. Knowing how desperate the Italians were to have Maradona, they decided to squeeze them some more. An exasperated Ferlaine exploded with rage when informed that Barca had suddenly demanded an extra $600,000. There was no more money in the pot. In a desperate plea to save the deal he appealed directly to the people of his home city. The Neapolitans, in their desire to have Maradona amongst them, would have sold their souls to the devil. Old people pulled their life savings out of banks, others sold wedding rings. Children gave up their precious toys. For a city like Naples, which suffered terribly from crippling unemployment, these events were nothing short of miraculous. Diego Maradona dared not let them down.

Maradona's unique talent was spotted as soon as he was old enough to kick a ball. He was blessed with whiplash pace, blinding skills and an uncanny ability to go past opponents. He was also as strong as an ox. Although diminutive and stocky, he had astonishing upper body strength. Proving almost impossible to knock off the ball, Maradona would swoop down on defences causing untold terror. When on top of his game he was impossible to contain. Along with Pele and di Stefano he was without doubt one of the greatest players ever to emerge from the South American continent. Napoli had got themselves a winner. The newly crowned king of Naples was ready to pick up the mantle for his kingdom and lead the southern hordes against the might of the giants in the north. In the striking light-blue shirt of Napoli, Maradona took instantly to the theatrical opera of Serie A. Every game was sensational drama. With the ball seemingly glued to his left foot, the Argentinian led a Neapolitan revival. Inspired by Maradona, players who had been doing little more than sleepwalking in the southern outpost began to earn their wages. The Brazilian Careca, plus some superlative Italians such as de Napoli, Francini and Crippa, finally woke up. With Maradona's mother being of Italian origin, allied with his own dark, swarthy looks, this 24-year-old Argentinian became the idol of all young Neapolitans. His name was scrawled down every alleyway in Naples. Every bedroom had a photo of the fresh-faced Diego on its wall. It was not, however, just his looks and talent that appealed to these rebellious southerners; for like themselves, Maradona was impossible to control. His total lack of respect for authority and his habit of speaking his mind, whatever the consequences, matched perfectly their own outlook on life. Most Neapolitans saw themselves as a separate state from the rest of Italy. The utter contempt in which they were held by the rest of their country was returned ten-fold from Naples. Their city raped by crime and unemployment whilst the northern cities of Milan and Turin prospered only helped to fuel their anger. This young man would help to give them back their pride. Their ongoing battle in the eternal struggle with the north was suddenly a winnable one, if only in the footballing sense.

Maradona was born to entertain. The dramatic, passionate gestures and the theatrical manner in which he went about his game endeared him to the Napoli supporters. The celebration of a goal by wheeling away in triumph towards the terraces, almost in tears of joy and making the sign of the cross, was pure Neapolitan street theatre. If there was ever an actor born to play such a role then it was Diego Maradona. Naples was his theatre, and the San Paolo was his stage. In 1986 Maradona confirmed his position as the best player in the world when he led Argentina to victory in the World Cup finals. In a four-week period his blazing talents set the tournament alight. Almost single-handedly Maradona led an average Argentinian side to glory. His performances throughout were stunning as he took on and destroyed the best defences in the world. During the quarter-final against England, Maradona scored one of the greatest goals ever in the competition. A run from his own half ripping to pieces an England team was followed by a typical piece of malevolent genius as he flicked the ball with his hand over an outraged Peter Shilton, fooling the referee. Back in his adopted city, this goal was greeted with as much acclaim as his astonishing second, the sly and the sordid equally appreciated with the beautiful and the brilliant. That night mopeds screeched down Neapolitan alleyways, their owners roaring out their hero's name. Argentina's victory was not only theirs alone, it belonged also to the people of Naples.

Diego Maradona returned triumphantly to Naples via Buenos Aires. His home city was gripped by the World Cup success. Maradona was met at the airport and driven in a cavalcade through the city streets. From every window Argentinians leaned out to catch a glimpse of the returning hero, blue and white confetti filling the sky as 'el Diegrito' took the acclaim of his blood nation. Maradona had been invited by the Argentinian President to share his palace balcony and show off the World Cup trophy. As Maradona lifted it high Buenos Aires erupted with delight. These events would pale into insignificance when compared to what was about to happen in Naples.

On 24 May 1987, Napoli were playing at home to Fiorentina. The Neapolitans held their breath. With seconds remaining, the home side were drawing 1–1 with the team from Florence. Napoli required just a single point to claim their first-ever Italian title. Their patron saint San Genaro was being forced to work overtime in order to deal with the thousands of Neapolitans praying their side would not blow it. For so many years the butt of the nation's jokes, redemption was almost upon them. The referee blew his whistle and the city of Naples began the party of all parties! Neapolitans took to the streets and indulged in their biggest celebration since liberation by the Americans in the Second World War. Every alley, street and doorway was transformed into a mass of blue and white confetti.

A week-long carnival got under way. At last the jibes that had been aimed in their direction ceased; for now they were the champions. The inferiority complex which at one time had threatened to strangle the life out of Napoli FC had been eased. It was pay-back time. Mock funerals were held for the northern clubs. Maradona was renamed Santa Maradona whilst their patron saint San Genaro found his name changed to San Genmaradona. Photographs of San Genaro dressed in the blue and white football kit of Napoli were sold on every corner. The Neapolitans were in no way mocking their holy one, they were simply allowing him to join in the fun! Bottles filled with the alleged tears of the hated AC Milan supremo, Silvio Berlusconi, were also popular sellers. Strangely, this epic celebration was also enjoyed by Neapolitans no longer on this mortal coil. Graffiti was spotted on a graveyard wall with the words, 'You don't know what you missed!' The next morning, scrawled underneath this was written, 'How do you know we missed it?' Diego's magic knew no limits!

The one who more than all made this possible? Well, he partied as long and as hard as the most drunken, ecstatic Neapolitan! Diego Maradona was to find countless babies and streets named in his honour. The king of Naples bathed in the warm glow of his adoring followers; but just when Maradona was enjoying the fruits of his labour, dark rumours began to emerge regarding his private life. Whilst he publicly paraded the image of a good family man and devoted Catholic, the reality was somewhat different. Maradona had become involved with a local girl called Cristina Singrita. Cristina claimed that the idol of all Neapolitans was the father of her baby child. This Maradona denied wholeheartedly. Later, tests showed that he had been lying. This incident caused a rift between the king and his subjects. Maradona had crossed a line. In Naples children are sacred. They had a saying: '*I figli, so figli.*' Translated this means roughly, 'Children are children and must be looked after, no matter what.' Maradona's insistence that the child was not his did him no favours with the locals.

There was also the involvement with the Camorra. Ever since Maradona had arrived in Naples the Camorra had made a point of being seen in public with him. There exists a photograph of Diego arm in arm with three of the

Guilliano brothers. The Guillianos played a huge part in the Argentinian's transfer from Barcelona. Their illegal activities included murder, prostitution, drug-running and bootlegging; and the profit to be made out of Maradona was enormous. As matters threatened to spiral out of control off the pitch, on it Maradona was still producing the goods. In 1989 the UEFA Cup was brought home to Naples after a magnificent performance, defeating Stuttgart in Germany. The Germans, with Jurgen Klinnsman in their line-up, were totally outclassed on home soil. With Maradona leading the Neapolitans in all-out attack, they romped home to a stunning 5–1 victory.

In 1990 the championship was reclaimed after they had lost to the Dutch-inspired AC Milan the previous season. However, as always seems to be the case with the Neapolitans, the title win was shrouded in controversy. The league was won after a coin-throwing incident at Atlanta. Their trainer was caught by the television cameras screaming at his supposedly stricken Brazilian goalkeeper Alemao to 'stay down, stay down'. This incident infuriated the rest of Italy. The Milan president Berlusconi, whose team had been robbed of a prospective second successive title, went public with his outrage and his contempt for the Neapolitans. For many the southern hordes had overstepped the mark. The time was drawing close for them to be put in their place. As for the great man himself, he dedicated the title success to his father. Naples once more celebrated long and hard – almost too hard. It was as if they had experienced a premonition of what was to come. With every wish there comes a curse. Diego Armando Maradona's world was about to get extremely complicated. Next on his agenda was the 1990 World Cup finals and the first faltering steps to everlasting football infamy.

REBELLION

Only Diego would have the nerve to try such a trick. In an unashamed attempt to persuade Neapolitans to change sides and support the blue and white of Argentina, Maradona sent forth his battle cry. He had dragged his country kicking and screaming to the semi-final stages of the World Cup. After an opening-day mauling by the lions of Cameroon, Argentina battled back to scrape through. Now they would face the host nation in Naples . . .

It had been a rocky road. They had staggered and stumbled but somehow kept their feet and managed to find a way past Yugoslavia and arch rivals Brazil. Whilst Yugoslavia were despatched on penalties, the Brazilians were seen off with a touch of archetypal Maradona genius. Despite not being fully fit and looking overweight, the Argentinian captain soared through

Brazil's defence to lay the ball off for Claudio Cannigia to fire into the net.

On 3 July 1990, Neapolitans woke to find their volcano shrouded in fog. A thick mist engulfed the bay of Naples. It was the dawn of the Italy–Argentina semi-final. The cafés and bars of Naples buzzed with the locals deep in conversation about Maradona's sensational outburst. This was a city at war with itself on who to support. Heated discussions on the merits of each took place. Old women hanging out their washing on balconies would gossip loudly about 'Diego's nerve'. Around Naples the flag of the Azzuri flew from passing cars and mopeds; but there was also a conspicuously high number of Argentinian flags. In his own inimitable way Maradona had lit a fuse. He knew well what he was doing. His asking the Neapolitans to cheer for himself and Argentina had caused outrage throughout Italy. Throughout the competition the Azzuri had received magnificent support in Rome and Milan. It was inconceivable that Italians (even low-lifes such as the Neapolitans) would not get behind their national side in their hour of need.

Azeglio Vicini's men had played marvellously skilful football on their march towards the semi. Italia 90 had presented them with a chance for a historic fourth World Cup triumph. Vicini had a rich array of talent to pick from, including a prodigious young midfielder who was being touted already as being among the world's best. Baggio, however, was not fully trusted by his manager. Vicini doubted whether his young star had the mental toughness to deal with the fearsome tackling of the Argentinians. The world champions had shown throughout the competition that they took no prisoners. Instead the Azzuri manager chose the more resilient Gianluca Vialli of Sampdoria. It was a massive gamble by Vicini. The lethal Vialli had failed to show his true form in his previous performances. In the first round Roberto Baggio had scored the goal of the tournament when he took on the entire Czech side and beat them. This magical effort would return to haunt Vicini. He did, however, possess in his starting line-up the man with the Sicilian eyes, Salvatore Schillachi.

Schillachi had been the find of Italia 90. The son of a Sicilian bricklayer, he emerged from a struggling season with Juventus to ignite the World Cup scene. A small, dynamic forward, Toto captured the hearts of Italians everywhere. It was during the Azzuri's first match against an ultra-defensive Austria that Schillachi first came to the fore. Coming on as a late substitute, Toto sent the 70,000 home fans in the Olympic stadium delirious when he headed home the winning goal. His celebration, with his mad staring eyes almost bulging out of his head, became an endearing memory of Italia 90. As the Azzuri made steady progress, Schillachi's goals became increasingly important. A memorable wonder strike against the Uruguayans in the second round was one that would be remembered; a fierce, snarling drive hit with pace that slammed violently into the roof of the Uruguayan goal. Every World Cup brings forward a new star. The new star for 1990 was without doubt Salvatore Schillachi.

On the evening of the showdown, a feeling of slight unease pervaded the sweltering Neapolitan air. The drums of the Argentinians beat loudly. From out of their mouths came a war cry so familiar to the locals, 'Maradona, Maradona!' The South Americans, with their faces painted in the light blue and white of their country, had arrived in Naples in large numbers; but the array of flags outside the San Paolo consisted mainly of the Azzuri tricolour. Early signs were that the Neapolitans had stayed loyal to Italy; but the night was young. Inside the stadium the atmosphere was intense. The teams were announced over a booming tannoy. The Italian line-up consisted entirely of northern-based players. The reaction of the 60,000 crowd was mixed. There was much jeering amongst the roars for each player. When the Argentinian team was read out the San Paolo erupted into a cacophony of booing and catcalls, but when it came to Maradona's name there were massive cheers, mingled with the derisory chants from the Azzuri followers. There were banners both for and against him. Naples was a city in deep and bitter turmoil. No city in World Cup history had ever had to face such a dilemma. It could only happen to Naples! As the teams came out to do battle it was obvious that the support for the Italians was not all that it should be. Many Neapolitans had decided not to cheer for either side. Others thought differently. Some Napoli fans were clearly visible amongst the Argentinian fans, joining in with their songs and chants. With all of Italy watching on television, the chance to show their contempt for all things outside the southern peninsula was too much to resist.

Diego Maradona bounced up and down full of nervous energy, his face a mix of passion and determination. From the referee's first whistle the Argentinians hunted down the Azzuri forwards. Throughout the tournament they had shown no mercy in their determined, and sometimes brutal, defence of their crown. But this was Italy. Themselves masters of the sly kick and debilitating tackle, they would stand up to the intimidation of the South Americans. If it came down to a fight they would not be found wanting. The Italians would meet foul with foul. On 17 minutes, Vialli's well-hit drive was kept out by the goalkeeper Goycochea, only to rebound to the feet of Toto Schillachi. From eight yards out Schillachi followed in and hooked the ball into the back of the goal.

Inside the stadium thousands of Azzuri tricolours waved in salute of the Azzuri goal. The home bench were on their feet as Vicini was smothered with hugs by his coaching staff. Italy at that stage looked set for the final; but the night was still in its infancy. There was a long way to go. Maradona fished the ball out of the net and sprinted back to the centre circle. Argentina restarted the game. The Azzuri were in a quandary. Should they continue to go forward and kill off the world champions, or should they, in true Italian manner, lock up shop? The remainder of the first half was a violent, niggly affair. The referee, Mr Michel Vautrot from France, required eyes in the back of his head as flare-ups raged off the ball. The Argentinian winger Cannigia had spent the entire period diving in and around the Italian penalty area, much to the disgust of the Azzuri defenders, Baresi, Maldini and Bergomi. It was a hard and physical encounter that was lightened every so often by moments of sweet skill. Slowly, as the second half wore on, Argentina began to gain momentum. A full moon shone in all its glory over Naples. Could Maradona supply the silver bullet?

The Azzuri were growing nervous. Even the great Franco Baresi was showing signs of strain as he marshalled his edgy defence. The Argentinians had by this time opened up, and for the first time in Italia 90 began to play football befitting their status as reigning world champions. Time and again, with the Italians retreating en masse, Argentina swept forward. The Azzuri supporters watched with fear etched on their faces as Maradona and his compadres attacked from all angles. Their manager, Carlos Bilardo, screamed out his orders from the touchline, imploring his players to give the ball at every opportunity to their captain. The normally so solid and reliable Italian defenders had been reduced to a dithering shambles. Individual errors had their fans closing their eyes in horror as the South Americans searched desperately for an equaliser. On 67 minutes, to the abject misery of all Italy, they got their wish. It was Maradona who fed Olarticoechea wide on the left. Olarticoechea's cross was met by the glancing head of Cannigia. The Azzuri goalkeeper Zenga misjudged badly as the leaping Cannigia dipped his header to send the ball gliding into the Italian goal: 1–1, and game on.

Around the stadium from Argentinian and Neapolitan alike there was massive acclaim for the equaliser. Vicini played his joker. On came Serena and at last, to a massive roar from his supporters, Roberto Baggio. With both sides happy to play for extra time, Mr Vautrot blew his full-time whistle and gave everyone a chance to rest. All 22 players slumped to the ground. They were exhausted. The dreaded lottery of a penalty shoot-out looked a distinct possibility. On 109 minutes the Argentinian Giusti was sent off for flattening Baggio. Chaos reigned in Naples as Maradona led the protests of his team-mates. With his hands raised in prayer, the Argentinian captain pleaded Giusti's innocence, but Mr Vautrot was not for turning. The South Americans would have to play out the match with ten men. In the final 15 minutes Argentina settled for penalties. They got their wish. The referee's whistle cut like a knife across the length and breadth of Italy. Their dreams of glory now hinged on the nerve of their players. It was Franco Baresi first. With all the participants watching from the centre circle, Baresi stepped forward and ever so calmly shot the ball past Goycochea.

Up came the Argentinian defender Serrizuela. His effort was despatched with some aplomb past Walter Zenga. Now came Baggio. The Italian substitute smashed his country back in front. Burruchaga made the long walk from the middle of the park. This was the man who four years earlier had scored the winning goal in the World Cup final. He would not let his country down: 2–2. Di Agnostini raised the stakes for Italy: 3–2. Olarticoechea appeared for Argentina. At 3–3 the tension inside the San Paolo stadium had reached fever pitch. Many supporters turned their backs, unable to watch. Donadoni was next up for the Azzuri. Donadoni stepped forward and hit his penalty straight at Goycochea. The line had been broken. It was advantage to Argentina.

The gods of football have always possessed a wicked sense of humour, for now it was Diego Maradona to shoot. This man who could cause a riot in the Vatican was next up for the Argentinians. If Maradona was successful the Azzuri would have to score the next penalty or face being knocked out of their own World Cup. Diego carefully placed the ball on the spot. Here on his own personal stage with a packed house watching his every move, Maradona milked the moment. The people of Naples held their breath. Up he strode to put the ball past a stranded Zenga into the net. Irony is not a strong enough word for these events. As Diego wheeled away in triumph and relief Italy stood on the brink. It was down to Serena to keep the Azzuri in the competition. The omens were not good as he appeared ready to collapse with nerves. His walk from the centre circle resembled a man on the way to the gallows. The penalty was awful, a weak effort which Goycochea easily blocked. Serena dropped to his knees. The Azzuri were out. Their supporters watched in horror as Maradona and his team-mates cavorted wildly on the pitch. The king of Naples raised his hands in salute of his followers, for it was not just Argentinians who laughed and sang on the terraces of the San Paolo that night. Many locals celebrated with equal glee at the unfortunate exit of their own countrymen.

It did not take long for the recriminations and the bloodletting to begin. Vicini slammed the lack of support his team had been forced to endure in Naples. He claimed that it was nowhere near the passion and desire of the Rome and Milan crowds. Journalists present at the San Paolo also detected a hidden agenda amongst the Neapolitans. There was no doubt that a restraint of support for the national side had existed on that fateful night. Maradona's act of psychological warfare had proved to be a master stroke. On 3 July 1990 the king of Naples had clicked his fingers and his people had obeyed the command.

After losing to the Germans in a horrendous final marred by Argentinian violence, Diego Maradona's world went downhill fast. Like a runaway train careering off track, events hurtled wildly out of control. An article appeared in the prestigious Italian sports newspaper *Gazette della Sport*. It spoke of a dark evil overcoming the Argentinian, and of how physically he had become nothing more than a rag. This was widely regarded throughout Naples and the whole of Italy as a veiled attack on Maradona's addiction to cocaine. On 17 March 1991, Diego's world collapsed around him. Following a home match against Bari he was drug-tested. The test proved positive and Maradona's urine was shown to contain traces of cocaine. Retribution was swift and merciless by his many enemies. An eager Italian Football Federation wasted little time in placing an immediate ban on this troublesome little Argentinian. With huge relish they prepared their case against the southern upstart. Diego Maradona was in big trouble.

He received little help from Napoli. After falling out with the president, Corrado Ferlaine, and suffering a bad loss of form and countless alleged niggling injuries, he found his Neapolitans were no longer in love with him. All of Naples knew of their captain's antics. Whilst he was performing miracles on the pitch almost anything could be forgiven, but as soon as this started to affect him on the field? By now allegations regarding Maradona's private life were rife. As if in a concerted effort to finish him once and for all different scandals came to light daily. Pimps, prostitutes, drug-dealers, all appeared out of the gutter to dish the dirt on the under-fire Maradona. They claimed he had taken part in orgies and wild drug-taking sessions. With his world in ruins and the Neapolitans all of a sudden disgusted with his antics, Maradona decided enough was enough. His reign in the south was over. It was time to go home.

On the night of 1 April 1991, Diego Armando Maradona sneaked away under the cloak of darkness. He had made up his mind to return to Argentina. By now a sad deflated character, Maradona gazed wistfully through the aeroplane window at the beautifully lit-up bay of Naples. Swooping upwards his private jet veered high above the southern peninsula and off into the dark Neapolitan night. The treasure of San Genaro fought to hold back the tears, but still they fell. In the end he had proved mortal after all.

On 12 April 1998, Napoli Football Club was relegated from Serie A. After

33 years in the top flight of Italian soccer this proud city finally succumbed to the horror of Serie B. A 3–1 defeat at Parma was the final spear through the heart for the beleaguered Neapolitans, a game which ended with the Napoli players in floods of tears. Their keeper Tagliatella sobbed uncontrollably. Tagliatella was helped off the pitch by Parma's Carnivarro. Himself a native of the south, he also wept for the city of his birth. As the Parma forward Crespo finished off Napoli with an easy tap-in, the shudder could be felt in Naples itself. The city that sits in the shade of Vesuvius had been rocked in a style that its famous volcano could not equal. A 20-game run in which a desperately poor Napoli had failed to win could have only one ending.

Their plight was greeted with joy elsewhere in Italy. The Neapolitans talked of refereeing conspiracies and of a northern bias against their team. A traumatised city struggled to come to terms with the shame of their situation. As the streets filled with Neapolitans distraught at their drop into the abyss, thoughts returned to happier times. Down many of Naples' alleyways there still hang to this day pictures of Naples' glorious title-winning team; a reminder of a time when they stood tall over the northern giants, of the time when the little Argentinian arrived like a gift from the gods, of how Maradona raised the banner of the south and led them through the gates of heaven. Now all that remained for Neapolitans were fading memories. Whilst Maradona reigned, the city of Naples ruled the roost. Those days were well and truly gone. But what times! On walls throughout the city his name is still scrawled. Maradona. The king who fell from grace.

18.

DANCING WITH TEARS IN RED EYES

MANCHESTER UNITED V BAYERN MUNICH

1999 EUROPEAN CUP FINAL

Football, bloody hell!
– Alex Ferguson

The time was way past midnight when the last light was dimmed in the Nou Camp. High above, the skies over Barcelona glittered with stars. Across the city there was riotous celebration. The unmistakable tones of Mancunian accents rang out in tribute to the memory of the man known universally as the father of their football club. For 26 May was the birthday of Sir Matt Busby, and in his honour thousands of bleary-eyed, drunken, ecstatic United fans sung boisterous renditions of 'Happy Birthday' to Sir Matt. Many were convinced that it was divine intervention on his part which finally brought the Germans to their knees.

'We'll score over there, there is no question about that.' If Alex Ferguson was concerned that his side had only managed to draw 1–1 at home with Juventus in the first leg of the European Cup semi-final, he was doing a grand job of hiding it. In the post-match conference Ferguson exuded confidence. The Italian journalists appeared nonplussed at the United manager's attitude. He worried them. After having seen Juve hand out to the Mancunians a footballing master class they expected the English to be at least a little down. Far from it. The man from Govan was shrewd enough to send out the right type of positive waves to his players as well as to their opponents. Ryan Giggs's life-saving, last-minute equalising volley from close range had almost ripped the roof off Old Trafford. An exasperated crowd had watched in frustration for the first hour as Deauschamps, Zidane and Edgar Davids ran United's much vaunted midfield ragged. The general consensus before the game in the media was that Juventus were ripe for the taking. Well, nobody bothered to tell their players. For the 'old lady' came to Manchester and in a rousing first

45 minutes outclassed the home side. Antonio Conte gave them a well-deserved 1–0 lead at the break; scant reward really for their overwhelming superiority. Ferguson looked a man deep in thought as he headed off towards the tunnel at half-time. His team were being overrun in midfield. In an effort to stem the tide he moved wide man David Beckham into a central position alongside Roy Keane.

United appeared for the second half on fire. In typical swashbuckling manner they stormed forward, but Juve held firm. It was only after a Teddy Sheringham header was controversially disallowed that a breakthrough occurred. Beckham's lob found a waiting Giggs who gleefully smashed home from eight yards: 1–1. But would it be enough? The Italian goal scorer Antonio Conte claimed after the game that the tie was already over. 'Manchester United must accept that we are the better team and that it will be the "Old Lady" who will be going to Barcelona for the final.' Dangerous words, especially considering their opponents, for this was a team that refused to give in, no matter what the odds. Ferguson's newly appointed right-hand man, Steve McClaren, once commented that 'this United team are never beat, they just run out of time'. A typical example had occurred earlier in the season, in an FA Cup tie against bitter local rivals Liverpool. United found themselves trailing at home to an early goal from Michael Owen. After laying siege to Liverpool's goal, it appeared that it was not to be their day. Then, with only minutes remaining, Dwight Yorke struck from close range. It appeared to all that a replay was on the cards. United would have to make the short journey down the East Lancs road to battle for their very lives in hostile Merseyside. But then again maybe not! With the referee glancing at his watch, substitute Ole Gunnar Solskjaer took aim and from 12 yards broke Liverpool's heart and sent Old Trafford into a frenzy. Solskjaer was the substitute from Heaven. This was a player capable of scoring from anywhere at any time.

Now all thoughts turned to the Stella delle Alpi in Turin. Juventus were odds-on favourites to go through. Whilst events unfolded at Old Trafford, far away to the east Bayern Munich launched a typically resilient comeback against a formidable Dinamo Kiev team, to grab a 3–3 draw. Coming from 1–3 down in Kiev, Bayern resembled a team on a mission as they clawed back the Ukrainians' lead. After such a courageous performance the Germans became convinced their name was already on the trophy. They prepared to finish off Dinamo on home ground in Bavaria.

Before the second leg with Juventus, Manchester United took part in an epic FA Cup semi-final clash with their great rivals Arsenal. After a 0–0 clash at Villa Park, Ryan Giggs settled a momentous replay in extra time with a goal unprecedented in FA Cup history. With United down to ten men after captain Roy Keane had been dismissed, Giggs set off on a mazy run which saw him slice through the legendary Gunners' rearguard and crash a magnificent rising drive past David Seaman. The young Welshman's celebrations were almost as memorable as the goal itself. Giggs tore off towards the United supporters, ripping off his shirt and swirling it above his head, to be swamped by fans as they rushed to congratulate him; all this after Peter Schmeichel had saved a last-minute Dennis Bergkamp penalty. It was a tumultuous occasion. At the final whistle United supporters invaded the pitch and raised high their heroes. A remarkable treble was suddenly a possibility. Ferguson refused even to contemplate such an achievement. He knew well the pitfalls that lay ahead. A season that promised untold glory still held the potential for heartache and utter humiliation. The league championship would be a fight to the death between themselves and Arsenal, whilst an FA Cup final against Ruud Guillit's Newcastle still awaited. As for the Champions League? Well, Juve stood waiting to end United's interest in that particular competition. This was not a season nearing its end, it was merely beginning.

In all his years as manager of Manchester United, Alex Ferguson never ceased to be amazed at how difficult his club made life for themselves. Events in Turin again proved his point. With only 11 minutes showing on the electronic scoreboard in the Stella delle Alpi, Juventus had struck like lightning not once but twice, to send their fans delirious. Amidst the blurry red mists of the flying flares and erupting smoke bombs, it took only six minutes for Zinedine Zidane to curl in a wickedly deceptive cross for centre-forward Inzaghi to score from six yards out. Worse followed shortly afterwards when Edgar Davids fed the on-fire Inzaghi, whose shot took a frightful deflection off Jaap Stam to beat Schmeichel. With the Italians already making their travelling arrangements for the final, United fought back. This was a team built and moulded in the manager's image. Shaking off their horrendous start, they poured forward. Juve appeared happy to sit back and try to hit the English team on the break, for one more goal would certainly kill the tie stone dead. Another goal was forthcoming, but it was for Manchester United. David Beckham's corner was met perfectly by the flying figure of Roy Keane. The United captain's barnstorming header flew past Peruzzi into the Juventus net: 2–1, and game on. Dwight Yorke and Andy Cole were terrorising the Italian defenders, their pace and movement causing untold problems. On 34 minutes the Mancunians drew level. A devastating combination between United's front two saw Yorke leap high to send the travelling supporters into raptures. Now the cards were stacked in their favour. If the score remained the same it would be Ferguson's men in red who would go through on away goals.

Four minutes later and Yorke almost scored again when his effort rebounded ferociously off the post, but United received a knock-back when Keane was booked for an innocuous-looking challenge on an over-acting Zidane. This meant a suspension for the Irishman, and if by chance his team made it to the final he would be out of contention. Such adversity only served to inspire Keane. Ferguson watched on stern-faced but proud, as his captain put aside his personal heartache to make sure his team made it to the final. Money could not buy what Roy Keane meant to Manchester United.

Half-time came and went and still United charged at the wilting home side. The Juve supporters could not believe their eyes as their team hung on by the merest of threads. Many could hardly bear to watch as Dennis Irwin marauded forward and crashed a low drive against the inside of Peruzzi's post. It was an exhilarating, brave performance by the men from Manchester. Their just reward arrived five minutes from time. Again Yorke and Cole combined to beat the Juve defence, leaving Cole to slot home after Yorke had been blatantly brought down by Peruzzi: 3–2 and Manchester United were home and dry. The celebrations that followed would live long in the memory, the United players ran off to salute their joyful fans. The chants of 'Keano, Keano' rang out in tribute to their captain, who would be absent when United strove to bring back to Manchester the most coveted prize of all. Also missing from the final showdown would be Paul Scholes. The flame-haired little midfielder was booked for a clumsy tackle in the second half. The sporting Italian fans stayed in their seats to applaud the victors. For the first time since 1968 the 'Old Lady' had lost a meaningful home match in this competition. They realised the full extent of United's victory and wished them well for Barcelona. A full hour after the final whistle the Manchester fans were still locked inside the ground, singing and dancing for all they were worth. Their plea for Alex Ferguson to take a bow was heeded when the granite Scotsman appeared and strode across the turf to applaud their support. It was an inspiring moment and a fitting way to conclude an unforgettable evening.

Courtesy of a Mario Basler wonder goal, and a superlative display from goalkeeper Oliver Kahn, Bayern Munich survived by the skin of their imperial teeth the wrath of a rampaging Dinamo Kiev. On three occasions Kahn's bravery had prevented certain goals. Kiev's wonderful attacking duo of Shevchenko and Rebrov repeatedly carved through the Germans' defence, only to be foiled at the last by Kahn. The final whistle was greeted with massive relief by the Bayern supporters. The scene from Turin had been flashed throughout on their giant electronic scoreboard. There were looks of incredulity as well as admiration on German faces as the English fought tooth and nail to stay alive in the competition. They had already faced United twice in the qualifying stages. Both games had ended all square. The return match at Old Trafford saw both safely through to the quarter-finals. The final ten minutes were a farce as the message got through that a draw would be sufficient for each side. At the final whistle Alex Ferguson and the Bayern manager, Ottmar Hitzfeld, left the field with arms round each other's shoulders. Half-joking, half-serious, Hitzfeld remarked: 'We will see you in the final!' Prophetic words. With their place in the Champions League final assured, Manchester United concentrated on wrapping up matters at home. The league championship was clinched with a victory at Old Trafford on the final day of the season against Spurs. Roy Keane raised the premier league trophy in front of an ecstatic home crowd. From the pitch Peter Schmeichel addressed the United supporters. For the big Dane it would be his final appearance in Manchester. He, like Eric Cantona, had decided to vacate the stage. His last two appearances would now be at Wembley against Newcastle and in Barcelona. Not a bad way to bow out after a wonderful career in England.

One week later Schmeichel had a relatively quiet afternoon as United put paid to a woeful Newcastle side with alarming ease. The only black spot on a perfect day was an injury to Roy Keane, forcing him off the pitch within ten minutes. It mattered little as his team-mates romped away with the cup, a 2–0 scoreline hardly doing justice to the manner of their victory. It was a hobbling Keane who made it up the royal steps to lift yet another piece of silverware. Now all eyes turned towards Barcelona, and a date with destiny.

BARCELONA

With Manchester United it is never over until
the fat lady has had a heart attack!
– Hugh McIlvanney

Wednesday, 26 May 1999; a day forever etched in Manchester United folklore. Ringway airport was decked out in red, white and black. Thousands prepared to travel to Barcelona. The charter flights hurtled off the runway in the direction of Spain. Already countless reds were descending upon Catalonia. From across the continent, and indeed the world, they came, drawn as if by an invisible string to the Nou Camp; all with one wish only – to see their team crowned European champions. Thirty-three years was a long time to wait for a club such as theirs. Bobby Charlton gave a rallying call. He declared that 'it is about time we put something on the table again'. Hopes and expectations were high. However, there were many who feared the worst. The double was already claimed. Surely it was asking too much for the gods of football to grant them yet more glory? Bayern Munich were not coming to Barcelona to lie down and die. They themselves were on course for a historic treble. Ottmar Hitzfeld had a good record against Alex Ferguson. It was he who had masterminded Borussia Dortmund's semi-final triumph against United two years previously. Hitzfeld felt his tactics were good enough to thwart the attacking instincts of the Mancunians. He placed huge faith in his defensive players. Cole and Yorke would be shackled by Thomas Linke and the Ghanaian international Samuel Kuffour, whilst his wing-backs Markus Babbel and Michael Tarnat would be expected to tame the threat of Giggs and Beckham. Tidying up behind these four would be the unmistakable features of the legendary Lothar Matthaus. During his exceptional career the 38-year-old Matthaus had won every honour in the game; everything that is except the European champions cup. This would undoubtedly be the last chance for this magnificent player to fulfil his ambition. Matthaus was not about to let such an opportunity pass. The man every English football supporter loved to hate, but secretly admired, prepared to bring home to Munich a fourth European Cup, and no one was going to stand in his way. Little did Matthaus realise what lay in store for him and his team.

The night before the final, Alex Ferguson took United's last training session wearing a replica shirt of the 1967 European Cup-winning team. It was a poignant act on Ferguson's part and showed his knowledge of just what victory in this competition meant to Manchester United and their supporters. This was a club steeped in the history and tradition of the European Champions' cup. The loss of the Babes on that infamous Munich runway still cut deep into the emotions of all connected with the club. The final would also fall on the 90th birthday of Sir Matt Busby. Ferguson more than any other was viewed as a worthy successor to Busby. His inclination to give youth its fling bore more than a passing resemblance to Sir Matt's way of doing things. For Edwards, Colman, Pegg, Taylor and Charlton read Scholes, Neville, Butt, Beckham and Giggs. Busby's Babes never got the chance to win the European Cup. Fate decreed it was not to be. Come kick-off at the Nou Camp, Alex Ferguson would ensure that his Manchester United team were playing for more than a simple trophy. They would be playing for their history. As birthday presents go it would suit Sir Matt and his lads quite nicely if they were to succeed. Make no mistake, they would be watching!

The loss of Roy Keane and Paul Scholes forced Ferguson into desperate measures. David Beckham came in from the wing to cover his captain's absence, whilst Ryan Giggs would switch wings and Jespar Blomqvist would play on the left. He was convinced that his team possessed enough firepower to counteract the loss of two such influential players. Although a huge gamble, it was one in which Ferguson felt justified. Besides, if the match was not going to plan he could always call on the talents of Sheringham and Solskjaer to come off the bench. For the man born at 667 Govan Road, immortality beckoned. Fifty-seven years previously, on 31 December 1941, the city of Glasgow had given birth to Alex Ferguson. Now, in the early Catalan evening, the Nou Camp, daubed three-quarters blood red with the legions of United followers, prepared to make him a legend.

The pre-match entertainment laid on by Barcelona was quite surreal. An overweight Montserrat Caballe was ferried onto the pitch by motor vehicle to perform a rather disturbing duet with the deceased Freddie Mercury, who appeared on a gigantic video screen. Together they belted out their classic hit 'Barcelona'. Deep below, in the bowels of the stadium, the teams nervously prepared. For the managers this was the worst time. Their job was almost complete. Now it was down to the players. Ferguson gathered his clan. He called for their attention. 'There is not a team in the world who can beat you,' he said. 'And that is why you must not be afraid. I am proud of you, and honoured about what you have already given for me and the club. The only thing I regret is that I can't send you all out onto the pitch, because without exception you all deserve it.' With this he looked across at the forlorn features of Roy Keane and Paul Scholes. Glancing around at the rest of his lads, Ferguson realised his job was done. He wished them all the best of luck. He could do nothing more. Ottmar Hitzfeld too gave his final instructions. His players were briefed and everyone knew exactly what was expected of them. Hitzfeld had already been quoted in the German media saying that this would be their year. The absence of Keane and Scholes was a huge bonus for Bayern Munich. Their midfield duo of Jeremies and the powerful Stefan Effenberg fancied their chances against Beckham and Nicky Butt. The inclusion of Blomqvist had momentarily taken Hitzfeld aback, but he recovered quickly to realise it mattered little. The plan was in place. Babbel would take the Swedish winger and victory would be theirs.

Led by their goalkeeping captains the two sides came onto the pitch. The sheer size of Manchester United's support became apparaent. Apart from one section the whole of the Nou Camp's vast sprawling terraces were bathed red and white. Flags and banners were draped over every surface of this wonderful footballing arena. The reception for Ferguson's team was overwhelming. Outside the ground there were a further 5,000 supporters who were forced to follow proceedings from the noise of the crowd and a half-sighted video screen. Manchester United dared to let such a raw passion go unrewarded. All shook hands before battle commenced. Stefan Effenberg glanced round the ground, as if to say 'Where are our supporter?' Finally the players broke ranks and began their short warm-up. Peter Schmeichel and Oliver Kahn shook hands in the centre-circle. The highly respected Italian referee Pierluigi Collina prepared to get the match under way. The bald-headed Collina wished his linesmen a good game and with the stadium close to collective heart failure steadied himself. For obvious reasons the city of Munich had always been synonomous with Manchester United Football Cub. The events of 26 May were to make it even more so. United kicked off. The 1999 European Cup Final began.

The early stages resembled a jousting match. A half chance appeared for United when Ryan Giggs, operating on the right, saw his cross go beyond a stretching Andy Cole. A surging run from the back by Babbel came to nothing as his manager screamed at him to get back into his position. To the roar of the United supporters Giggs took off on a charge but found himself blocked by a rush of grey shirts. Bayern had settled quickly into their defensive set-up. However, on six minutes they received a wonderful tonic when Jeremies fed his huge bustling centre-forward Carsten Janker to break clear on goal. Ronnie Johnsen was forced into grounding him on the edge of the area. As the German supporters screamed Collina awarded them a free kick. United formed their defensive wall. Beckham took directions from Peter Schmeichel. It was Stefan Effenberg and Mario Basler who stood over the ball. As the Nou Camp held its breath Basler stepped forward and hit a fine shot through the wall, totally hoodwinking Schmeichel. The ball skidded low into the back of the net. Bayern had the lead. Basler slid away on his knees in celebration, soon to be joined by his jubilant team-mates. The first to embrace him was the Ghanaian Kuffour. First blood to Munich.

United tried to hit back straightaway. Cole fed Blomqvist, whose cross into the box came to nothing when Yorke was penalised for knocking over his marker Kuffour. The Germans looked supremely confident. Mario Basler strutted around. Known for his arrogance both on and off the field, this immensely talented midfielder was bossing the middle of the park. David Beckham tried to pick holes in the watertight Munich defence, but the German markers were on top of their game. Every loose ball fell to a grey shirt. On 14 minutes a half chance occurred when, from a Jaap Stam header, Andy Cole tried desperately to control a bouncing ball, but was forced to watch as it spun wide of the net. Giggs and Beckham were looking for a way through. Chances appeared at a premium. A snap-shot from Cole was saved acrobatically by the magnificent Oliver Kahn, but this apart Bayern seemed to have the measure of the United forwards. Jespar Blomqvist was repeatedly coming unstuck against the snapping, fierce challenges of Babbel, whilst in the middle Kuffour and Linke were not giving Cole and Yorke room to breathe. Lothar Matthaus was dictating events from behind the two centre markers, but this was not simply a defensive role. Matthaus still had enough left in the old tank to move forward when required. On the half-hour it was he who led a German breakout which ended with Alexander Zickler shooting narrowly wide. It was a warning to United that Bayern, when given the chance, would be straight down their throats. Giggs again tried to run up a head of steam against his marker Michael Tarnat, but once more the German kept his concentration and led the Welshman into a blind alley. Matthaus broke again. Throwing off the years, he stormed over the halfway line before letting fly from 30 yards. Schmeichel watched in relief as Matthaus's effort flew harmlessly over. The great Dane was not enjoying himself. His nervous first half continued when he mishit a clearance straight to the feet of the marauding Basler. The Germans had done their homework on the United goalkeeper. They constantly rushed him to play the ball out on his left foot. Four minutes from half-time, Schmeichel once more miskicked to Basler, who could only manage to shoot wide of the goal. The half-time whistle blew with Bayern Munich in total control. Hitzfeld's plan was working to perfection. His tactics had strangled the life out of Manchester United.

Alex Ferguson was a man with a lot on his mind as he entered his team's changing-room. He told his players, 'Keep your shape, keep attacking and the goal will come.' Just as they were leaving to go back on the pitch he played his ace card. 'Lads, when you go back out there, just have a look at the cup. It will be about five yards away from you, but you won't be able to touch it. I want you to think about the fact that if you lose this game you'll have been so close to it. You will hate that thought for the rest of your lives, so just make sure you do not lose!' The second half began. The Germans started as they left off; confident, determined and hunting down the United forwards in packs. It appeared to be business as usual. The Manchester fans fought desperately to lift their side, but try as they might the spark appeared to have gone out of their young team. Something needed to happen. Teddy Sheringham began to prepare to enter the action. Whilst warming up, Sheringham crossed swords with Mario Basler, who even at this early stage was conducting the Munich supporters in what resembled a victory celebration. The midfield battle was beginning to even up. Beckham and Butt at last began to dominate. The Germans retreated en masse to defend their slender lead. Finally, a clear-cut chance arrived for United when Giggs's cross found Blomqvist, only for the Swede to stab his effort over the bar. The spirits of the Manchester supporters were lifted. Another surge by Giggs from his own half was brought to a crashing end by a scything tackle from Effenberg. For this he was booked. Just after the hour Basler stormed clear into the United half and from full 40 yards attempted to chip Schmeichel. He missed by a whisker. The clock was running down, the tension was rising. With 23 minutes remaining, on came Teddy Sheringham for a terribly under-par Jespar Blomqvist.

Another opportunity arrived for Andy Cole when Dwight Yorke headed down to him in the penalty area. Cole's overhead kick fell miserably wide of the goal. It had been a very low-key evening for United's front two. Kuffour and Linke had handled them magnificently. The Germans made a charge. On came the raiding midfielder Helmut Scholl for the tiring Zickler. Scholl made his presence felt almost immediately as he set up Effenberg to shoot high over Schmeichel's bar. Ferguson checked his watch, 15 minutes remained. The night looked set to end in tears. A bad pass by Nicky Butt was seized on by the Germans, and Effenberg sent Basler flying clear into the United half. Basler bore down on Johnsen and Stam before laying the ball off for Helmut Scholl. Scholl took aim, and from the edge of the box clipped a wonderful shot over Schmeichel which struck the inside of the post and bounced back into a relieved keeper's hands. The Munich supporters held their heads in their hands. It should have been 2–0. With ten minutes left, Matthaus departed the scene of battle. His contribution had been immense. It was only his sheer exhaustion that decided Hitzfeld to make the substitution. On came Thorsten Fink to replace the great man.

United were straining every sinew to get through. A Beckham slide pass to Sheringham resulted in a one-two between Yorke and Nicky Butt. Butt's final cross flew across the face of the Bayern goal finally to be put behind for a corner. To a huge roar from the Manchester supporters Solskjaer was brought into the fray. Off went Andy Cole. From the resulting corner the little Norwegian smashed in a header which forced Kahn to dive low and save. The tension was becoming unbearable. As another United attack broke down the Germans once more swarmed away on the break. Scholl hit a wonderfully low, snarling drive which Schmeichel tipped away for a corner. Basler took his time in taking it. It came to nothing. The United keeper cleared his lines, only to see Munich again claim possession. Gary Neville was forced to concede another corner. As if in slow motion Basler finally put the ball into the crowded penalty box. Scholl's header back found the huge bulk of Carsten Janker. From six yards out Janker thundered an overhead drive against the Manchester United crossbar. The shudder could be felt back in Munich. Ferguson's men were still alive. They cleared their lines. Six minutes remained. Still United pressed. Solskjaer's cute back-heel let in Sheringham to hammer a low shot which Kahn managed to block. Again the noise level was raised.

The English champions were fighting to the very end. Urged on by the deafening roars of their supporters, they kept going. The Germans looked weary. The effort put in by their defenders at last began to show. Beckham broke clear into the Munich box and crossed deep for Yorke. Unfortunately for him his header back into the six-yard box found only a German boot. The pressure from the red shirts was now forcing the Bayern players to defend for their very lives. David Beckham set up his best friend Gary Neville, whose cross landed at the feet of Dwight Yorke. From nine yards out Yorke mishit and 65,000 hearts sank. Hitzfeld decided to waste vital seconds. Off would come his goalscorer. Basler saluted the German supporters. He gestured that the job was done. It was time to celebrate. There were fewer than 60 seconds remaining. The European Cup was on its way to Munich.

There were three minutes of time added on. The Germans looked dead on their feet. United tried one last time to get the ball forward. Linke found himself hounded by Solskjaer and forced to concede a throw-in level to his own penalty area. Across came Gary Neville to hurl it in. The immense Kuffour managed to head it clear, but only as far as Beckham. The young midfielder, controlling wonderfully, played it back out wide to Neville. The full-back's attempted cross into the area was blocked by Effenberg and deflected behind for a corner. There was still hope. Beckham sprinted over to take it. To the disbelief of the Munich defenders, Peter Schmeichel was making his way over the halfway line and into their box. Ferguson screamed at him to stay back, but the big Dane ignored him. Desperate times called for desperate measures. Over came Beckham's cross. Schmeichel's presence caused havoc. A mad scramble ensued. The ball fell loose to Dwight Yorke. Yorke headed it back into the danger area. A German leg managed to clear, only to see it fall at the feet of Ryan Giggs. Giggs screwed his shot towards goal and onto the waiting toe of Teddy Sheringham. Sheringham pivoted and poked the ball low into the Bayern goal: 1–1! Manchester United had saved it at the last. Across the Nou Camp the explosion of noise told its own story. The prayers of the many had outweighed the wishes of the few. The 1999 European Cup final was all square. Red flares exploded like dynamite amongst the United fans, as the English PA announcer gave out the name of the goalscorer to deafening cheers. Bedlam reigned in Barcelona!

Back on the field United were again on the rampage. Irwin smashed a long ball clearance down into the German half. Solskjaer teased his opponent into giving away a corner. Ferguson turned to his assistant Steve McClaren and exclaimed, 'Steve, this game isn't finished!' David Beckham prepared to take it. Behind him pandemonium reigned on the terraces. Once more Beckham's flighted ball came into the Munich goal area. It was met perfectly by the head of Sheringham, whose precise flick found the prowling Ole Gunnar Solskjaer. Solskjaer's right foot did the rest. From six yards out the Norwegian flashed the ball high into the German net. Solskjaer skidded away in delight on his knees. Up the other end of the field Peter Schmeichel performed an extravagant cartwheel as he danced around his penalty area in sheer disbelief. What followed were scenes of unadulterated joy amongst the United supporters. Many were still celebrating the equaliser when Solskjaer swooped to hit home the winner. On seeing the ball hit the net, all of the United substitutes sprinted madly down the touchline to leap on their Viking hitman. Alex Ferguson hugged and embraced all around him. Somebody was keeping a special eye out for Manchester United, there could be no other explanation. A miracle had occurred at the Nou Camp.

The Bayern Munich players were scattered in grey heaps across their penalty area. Michael Tarnat sat slouched against one post, whilst Markus Babbel stood resting his head against the other. Oliver Kahn curled up in a ball with his head between his knees behind the goal-line. Stefan Effenberg lay on the ground. The worst by far, though, was Samuel Kuffour. Kuffour was distraught. He pounded the ground in agony. It had been his task to pick up Solskjaer at the corner. He had failed, and this was the result. At first he was angry, swinging his arms madly in the air and screaming abuse at himself. But as the realisation struck home the tears welled in his eyes. Lothar Matthaus sat open-mouthed on the bench, his face telling the story of the thoughts swirling around in his head. But the game was not yet over. Pierluigi Collina helped the Germans. There were still six seconds to play. For the Munich players these few seconds were torture and couldn't end soon enough.

Sweet memories are made of this. After a 33-year wait the European Cup was on its way back to Old Trafford. The United bench ran onto the field to celebrate. Alex Ferguson had the look of a man whose life-long dream had come true. Ryan Giggs came bounding up towards him and the two embraced. Giggs had been with Ferguson since he was 13 years old. It was a special moment for both. The Nou Camp danced and swayed. Amongst the United supporters there was a smile for every tear. Emotions overflowed, many stood misty-eyed in complete shock. From despair to ecstasy in the blink of an eye. Amidst the rejoicing Sheringham had a quiet little word in the ear of the previously cocky Mario Basler. 'Congratulations,' said the United hero. 'You have just been Man U'd!' As the stage for the presentation was prepared the carnival on the field continued in full swing. All the players linked arms and sang along with the fans. This had been a long day in coming. Such were the feelings stirred that night in the Nou Camp, there would always be, forever more, a little part of Manchester in Barcelona.

As bad nights go this was up with the best of them for the Germans. UEFA were not about to let them slip away quietly and wallow in self-pity. First up on the podium was Oliver Kahn. He and the others who followed behind him could not even bear to look at the trophy. Alex Ferguson's wise half-time words had in the end proved true. Last but never least for the Germans came Lothar Matthaus. He accepted his medal, shook a few hands and headed swiftly down the steps. Feeling sick to the stomach, he ripped the consolation prize from around his neck. No prizes for guessing where that particular medal would finish up at the end of the evening. To Matthaus's eternal credit he was the only Bayern player to congratulate the Manchester United team on their victory. Barcelona would be his final encore. It would be one worthy of his memory.

Back in England, Manchester had gone berserk! The city centre and the forecourt of Old Trafford were flooded with supporters within minutes of the full-time whistle. Car horns sounded in triumph long into the night. The next day close to one million people would turn out to welcome their side home. Amidst scenes of mass hysteria the players and coaching staff showed off all three trophies. The entire city was a sea of red. As far as the Mancunians were concerned the European Cup was back where it belonged. It was the time for the crowning of the European champions. On his final appearance, Peter Schmeichel was handed the honour of accepting a trophy which meant everything to Manchester United and the city they so proudly represented. In 1968 Matt Busby's magnificent team had helped to lay the ghost of Munich by overcoming Benfica at Wembley. Victory was seen by many as the end of an era, the closing of a chapter, if not indeed a dramatic novel. Barcelona was different. The '68 team was ageing, Ferguson's class of '99 had yet to reach their peak. It was only fitting that Peter Schmeichel should signal for his manager to raise with him the measure of their dreams. Hundreds of cameramen and photographers stood primed. Amidst a blinding array of dazzling flashlights, the European Champions' cup was lofted high. All around the Nou Camp, United supporters danced with tears in red eyes. High above in the dark Catalan skies a shooting star appeared to do a victory roll. Surely it couldn't have been: could it?